MW00824047

Narratives of Persistence

ARCHAEOLOGY OF INDIGENOUS-COLONIAL INTERACTIONS
IN THE AMERICAS

Series Editors
Liam Frink
Aubrey Cannon
Barbara Voss
Steven A. Wernke
Patricia A. McAnany

Narratives of Persistence

Indigenous Negotiations of Colonialism in

Alta and Baja California

Lee M. Panich

**THE UNIVERSITY OF
ARIZONA PRESS**

TUCSON

The University of Arizona Press
www.uapress.arizona.edu

ISBN-13: 978-0-8165-4077-8 (hardcover)

Cover design by Sara Thaxton
Cover photograph courtesy of the National Anthropological Archives, Smithsonian Institution,
John P. Harrington photo of "Maria de Los Angeles Coloa" (August 1921), Image 91-30287

Publication of this book was made possible in part by financial support from Santa Clara University.

Library of Congress Cataloging-in-Publication Data are available at the Library of Congress.

Printed in the United States of America
♾ This paper meets the requirements of ANSI/NISO Z39.48-1992 (Permanence of Paper).

This book was written in the unceded homelands of the Ohlone people. It is dedicated to their enduring efforts toward the restoration of federal acknowledgment.

Contents

Illustrations

Figures

Tables

Acknowledgments

MANY PEOPLE HAVE HELPED SHAPE this book. First and foremost, I thank the Paipai Indian community of Santa Catarina, Baja California, who hosted my dissertation project at the site of Mission Santa Catalina. I am forever grateful to everyone who welcomed us into their community and homes. Feliciano Cañedo was instrumental in setting up the original project and making sure that fieldwork ran smoothly. Abelardo Ceseña and Daria Mariscal were kind enough to let us stay with them and their extended family over three field seasons of research. Through their longstanding relationships with local Native groups, Mike Wilken and Moisés Santos Mena provided invaluable support and insight. The research in Santa Catarina was approved by the Instituto Nacional de Antropología e Historia (INAH) and supported by Julia Bendímez Patterson, director of the Baja California INAH Center, and archaeologist John Joseph Temple. Through my work in Santa Catarina, I also had the good fortune to meet archaeologist Antonio Porcayo, with whom I have had many adventures in the years since. *Mil gracias a todos.*

A number of other people have aided my research in Baja California. During field and laboratory research, fellow Berkeley graduate students David Cohen, Rob Cuthrell, Esteban Gómez, John Matsunaga, Mark McCoy, and Tsim Schneider all made significant contributions of their own time and expertise. My understanding of the archaeology and anthropology of the region has benefitted from discussions with Richard Carrico, Loren Davis, Matt Des Lauriers, Bill Eckhardt, Horacio González Moncada, Andrea Guía Ramírez, Don Laylander, Eric Ritter, Olimpia Vázquez Ojeda, and others at the annual Balances y Perspectivas conference. Financial support for my research in Baja California was provided by a National Science Foundation Doctoral Dissertation Improvement Grant (BCS 0742062) and a Dissertation Grant from the University of California Institute for Mexico and the United States (UC MEXUS). A UC MEXUS Faculty Grant awarded to Kent Lightfoot also provided funding for initial field research at Mission Santa Catalina.

North of the border, I value the insights into Ohlone perspectives offered by Andy Galvan and members of the Muwekma Ohlone Tribe, notably Monica Arellano, Rosemary Cambra, Vincent Medina, and Charlene Nijmeh. This book builds on projects examining Mission Santa Clara on the campus of Santa Clara University (SCU) and Mission San José. I appreciate the generosity and collaborative spirit of other archaeologists who have worked at these sites, including Rebecca Allen, Scott Baxter, John Ellison, Mark Hylkema, Alan Leventhal, Sara Peelo, Seetha Reddy, and Russ Skowronek. Their research has added significantly to the argument presented here. My broader understanding of the archaeology and ethnohistory of Alta California has been enhanced by friendships with John Douglass, Glenn Farris, Gustavo Flores, Sara Gonzalez, Kathleen Hull, Roberta Jewett, Peter Nelson, Matt Russell, Nick Tipon, and Mike Wilcox. Aspects of my research on Native persistence in the greater San Francisco Bay Area were conducted with Tsim Schneider and funded by a collaborative research grant from the National Science Foundation (BCS 1558987 and 1559666).

At Santa Clara University, I owe a debt of gratitude to Lisa Kealhofer and Michelle Bezanson who, as chairs of the Department of Anthropology, have tirelessly advanced the uphill battle to involve SCU students and faculty in the archaeology of our own campus. I am especially proud of the efforts of the student researchers who have contributed to these projects over the years, particularly Helga Afaghani, Molly Bonney, Tyler Downing, Ben Griffin, Emilie Lederer, Nicole Mathwich, and Maggie Sorem. Funding for my research and publishing has come from the SCU Department of Anthropology, College of Arts and Sciences, Office of the Provost, and Office of the President. In particular, I thank Debbie Tahmassebi and Fr. Michael Engh for their support.

It has been a pleasure working with the University of Arizona Press and their team on this book. I am thankful for the guidance of Allyson Carter, who has patiently offered advice about the argument and scope of the project for several years. I also appreciate the support of the editors of the Archaeology of Indigenous-Colonial Interactions in the Americas series. It is an honor to have this book appear alongside so many important volumes. Two anonymous reviewers offered detailed comments and suggestions on the original manuscript, all of which have strengthened the final product.

The contributions of several people warrant special mention. Kent Lightfoot has been a trusted mentor and friend for the better part of two decades, and I thank him for helping me choose the path that led to this book. Tsim Schneider has also been there for the long haul. From Marin to Mexico and a surprising number of places in between, I have enjoyed his steady presence and insightful perspective on the field of archaeology. My mother-in-law, Emily Boochever, went above and beyond the call of duty to read and comment on earlier drafts. Most importantly, I thank my family—especially Lucy, Tessa, and Oliver—for all of their love and encouragement.

Narratives of Persistence

Introduction

Rewriting Indigenous and Colonial Histories

A LARGE PORTION OF MY day job involves teaching young people about the complex history of the place they call home. As an archaeologist studying the long-term histories of the Indigenous peoples of western North America, I often focus on case studies that resonate with my students at Santa Clara University, who, if they are not from the West Coast originally, are at least spending four of their most formative years here. They are frequently surprised to learn that some of the first people to arrive in North America made their way down the Pacific Coast and that today remains of these early voyages are still being found from British Columbia to Baja California. The majority are also unaware that several thousand years later, Native people constructed over four hundred shell and earth monuments all around San Francisco Bay—huge shell mounds, most of which are today hidden beneath the shopping malls and office parks of the nine-county Bay Area megalopolis. And it is a revelation for many that from the 1780s through the 1840s, thousands of Native Californians lived on what eventually became our own campus. They were residents of the Franciscan mission of Santa Clara de Asís, part of California's most controversial colonial institution: the Spanish mission system. Yet, what my students find most thought provoking is that the Indigenous people of the Bay Area are still here, fighting against deeply entrenched cultural stereotypes and narratives of Indian extinction.

The Native inhabitants of the central and southern portions of the San Francisco Bay Area are known collectively as the Ohlone. Before being lumped together by Spanish colonists and later anthropologists, the Ohlone organized themselves into multiple village communities that spoke variants

3

of a common language. Today their descendants are caught in a double bind. To survive, let alone thrive, in twenty-first century Silicon Valley, they must contend with the same traffic congestion and astronomical housing costs as any other Bay Area resident. In so doing, they often pay a price in the form of perceived cultural authenticity. Directly descended from the Native American groups living here at the time of the first European expeditions to the region, they are constantly challenged to prove their Indigenous heritage. In fact, not a single contemporary Ohlone individual living in the Bay Area is considered an authentic Native American from the vantage point of the United States federal government. And the largest Ohlone group, the Muwekma Ohlone Tribe, has been repeatedly denied restoration of federal acknowledgement despite detailed genealogical and ethnohistorical research demonstrating connections dating back to precolonial times.

This is all new to the vast majority of my students, who have unconsciously absorbed the entrenched myth of Indian extinction that pervades popular culture, textbooks, and even their own college campus. Of course, the reality is that tens of thousands of Native Americans live in California today. In addition to the dozens of unacknowledged tribes, who like the Muwekma Ohlone are fighting for federal acknowledgement or its restoration, California is home to 109 federally recognized tribes, nearly all of which live outside of the region that saw the heaviest mission influence between 1769 and the 1840s. Unbeknownst to most Americans, another eight Indigenous communities live just across the international boundary in Baja California, Mexico. These groups are culturally and linguistically related to California Indian groups residing in the United States but have been cut off from their compatriots by an arbitrary and increasingly militarized border.

These remote reserves, comprising the southernmost extent of Native California, offer a counterpoint to the frustrations of the Ohlone. Arrayed from the western foothills and high plains of the rugged Sierra Juárez to the low desert of the Colorado River Delta, several hundred individuals continue to live in multiple enclaves, each of which is associated with one of the region's four primary ethnolinguistic groups. Perhaps the best known are the Paipai, who continue many of the traditions of their ancestors within the roughly seven thousand tribally controlled acres of the Sierra Juárez and adjacent lowland desert. There, many families still group themselves according to their ancestral clans, women continue to make hand-modeled pottery, and hunting and gathering supplement household incomes and diets. The principal community is called Santa Catarina, an apparent malapropism of Santa Catalina, which was the name of the Spanish mission established there in 1797 by friars of the Dominican order. Nevertheless, the Paipai refer to themselves as the *Jaspuipaium*, or "those who have not bathed," highlighting their rejection of baptism during the late eighteenth and early nineteenth centuries. This defiant stance continues to characterize the Paipai, whose community of Santa Catarina has served as the nexus of Native life in the Sierra Juárez for over two centuries.

At first glance, then, the Ohlone and the Paipai appear to occupy opposite ends of the spectrum of California Indian identities. The Paipai maintain a close-knit, socially isolated community where important components of precolonial kinship practices continue to structure daily life and where outward signs of Native identity, such as traditional arts and crafts, are clear to external observers. The Ohlone, in contrast, have been alienated from their ancestral lands, and though they too maintain close family ties, these connections are more difficult for outsiders to see against the backdrop of the Bay Area's cultural diversity and suburban sprawl. Yet, the Ohlone and the Paipai also share a common colonial history: both groups were subject to forced relocation and directed enculturation during the Spanish mission period (ca. 1770s–1840s) and both groups later navigated successive waves of ranchers, miners, and settlers who frequently saw Indian people as impediments to their emerging visions of California.

Given their commonalities, why do these two tribal groups stand in such stark contrast today? This book illuminates how the ancestors of today's Ohlone and Paipai people accommodated and negotiated successive waves of colonialism in light of their distinct cultural traditions. Through a long-term perspective on persistence, I trace Indigenous social agency from first contact situations through the mission period to the more entrenched forms of settler colonialism that followed. Despite their shared histories, the Ohlone and Paipai traveled complex pathways to the present, negotiating local manifestations of global colonialism. In teasing apart how Native people themselves understood and dealt with colonial impositions, it is possible to illuminate the historical roots that anchor the broad spectrum of Indigenous identities visible today in California and across North America. Indeed, a guiding principle of this book is that both the Ohlone and the Paipai constitute equally valid forms of being Indigenous—in other words, to be Native does not require one to live (or speak or eat or work or pray) exactly as one's ancestors did at the onset of colonialism (Raibmon 2005). As these two case studies demonstrate, continuity does not require stasis.

Privileging Indigenous Histories

It can be difficult for outsiders—myself included—to understand how contemporary Native communities weigh the experience of colonialism within the context of their own histories. This point was made clear to me the very first day that I arrived in Santa Catarina in 2005. I was there to begin research for my dissertation project which I initially designed to assess the impacts of the Dominican mission system on the Native people of northern Baja California, primarily the Paipai. Our host, a tribal leader named Abelardo Ceseña, accompanied me on some errands while the rest of the Berkeley crew set up our field house. As we drove along a winding two-track road, Abelardo took the opportunity to probe my understanding of the history of his tribe (Panich 2011a). What gradually became clear to me was that the facts and figures regarding the mission padres, the crops grown, and the animals raised—the kind of information found in most traditional mission histories—held little interest for him. Instead, we talked about how his ancestors lived prior to the founding of the mission and the various events that occurred in the wake of its destruction by Indigenous rebels in 1840. I was somewhat surprised to see the mission period (and by extension, my project studying Mission Santa Catalina) so easily discounted by an important member of the descendant community. But, as I learned, this sentiment was commonplace in Santa Catarina. As Feliciano Cañedo, another tribal elder, adamantly pointed out to me: the mission is today nothing more than ruins whereas the Paipai are still here (Panich 2010a, 254).

We are still here. This phrase resonates in various ways across Native California. It is a declaration of the enduring presence of Native Californian communities at the same time that it acknowledges the struggles of earlier generations. Abelardo and Feliciano wanted to make sure I understood that the mission period was just one moment in the broader scope of Paipai history, a history in which they and their ancestors maintained autonomy despite considerable adversity. In neighboring Cucapá territory, along the Colorado River Delta, the phrase encapsulates a similar sentiment—after a history filled with hardship, the Cucapá are "still there carrying on with their lives" (Muehlmann 2013, 26). For both of these Baja California communities, the emphasis is often on the final word—*here*—giving the phrase a more carto-graphic meaning. The Paipai, like the Cucapá, continue to live in many of the same places their ancestors occupied when they first encountered European explorers and later Euro-American settlers.

North of the border, the meaning of "we are still here" has a slightly differ-ent valence, particularly in the formerly missionized regions of the south and central coasts. In this vast territory, the myth of Indian extinction is baked into the very fabric of everyday life from the physical landscape to vacation souvenirs (Kryder-Reid 2016; Thomas 1991). Take, for example, the experi-ence of Deborah Miranda, an Ohlone/Costanoan-Esselen scholar who shocked a family visiting one of the iconic California missions by revealing that she was a descendant of the Native people who originally built the church more than two centuries ago—people whom the visitors assumed were extinct (Miranda 2013, xviii–xix). This encounter is not surprising given that the interpretive materials at most of the twenty-one Spanish mission sites in California largely relegate Indigenous people to a romanticized past. Meanwhile, the state's primary school curriculum often reinforces the idea that the founding of the missions marks the end of Native Californian history (Dartt-Newton 2011; Herrera 2019; Kryder-Reid 2016; Lorimer 2016). Thus, in Alta California, the focus on continued Indigenous presence is framed in contrast to the missions themselves. In the words of Salinan/Rumsien Ohlone writer Gregg Castro (2014–2015), "the missions did not succeed."

Few tribes in the United States whose ancestors were impacted by the mission system, however, have federal recognition today. This injustice is directly linked to the events of the relatively short period—roughly seventy years—during which their ancestors toiled at places like Mission Santa Clara, just steps away from my office at Santa Clara University. According to early anthropologists and government officials, the Indigenous groups of Alta California who entered the missions became so intermixed and degraded that their descendants can no longer be recognized as legitimate Native American groups. Although many scholars have demonstrated that these earlier proclamations were based not on fact but on outdated understandings of cultural identity and the processes of colonialism, the outcome for Native communities remains the same (Field 1999; Lightfoot 2005; Lightfoot et al. 2013b; Montenegro 2019; Panich 2013). For these Native Californians, then, affirmative statements of their continued presence in the region also stand in direct contradiction to their lack of federal acknowledgement. As discussed by Olivia Chilcote (2015), a member of the San Luis Rey Band of Mission Indians, the bureaucratic nature of the federal recognition process leaves little room for active participation. Instead, community events like pow wows offer ways to reclaim colonial spaces and broaden the public visibility of the so-called unacknowledged tribes. They are still here despite the government's refusal to recognize their existence.

These challenges are not unique to California. Centuries of entanglements between diverse Native American groups and agents of missionary, mercantile, and settler colonialism have left archaeological and documentary evidence that has been used to tell many stories. But the one story that has been told most often is the story of decline. Native American histories across the continent have been written as the passing of ancient cultures into a mythical past. This is what archaeologist Michael Wilcox (2009) calls "terminal narratives," tropes that infuse both popular and scholarly understandings of the colonial period throughout North America (Cipolla 2013; King 2012; Mrozowski et al. 2009; O'Brien 2010). These narratives, moreover, support the logic of settler colonialism, a form of colonialism that requires the elimination of Indigenous people through violence, removal, or popular mythology (Wolfe 2001). Like the appropriation of Indigenous land, traditional histories of colonial America reinforce the idea that the continent's Native peoples are gone. According to the Muwekma Ohlone Tribe, these are "the politics of erasure" (Field et al. 2013).

Native Californians continue to resist their erasure in various ways, a point demonstrated during the canonization of Franciscan missionary Junípero Serra in 2015 (Panich 2016a). As at other times along Serra's path to sainthood, Native Californians expressed deeply held convictions about the negative outcomes of the Spanish mission system for their communities. Part of that story was about perseverance, but many also demanded a public acknowledgment of the suffering of their ancestors—forced relocation, heavy labor, and cultural suppression in the Franciscan missions that operated under Spanish and Mexican rule and then worse, the genocide committed by American settlers in the mid-nineteenth century. Valentin Lopez, the chairman of the Amah Mutsun Tribal Band, put it bluntly, stating that the canonization of Serra revealed that the Catholic Church "does not care about our true history or our historic trauma" (Lopez 2015). Mark Marcarro, the tribal chairman of the Pechanga Band of Luiseño Indians similarly wrote, "The only benefit of Serra's sainthood will be the platform it creates for us to tell the real, whole and true story of Fr. Serra and to do so in our voice" (2015, 2). Their remarks converge with those offered by Anishinaabe-Ojibwe anthropologist Sonya Atalay (2006) who critiqued the inaugural exhibitions of the Smithsonian's National Museum of the American Indian for failing to give a "sense for the struggle." While the museum effectively highlighted vibrant, contemporary Indigenous communities throughout the Americas, visitors were not challenged with the horrors endured by Native people at the hands of Euro-American colonists.

This balance can be difficult to achieve, particularly when the tragic effects of colonialism are mobilized by the dominant society to undermine efforts to restore federal acknowledgment or even to implement Indian gaming compacts. As detailed by Coast Miwok archaeologist Tsim Schneider (2019), part of this issue is a misunderstanding about how Native people persevered in the times "in between" the early colonial period and the present day. Given the overarching narrative of loss that suffuses most understandings of Indigenous experiences in the Spanish mission system, casual observers are often unaware of the various ways that California Indian communities regrouped and reestablished themselves in their homelands during the nineteenth and twentieth centuries. Yet, as historian William Bauer (2016a), a citizen of the Round Valley Reservation, argues, the history of Native California is a history of adaptation to changing environments, economic pursuits, and political structures. Thus, one of the key points made by Native Californian scholars and community members is that their ancestors persevered not by chance but through culturally situated knowledge. This knowledge, in turn, allowed them to make intelligent and meaningful choices despite the constraints of colonialism and its attendant struggles.

This important consideration is encapsulated in the concept of "survivance" coined by Anishinaabe scholar Gerald Vizenor (1999, 2008). Intentionally fluid, survivance stresses the active role of people in creating their own stories and self-reliant communities, rejecting the portrayal of Native Americans as mere victims of colonial domination. Frequently used within Native American studies, the concept of survivance has recently entered mainstream debate in archaeology and related heritage fields (e.g., Acebo and Martinez 2018; Atalay 2006; Kasper and Handsman 2015; Lightfoot and Gonzalez 2018; Nelson 2019; Silliman 2014; Walder and Yann 2018). In this context, survivance serves to highlight the active persistence of Native people who often worked simultaneously within and against the structures of colonialism in charting their own futures. By situating Native actors as neither completely unencumbered nor totally without agency, survivance pushes us to look for the ways that Indigenous people made pragmatic choices to resist, accommodate, or avoid various colonial impositions.

Contextualizing Colonialism

As argued by Atalay (2006), linking Indigenous pasts to contemporary Native presence requires both the acknowledgment of the persistence of Indigenous communities and an honest reckoning with the dark realities of colonialism. In California, Native scholars and their communities have long pointed to the struggles of those who were caught up in the Spanish mission system, where Indigenous people faced social controls, corporal punishment, and family separation, among additional injustices (Castillo 1978; Costo and Costo 1987; Norton 1979). For these and other scholars, the demographic effects of the missions have been of particular interest, with many concluding that missionization led directly to the dissolution of tribal societies throughout coastal California (Cook 1976; Jackson 1994; Jackson and Castillo 1995; Milliken 1995). Researchers have also documented the horrific violence that

American settlers unleashed on the Native groups who lived beyond the mis-sionized zone, capturing in grim historical detail the genocide of the early American period between the 1840s and 1870s (Cook 1976; Heizer 1974; Lindsay 2012; Madley 2016; Trafzer and Hyer 1999).

There is no doubt in my mind that these works represent important, fully substantiated documentation of the crimes perpetrated against Native Californians in the name of colonialism and Manifest Destiny. Such research, moreover, can help contemporary communities understand the historical trauma with which they are still coping. However, a single-minded focus on the "grisly statistics" related to violence and disease (Hurtado 1988, 1) also unwittingly perpetuates a top-down viewpoint of catastrophic colonialism. In this view, which characterizes much of the early critical scholarship on colo-nial California, Native societies were fundamentally altered by demographic changes and/or acculturation during a relatively short period of time—a "fatal impact" model that has a cascading series of ramifications for how scholars and government officials have treated, and continue to treat, Native people (Jones 2015; Silliman 2012). To be clear, the facts of the physical and structural violence faced by Native Californians are irrefutable, but a full accounting of the survivance of Indigenous communities throughout the region requires moving beyond a narrow focus on demographic and cultural loss.

Thankfully, numerous scholars are showing how to balance the struggles of the colonial period with the endurance of Native Californians. Many come from tribal communities themselves, documenting how their ancestors made do despite the constraints of missionary and settler colonialism (Bauer 2009, 2016b; Chavez 2017; Chilcote 2015; Cordero 2015; Nelson 2017, 2019; K. Schneider 2010; T. Schneider 2015b, 2018, 2019). One important branch of this recent scholarship focuses on how Indigenous people negotiated tensions over the symbolic nature of colonialism. The Spanish enterprise in California, for example, was predicated on the spiritual conversion of Native people, bringing with it new understandings of the divine and of personhood that left subtle traces in the documentary and archaeological records. While true religious conversion seems to have been rare (Cordero 2017), music, dance, and artwork were all domains of intercultural negotiation. By examining the historical and archaeological records for the ways that Indigenous people inserted themselves into these interactions, we can better appreciate the inge-nuity of Native Californians who resisted wholesale assimilation even as they incorporated aspects of colonial culture into their own (Chavez 2017; Haas 2014; Robinson 2013; Sandos 2004).

Recent scholarship also explores how Native people navigated inter-personal relationships—what historian Erika Pérez (2018) calls "colonial intimacies" (and see Barr 2007). While many scholars, particularly anthropologists, have used mission sacramental records to reconstruct Native Californian kinship networks, the documentary record also reveals how Indigenous individuals and colonists alike used marriage and other bonds, such as cohabitation and godparenting, to create a social foundation that helped them buffer the impacts of colonialism from the mission period onward. Importantly, many of these studies highlight the choices of women and their roles as cultural brokers despite colonial gender dynamics and pervasive sexual violence that shifted in various ways according to the laws and norms of Spanish, Mexican, and American societies (Douglass et al. 2018; Haas 1995; Reyes 2009; Sousa 2015). These fine-grained works highlight how the intimate decisions made by both Native Californians and newcomers relate to broader patterns of persistence including the continuation of kin relations, social organization, and gendered cultural practices.

Studies like these are the leading edge of a new wave of scholarship that has marshaled various combinations of archaeological investigations, material culture studies, and detailed reexaminations of the documentary record to paint a more nuanced picture of Native life in colonial California (Haas 2014; Hackel 2005; Hull 2009; Hurtado 1988; Lightfoot 2005; Newell 2009; Phillips 2010; Rizzo 2016). Though they approach the subject matter from different angles, an important connection among many of these scholars is that they each extend their investigations beyond tightly bracketed case studies by tracing the intersecting historical threads that connect the colonial period to the precontact past and also to our contemporary world. These lines are sometimes thin but together offer us a fuller view of how Native people made sense of their encounters with different colonial institutions and how those experiences structured the diversity of Native Californian groups that exist today.

Understanding these successive developments from the vantage point of Indigenous persistence—the approach championed by my Paipai interlocutors—requires contextualizing the short-term encounters of the colonial period within long-term trends in Indigenous history. More than two decades ago, archaeologist Kent Lightfoot (1995) argued against the artificial divide between "prehistory" and "history" that hobbles the nuanced investigation of long-term cultural trajectories. The intervening years have seen a proliferation of studies seeking to understand how the ancient past continues to have relevance for Native communities, particularly as they negotiate ever-shifting colonial structures (Cipolla 2013; Ferris 2009; Ferris et al. 2014; Gallivan 2007; Hantman 2018; Hull 2009; Jordan 2008; Oland et al. 2012; Panich 2013; Rubertone 2000; Scheiber and Mitchell 2010;

Silliman 2009, 2012). The result has been nothing short of the "death of prehistory" (Schmidt and Mrozowski 2013), at least in the archaeological study of colonial encounters. Even if some disciplinary hesitations remain, historians and ethnohistorians have likewise sought to move beyond the ethnocentric relegation of precontact Native histories to a space outside of world history (e.g., Barr 2007; Ethridge 2010; Hämäläinen 2008; Radding 1997; Reid 2015; Zappia 2014). As eloquently stated by Juliana Barr, "Time was not interrupted upon European arrival, nor did it stop (and then begin again). Rather, Europeans arrived and became caught up in the tide of Native events and processes, the currents of Native history" (2017, 204–205).

Reading these currents, assessing the unfolding of colonialism from the vantage of those who lived through it, allows us to work against the teleology of terminal narratives. This reorientation, however, also requires a framework for organizing the processes that we uncover in our investigations. For archaeologists and ethnohistorians, the broader processes that we seek to understand are reflected in the small-scale remnants of daily life that survive to the present, such as an arrow point made from imported bottle glass or the intertribal marriages recorded by a Franciscan missionary. When viewed in isolation, these data points may appear to suggest colonial disruptions to Indigenous life; yet, contextualized within the scope of Indigenous traditions, such practices can be seen to stem from the accumulated knowledge of particular individuals or groups. In thinking about how people draw on the past to anticipate the future, many scholars are informed by the writings of theorists such as Pierre Bourdieu (1977, 1990) and Anthony Giddens (1979), who argue that social life is structured by cultural dispositions but that such worldviews are also continually remade in practice. Applying these insights to long-term Indigenous histories, daily practices may provide evidence of "changing continuities" rather than continuity and change as separate, mutually exclusive phenomena (Ferris 2009). In other words, a long-term perspective on colonial entanglements can allow us to see how the developments of one era were simultaneously structured by what came before and served to structure what came after.

Yet, these threads may be difficult for some outside observers to appreciate. As put by Deborah Miranda, "Those who will not change do not survive; but who are we, when we have survived?" (2013, xiv). This is a particularly vexing question for groups like the Ohlone, who are often not considered "real Indians" by the government, the general public, or even other Native people (Ramirez 2007). Outside observers have long used legal definitions, blood quantum, or cultural traits to define what constitutes legitimate Indigenous identity. In the United States today, for example, legally defined

Native identity is equated with federal acknowledgement either as a recognized tribe or an enrolled member or citizen of such a tribe (Garroutte 2003; Miller 2004). Yet, as many Native Californians know all too well, the federal acknowledgment process is fickle, arbitrary, and fundamentally essentialist (Field 1999; Montenegro 2019). In contrast, many would argue that identity is, broadly speaking, socially constructed. Identities are ultimately forged both by outside perceptions and, importantly, by internal understandings of belonging and community, including shared ways of doing things, which themselves are passed from generation to generation through dynamic cultural traditions (Panich 2013, 107–108). Based in culture and history, identities are constantly constructed through the practicalities of daily life.

This book, then, seeks to weave these threads together by examining how Native Californians charted a course through increasingly entrenched colonial institutions. In taking the long view, we can trace the changing continuities from one historical moment to another, highlighting the connective tissue that ties generations together despite the past three centuries of colonial disruption. As we shall see, the Native people of the San Francisco Bay Area and the Sierra Juárez made many readjustments in realms of daily life such as diet or material culture, but such modifications are best understood as the interested actions of groups and individuals rather than externally imposed breaks with the past. By recognizing the dynamic nature of cultural traditions and identities, moreover, we must also accept that continuity cannot be equated with stasis; in the words of archaeologist Lara Ghisleni (2018), "continuity can be otherwise." As the following chapters demonstrate, the ancestors of the Ohlone and Paipai—like other Native people throughout the region—drew on existing cultural knowledge to navigate newfound circumstances, forging independent trajectories that together point toward observable patterns of persistence.

Sifting the Evidence

As anthropologist Michel-Rolph Trouillot points out, "History begins with bodies and artifacts; living brains, fossils, texts, buildings" (1995, 29). But how history is ultimately told depends on what is saved and what survives, on how things are classified, curated, accessed, and ultimately brought back to light. Countering terminal narratives, then, requires a careful sifting of the evidence, both to reveal silences and ethnocentric biases in the archive and to make the connections that bind Native communities past and present. The approach I take in this book can be characterized as historical anthropology, drawing on a wealth of archaeological, ethnographic, and historical data that offer an Indigenous perspective on missionary and settler colonialism in California. Of course, each of these lines of evidence has its own inherent strengths and weaknesses, and for each the record is fuller for some geographic areas or time periods than others. But taken together, they can help paint a more nuanced picture of how Native Californians actively persisted from their first contact with Europeans onward.

Archaeological data, for example, can provide a general picture of the precontact social and economic characteristics of Ohlone and Paipai societies that structured the way they dealt with the challenges of the region's first major colonial institution, the Spanish mission system. Here, ironically, the massive scale of urban development in the San Francisco Bay Area over the past fifty years proves to be something of an asset for understanding the long-term histories of Ohlone groups. Several major village and cemetery complexes dating to late precontact times have been professionally excavated, offering a picture of life prior to the arrival of the Spanish. In northern Baja California, the systematic investigation of the precontact past did not begin until the opening of the Baja California Center of the Instituto Nacional de Antropología e Historia (INAH) in the 1980s. Data from INAH projects can be supplemented by information collected from nearby San Diego County, California, where development pressure has similarly resulted in a boon for archaeologists.

Archaeological investigations have also been carried out at mission sites in both regions, notably at Mission Santa Catalina in one of the Paipai's Indigenous reserves and also at Missions Santa Clara and San José, where Ohlone people lived and worked during the late eighteenth and early nineteenth centuries. Scale is certainly an issue—the excavations at Mission Santa Catalina were explicitly designed to be low-impact whereas recent work at Mission Santa Clara has encompassed entire city blocks—but sufficient data are available to make meaningful comparisons in most areas of interest with local precontact patterns and between different colonial establishments. Although some might question the need for archaeological studies of post-contact Indigenous communities, the physical remnants of daily life offer a relatively unfiltered view of how Native people coped with missionization. Often excavated from within the missions' Native neighborhoods or even particular dwellings, these materials offer glimpses of what life was like away from the watchful eyes of the padres. The archaeological evidence illuminates practices, ranging from mortuary rituals to exchange networks to leisure activities, that were not well documented by Euro-American observers of Indigenous life in colonial settings.

To this trove of material evidence, we can add the rich documentary record for Spanish California, which can be examined for evidence about how people reinterpreted existing traditions and adopted new strategies in light of the constraints of missionary colonialism. Spanning from accounts of first contact between Spanish officials and Native people to detailed censuses and vital records, these documents have served as the foundation for generations of scholars. The record for Baja California is comparatively slim, many of the key documents having been lost over the intervening decades (Gerhard and Mathes 1995). In contrast, the detailed sacramental registers from Alta California have been meticulously digitized and are today available online through the Huntington Library's Early California Population Project (ECPP) database, giving instant access to information regarding key life events for tens of thousands of Native men, women, and children (Huntington Library 2006).

For the second half of the nineteenth century, Native people in both areas are only poorly represented in the documentary record. In the San Francisco Bay region, many former mission Indians passed as Mexican in order to avoid the ruthless violence against Native Californians that accompanied the American annexation of the region. In northern Baja California, Native groups enjoyed a period of relative autonomy, and though they largely lived beyond the archival curtain, they can be found through careful reading of documents related to ranching and mining concerns in the area. The embedded biases of contemporary observers combined with the prosaic nature of many documents can dull the cultural context for action in many instances, but this varied documentary record helps bring to the fore the lives of Native individuals during a particularly dark time.

By the early twentieth century, the young discipline of anthropology had trained its gaze on California Indians, who it felt were on the cusp of passing into obscurity. At the same time that some of the field's leading figures avoided formerly missionized groups to seize upon the last tribal people who could recall a time before the arrival of Euro-Americans, other scholars sought out the Ohlone and other groups in central California who had been subject to the full brunt of the Franciscan project. Perhaps due to their living south of the border, the Paipai and neighboring groups escaped sustained scholarly investigation until the 1920s, but their isolation and maintenance of key cultural traditions—despite their missionization—soon attracted a fairly steady stream of anthropologists over the rest of the twentieth century. It is tempting to use the robust ethnographic record from Baja California and the scattered accounts from central California to help build a baseline understanding of precontact Native Californian cultures. Yet, as I hope to demonstrate with this book, Indigenous societies are dynamic and have changed over time without losing authenticity. Thus, in most cases, the wiser course of action is to treat ethnographic accounts not as some kind of static ethnographic present revealing "traditional" Native culture but as direct evidence of Indigenous life at the time that the information was collected (Lightfoot 2005, 46–47).

The ethnographic record, particularly for Baja California, also contains an impressive number of Native narratives, both oral traditions that were passed down over generations and oral histories that detail events in the teller's own life. Here again, this information may most clearly relate to the period in which it was recounted. But in the case of oral traditions, we may be able to use these narratives to gain an insider's perspective into the way historical events are understood in different Indigenous societies. While many scholars still debate the validity of oral narratives, their usefulness for understanding the colonial past has been demonstrated on two fronts. The first is that they often contain historical facts; in the absence of written language, Native people developed sophisticated ways of passing historical information from generation to generation (e.g., Farris 1988). Second, oral narratives are not simply texts to be dissected for historical content but are in many instances active pieces of living cultures, narratives that ensure intergenerational transmission of values (Cavender Wilson 1998).

We must use these diverse datasets reflexively, however. Viewing the disparate sources as a series of windows on a historical timeline is perhaps too tidy. Many accounts from Franciscan missionaries in California refer to Native practices conducted in their "pagan state," and early ethnographers often sought to elicit information they believed represented California Indian societies before the corrupting influences of colonialism. These separate sources of evidence may better be viewed as a web of information that can be used to generate interpretations about the past. And just as a single thread does not reveal much about the structure of a web, neither does one line of evidence sufficiently illuminate past encounters. The goal, then, is to carefully consider the evidence of Native Californian life, to remove the chaff of observational biases and array the remaining kernels in a narrative that does justice to the lived experiences of people who endured the worst excesses of multiple colonial systems.

Reading This Book

This is a book about how Native Californians negotiated various colonial impositions from the earliest encounters with outsiders through the mid-twentieth century. It is not about those colonial systems per se. I do not treat in any substantive detail the hardships and bravery of the early European explorers who came to North America's West Coast or the institutional histories that brought three different missionary orders—the Jesuits, Dominicans, and Franciscans—to the Californian colonies. Nor do I fully examine the political wrangling that accompanied the transition from Spanish to Mexican rule or the push-and-pull factors that presaged the swift and brutal arrival of the Americans. Instead, I examine the cultural and historical trajectories of two particular Native groups, the Ohlone and the Paipai, who struggled against these shifting forms of colonialism, with an eye toward understanding their persistence over the course of the past two and a half centuries.

I employ a comparative framework to demonstrate that the consequences of colonialism we see today were at no point inevitable. As Hayes and Cipolla note, comparative approaches to colonialism call attention to "a series of scalar tensions: the specific versus the general, the historical versus the anthropological, the practical versus the theoretical, and the broad-brush perspective on human history versus the local and individual experiences constituted and oftentimes lost therein" (2015, 2). Rather than a flaw, the tensions revealed through comparison are a key feature of many illuminating examinations of colonial entanglements (Cipolla and Hayes 2015; Lightfoot 2005; Oland et al. 2012; Radding 2005; Scheiber and Mitchell 2010; Stein 2005). In California, terminal narratives effectively flatten the variety of colonial experiences, but as I hope to demonstrate, Native people moved forward against these hardships in various ways. Each Native Californian community has its own remarkable history of survival and endurance, and by holding up two such histories against each other, it is possible to diffuse both the fatal impact model of demographic and cultural collapse as well as the ethnocentric underpinnings of many conventional histories.

Building these stories around a comparative framework involves additional structural challenges for the book, but I have elected to proceed chronologically and to present the case studies in parallel fashion. Each chapter will begin with a broad overview of Native California during the period in question, structured around five areas of investigation—political organization, subsistence economies, technology, ceremonial life, and conflict—that highlight the changing continuities evident across the region. These sections are intended to foreground and give context to the more detailed examinations of the experiences of the Ohlone and Paipai that delve into the particulars of Native life in the San Francisco Bay region and the Sierra Juárez during the periods under consideration. Here, the intent is not to write an exhaustive account but to provide the reader with a sense of the motivations and

possibilities for action in different colonial settings. Each chapter will end
with a brief summary of the two case studies, calling attention to the threads
that tie one period to another. Taken together, this framework provides a
general history of Native-lived colonialism in Alta and Baja California, with
the two case studies showcasing the commonalities and divergences in how
particular groups persisted across the past 250 years.

The case studies begin in the following chapter (Chapter 1), which will
lay out the five areas of investigation discussed previously through a general
introduction to Native Californian societies. The chapter will also examine
what we know about the ancestors of the Ohlone and Paipai who lived in the
late precontact period through a consideration of regional archaeological, ethnohistorical, and ethnographic evidence. Chapter 2 will examine the initial
contacts between Europeans and the Native people of the San Francisco Bay
region and the Sierra Juárez. While this is not a book solely about the mission
period, it is worth examining how Native Californians interacted with outsiders during the early years of missionization (Chapter 3) and from the height of
the mission system to its collapse (Chapter 4). Arranging the chapters in this
way challenges the notion that the mission period was monolithic and instead
highlights the fact that people had different constraints and opportunities at
different times and places. Moving forward, this periodization also helps to
contextualize Native strategies under American or Mexican administration
which built more from the final stages of missionization rather than initial
years of sustained contact. Chapter 5 considers the decades after the closing
of the missions during which Native Californians suffered dispossession and
violence but nonetheless found ways to maintain their communities. Chapter
6 examines the strategies of Native people in the opening decades of the twentieth century when many of the social and economic patterns visible today in
the states of California and Baja California had solidified.

The chapters of this book bring the stories of the Ohlone and Paipai peoples up to the mid-twentieth century, which constitutes the childhood years
of many of the elders who have led the way for contemporary revitalization
movements in both regions. Members of each group no doubt hold a vast
amount of information on their respective histories, and I have sought here
to bring together the various threads in regional archaeology, ethnography,
and history in a way that makes the most of my particular skillset and expertise. It is by no means the definitive statement on the histories of the Ohlone
or Paipai but rather a jumping-off point for further exploration for those
who would seek to more fully understand the different pathways that Native
Californian communities have taken to the present. Accordingly, the mid-
twentieth century seems like a fitting historical moment to pass the baton to

those tribal people who work hard every day to maintain their communities within the ever-changing social and political environments of the twenty-first century. Much like their ancestors who first encountered Spanish missionaries and later Mexican and Anglo ranchers, miners, and settlers, they have a wealth of knowledge to draw upon.

A final note regarding terminology. The names "Ohlone" and "Paipai" are in many ways cotemporary constructions, as will become clear in the following chapters. I have chosen to employ them in this book because they are the terms used by the tribal communities today. In common practice, Ohlone is interchangeable with the linguistic designation "Costanoan," which has its roots in the Spanish *costaño*. This term, which some find offensive today, refers to the language family that subsumes several Native languages spoken from the San Francisco Bay to Carmel and inland to the Salinas Valley (Golla 2011; Levy 1978). For the sake of clarity, I reserve the term "Ohlone" for those groups whose ancestors lived in the U-shaped region stretching from the San Francisco Peninsula, south to the Santa Clara Valley, and up the East Bay. In the colonial period, these communities were most closely associated with Missions San Francisco, Santa Clara, and San José. For more information on the origins of the term "Ohlone," see Milliken et al. (2009). The name "Paipai" (variously, Pai Pai or Pa'ipai) is similarly complex, but like Costanoan, it is best understood as a linguistic term (Golla 2011; Winter 1967). In late precontact times, the Paipai language was spoken in a narrow east-west swath of northern Baja California, stretching from the Gulf of California to the Pacific Coast. Groups speaking this language were principally associated with Mission Santa Catalina but also lived at other regional missions consisting of San Vicente and probably Santo Tomás and Santo Domingo. In practice today, the ethnonym Paipai subsumes a relatively diverse set of interrelated lineages that are centered in the Sierra Juárez and the community of Santa Catarina in particular (Panich 2010a).

I

Situating Native California

WHERE DOES THE STORY OF Native-lived colonialism in California begin? Archaeologists tend to think in broad swaths of time. Most archaeologists working in California would agree that the story we collectively tell begins somewhere around 15,000 years ago. During that time, people with a distinct maritime adaptation appear to have arrived by sea, moving southward along the "kelp highway" that stretches from Alaska to Baja California—a 3,500-mile-long ecosystem teeming with life and which supported a relatively rapid migration of people into the region's coastal areas. Further inland, archaeologists have also documented scattered evidence of big-game hunters who used a telltale form of fluted spear point. Known as the Clovis culture, these people were part of a broad hunting tradition that existed across the North American continent some 13,500 years ago. The timing and relationship between these seemingly separate populations are sources of much archaeological debate (Braje et al. 2017; Des Lauriers 2011; Wade 2017).

Native Californians, by and large, take a different view of their origins. Across the region, they maintain a diverse set of narratives that have been passed down since time immemorial. Maligned or overlooked by colonial period observers—missionaries at Mission Santa Clara claimed that Native people there had "no knowledge of their remote ancestors nor of the land from which they came" (Geiger and Meighan 1976, 94)—such traditions endured despite the upheavals of the past 250 years and today remain important means of transmitting cultural knowledge across generations.

For example, a Kiliwa narrative told by Rufino Ochurte, who in his later years lived in the predominantly Paipai settlement of Santa Catarina, offers insight into the origin of the region's Native people: "Earth-Person created people and left. He went along setting the tribes in place; into their territories he spilled them. He made foods for them; the deer he made for them to chase and kill, to shoot and kill. He created the jackrabbit for them to kill and eat . . . He created the agave for them to pit-roast and eat. This chia [that] is here; he created chia for them to beat up and drink. Every little thing there is, he created for them. By Earth-Person these foods were given" (Mixco 1983, 45).

From the perspective of lived experience, the creation of the tribes by Earth-Person or the arrival of early hunters and fishers, as attested by archaeological evidence, took place in deep time. Although we archaeologists should carefully approach the temporal context of each case—rather than simply listing off thousands of years of culture history simply because we can (Silliman 2012)—different kinds of origin stories challenge us to reject the idea that Indigenous cultures were, at their core, unchanging and static (Lightfoot 1995, 199–200; Rubertone 2012, 269). Whether one views the past through oral narratives or through archaeological evidence, both vantage points support a long-term presence of Indigenous people in the places that today make up the states of California and Baja California. Both provide insight into the connections between people and place, as demonstrated through the plants and animals described in Native texts or through the animal bones and stone tools that allow archaeologists to reconstruct ancient diets and subsistence practices.

The following pages summarize what we know archaeologically about Native Californian societies in late precontact times. This synthesis should in no way discount the antiquity of Native presence in the region nor the validity of oral narratives as important windows into the past. As a matter of fact, they are often mutually reinforcing. As Kiliwa elder Rufino Ochurte remarked of his ancestors when relating traditional oral narratives, "The things they had been coming along doing, the way they lived, persist to the present. The places where they spit-roasted and ate are there. Their water jars are there still. Their mountains are there still" (Mixco 1983, 47).

Native Californians in Regional Perspective

When Europeans first encountered Native Californians, they typically noted two characteristics of the region's Indigenous people, both of which continue to structure the popular image of precontact California. First, Native Californians lived in small communities with minimal political hierarchy, and second, these communities supported themselves without recourse to agriculture, living off the bounty of the land and sea. While these observations have largely held up to the past century and a half of anthropological scrutiny, the realities of precontact life in California were in many cases more diverse and complex than early commenters realized. Here, I briefly examine recent research on five interrelated aspects of Native California in the late precontact era—political organization, subsistence economies, technology, ceremonial life, and conflict—that can highlight the structuring effects that precontact local political economies had for the unfolding of colonial encounters (Lightfoot et al. 2013b). After exploring these topics on a regional scale, I review the extant archaeological and ethnohistorical evidence for late precontact lifeways in the San Francisco Bay Area and northern Baja California.

Social-Political Organization

One of the most distinctive aspects of California prior to the arrival of Europeans was the sheer diversity of the Indigenous societies living there. By the late precontact era, the region was home to hundreds of independent hunting and gathering groups, distributed within several dozen major language families (Figure 1). Today, many people refer to Native Californian groups in general terms, typically as ethnic groups rooted in language classifications—terms such as Ohlone or Paipai—but these designations would have been functionally meaningless to people living in precontact times.

Throughout most of the region, Native people instead organized themselves into relatively small, autonomous land-holding units typically referred to as "tribelets." As envisioned by Alfred Kroeber (1932, 1962) and other early anthropologists, tribelets consisted of a primary village, which was often at the center of a broader territory containing stands of key plant resources, associated logistical sites, and other small hamlets or camps. The authority of political leaders was limited to the tribelet territory, which spanned a few hundred square kilometers and contained a population of between one hundred and five hundred individuals. Even within the territory of particular groups, the political authority of individual leaders was thought to have been weak. Of course, it must be stressed here that the classic tribelet model developed by Kroeber was the outgrowth of a very particular kind of research program. This work was based not on archaeological evidence but rather on the "memory culture" method of capturing supposedly untarnished and pure ethnographic data from elderly Native consultants who held information regarding precontact Indigenous lifeways (Lightfoot 2005, 32–33; Lightfoot and Parrish 2009, 78).

FIGURE 1. Map of Native Californian languages (after Lightfoot and Parrish 2009).

The term "tribelet" has recently fallen out of favor in some quarters due in part to its diminutive suffix and seemingly pejorative connotation (Leventhal et al. 1994) but also because many scholars feel it doesn't appropriately describe the political and social organization of Native Californian groups. One such critique emerged in the 1970s and stressed the hidden complexity of California's Indigenous polities (Bean and Blackburn 1976; Bean and King 1974). This research was spearheaded by anthropologist Lowell John Bean, who argued that the idea of Native Californians as living in the relatively simple small-scale societies described by Kroeber "has been replaced by a realization that they were peculiarly complex hunters-and-gatherers whose social systems were similar to those of peoples with presumably greater technological advances" (Bean 1976, 99). In this interpretation, tribelets were not isolated but were instead connected through ceremonial practices, economic relationships, and occasionally by political confederations. Bean and others also argued that Native communities were in fact subject to relatively complex social hierarchies, living under the rule of hereditary elites and their families who wielded considerable power over political, economic, and ceremonial life. Many groups also had spiritual leaders, bureaucrats, and craft specialists who enjoyed privileges greater than those afforded to the commoner classes (Bean 1976).

Recently, archaeologist Robert Bettinger (2015) has painted a still different picture of life in California in the centuries prior to the arrival of the Spanish. While Bettinger generally accepts the tribelet model proposed by Kroeber, he draws on a detailed review of archaeological and ethnographic data to examine the role of individuals and families in relation to the tribelet, which has over time come to signify a fairly cohesive political unit. Importantly, this new interpretation posits that tribelets operated not as unified societies living under a single leader, but rather as communities made up of a small number of loosely affiliated extended-family units. Families bonded together for mutual aid and protection, but the family—and not the tribelet—remained the most important vector of social identity.

This understanding of late precontact sociopolitical organization also introduces a temporal element by suggesting that the tribelet was in decline across much of the region at the onset of European colonialism. In the classic model developed by Kroeber and perpetuated for decades (Heizer and El-sasser 1980), tribelets were seen as internally oriented amalgamations of kin groups seeking to defend privately held resources and territory. As detailed by Bettinger, however, several relatively late developments, including the spread of shell-bead money and regional ceremonial complexes, prioritized multidirectional individual relationships at the expense of group cohesion.

These relationships were largely horizontal, promoting heterarchy, rather than vertical, promoting hierarchy. Thus, many Native Californian groups may have been in the process of rejecting the tribelet or village community in favor of widespread individualism by the eighteenth century (Bettinger 2015, 236–39). To Bettinger, these developments, which deemphasized social hierarchy despite relatively high population densities, might best be described as "orderly anarchy" (and see Allen et al. 2016 for a discussion of these points).

It is crucial to note here that Bettinger's analysis does not include the groups indigenous to the San Francisco Bay region or northern Baja California. Neither the Ohlone village communities of the Bay Area nor the Paipai-speaking patrilineal bands of the Sierra Juárez equaled the fully anarchic family groups that he describes for northwestern California and the Great Basin. Still, a key point to draw from recent debates about precontact sociopolitical organization in the region is that Native Californians did not live in an evolutionary eddy. Quite the contrary, in many areas of the broader region, they had developed relatively stable social institutions that favored small group size with minimal political hierarchy. These deceptively straightforward political formations had very real implications for how Native people interacted with particular colonial institutions, such as Franciscan missions that emphasized an ostensibly communal ethos or secular settlements that may have offered individuals the opportunity for unprecedented access to social prestige.

Subsistence Economies

Just as recent research has complicated the seemingly settled characterization of Native Californian political and social life, so too has a reexamination of Indigenous subsistence practices in California upended long-held beliefs. Many traditional accounts imagined California Indians as primitive peoples residing in a veritable Eden of wild plant and animal resources that supported a simple foraging lifestyle. Instead, new approaches point toward the complexity of Indigenous hunting and gathering practices across the region.

Beginning in the 1970s, the reexamination of Native Californian hunting and gathering practices proceeded in tandem with revisionist approaches to Indigenous political organization. Scholars such as Bean (Bean and Lawton 1976) and Florence Shipek (1977) argued that the political and social complexity they saw in the ethnographic and archaeological data was intimately tied to the intensification of subsistence practices, which increased yields and productivity of certain resources. This, in turn, resulted in surpluses that supported political and social complexity. Other researchers have focused less on the implications for sociopolitical structures and instead investigated the specific methods of how Native people actively managed the natural world to create anthropogenic landscapes (Anderson 2005; Blackburn and Anderson 1993). This research, based in large part on ethnographic information, details how Indigenous hunter-gatherers in California managed their environments through weeding, pruning, controlled burning, and in some cases, sowing and irrigation.

In the past decade, Lightfoot and other archaeologists have worked with various Native Californian tribal groups to take a fresh look at Indigenous subsistence and landscape management practices. Of crucial interest to this interdisciplinary team is the central role of fire in Native landscape management (Lightfoot and Parrish 2009; Lightfoot and Lopez 2013; Lightfoot et al. 2013a; Lightfoot and Cuthrell 2015). Current research suggests that Native Californian groups employed periodic, low-intensity burns to maintain a mosaic of different habitats at different stages of ecological succession within a single tribelet territory. This form of landscape management, dubbed "pyrodiversity" (Lightfoot and Parrish 2009), resulted in a rich patchwork of habitats available to members of a particular tribelet or village community. Still, hunting and gathering economies were not without risk. Some important resources, such as many species of oak that produce unpredictable acorn masts, could fail in a given year, and California is well known for its periodic climatic perturbations like droughts and El Niño events. Accordingly, most Native Californian groups stored important food resources as a buffer against risk at the same time that regional landscape management ensured a diverse array of plant and animal resources that they could draw on at different times of year or in the event of longer-term environmental changes.

The model put forth by Lightfoot and colleagues suggests that Native Californians employed a distinct approach to hunting and gathering. While they acknowledge some superficial similarities to agriculture—for example, the active management of the environment and the storage of surplus foodstuffs—these researchers make a clear distinction between the pyrodiversity practices of Native California and what others have seen as proto-agriculture. Lightfoot and Parrish stress that in contrast to farmers, "pyrodiversity practitioners emphasize resource diversification, landscape management at the regional scale, minimal seed sowing, flexible relationships with specific plant species and habitats, and relatively modest labor inputs throughout the year" (2009, 137). In other words, the subsistence economies of Native Californians were not on an evolutionary trajectory toward full-fledged agriculture; rather, the emerging picture of Indigenous landscape management reveals a distinct form of subsistence built upon particular relationships with plant and animal communities. These practices created what some might call "working land-scapes," which undermine the colonialist discourse of a precontact Californian Eden ripe for improvement or preservation by Euro-Americans (Diekmann et al. 2007).

In applying the pyrodiversity model to the late precontact period, two key points can be made. First, we now know that the highly productive environments described by early European observers were largely the result of active Indigenous management of the landscape. In particular, Indige-nous pyrodiversity practices would have resulted in a landscape encompass-ing highly diverse habitats even within relatively small tribelet territories. Second, these complex management practices extended beyond the staples—acorns, salmon, deer—recalled by Indigenous elders in twentieth-century eth-nographic interviews. Burning and other practices encouraged a wide variety of plant resources such as nuts, seeds, grasses, fruits, roots, and tubers, as well as animals that were attracted to them. Although scarcity and overharvesting were very real problems in late precontact times, the diversity of potential food resources nonetheless served as a buffer against the failure of any one particular resource and no doubt helped Native societies weather the peri-odic climatic events like droughts and El Niño cycles that continue to affect California. Similar strategies would prove useful during the disruptions of the colonial period.

Technology and Material Culture

Worldwide, hunters and gatherers are known for the relative simplicity of their lifestyles. Seasonally mobile people, in this train of thought, must make trade-offs between mobility and the accumulation of goods. To be sure, hunter-gatherer groups have developed strategies for minimizing the trans-portation of heavy or fragile objects. For example, many groups leave heavy stone milling equipment near particular resource patches and eschew pottery in favor of baskets, gourds, or other lighter and more durable containers. Yet, beyond these general observations, the richness of hunter-gatherer material culture is often overshadowed in archaeological and ethnographic accounts by the sophisticated technologies and craft specialization of agricultural societies.

As with hunting peoples around the globe, stone tools were a critical component of Native Californian technology. Throughout the region, In-digenous people manufactured tools from an array of raw materials. Many expedient tools were created from locally available stones, but carefully crafted projectile points, used to tip darts and arrows, required finer, more

easily controlled materials such as chert or obsidian. California boasts up-
wards of fifty discrete geological sources of obsidian, which Indigenous
people have used for millennia to fashion expedient cutting tools, numerous
types of projectile points, and impressively large blades for use in particular
ceremonies. Given its limited geological availability, only a small fraction of
the hundreds of late precontact village communities would have had ready
access to obsidian within their home territory. While some groups enjoyed
direct access to sources within the homelands of nearby communities speaking the same language (Basgall 1979), obsidian was more often conveyed
along far-flung exchange networks that cut across multiple linguistic and
geographic zones (Hughes and Milliken 2007; Jackson and Ericson 1994;
Panich et al. 2017).

Shell beads were also ubiquitous in Native California, having been used
from the earliest times. Among the most prevalent shell bead types in the late
precontact period are beads made from the shells of the olive snail (*Olivella*
ssp.) and those manufactured from various species of clam (e.g., *Saxidomus
nuttalli*, *Saxidomus giganteus*, and *Tresus nuttalli*). These two broad categories of shell beads—*Olivella* and clamshell—are linked to two distinct regional interaction spheres in late precontact times (Rosenthal 2011). *Olivella*
shell beads and similar beads made from the epidermis of the red abalone
(*Haliotis rufescens*) were manufactured in bulk in workshops along the Santa
Barbara Channel (Eerkens et al. 2005). Clamshell beads, in contrast, were
mass-produced by Indigenous people living north of San Francisco Bay. Shell
beads—particularly those crafted from *Olivella* shells—circulated widely
throughout California and into neighboring regions. In many parts of California, shell beads served as a form of currency, and Native people used beads
for the purchase of goods and services as well as to affirm individual status
in life and in death (Bennyhoff 1977; Gamble and King 2011; King 1990;
Smith and Fauvelle 2015).

Though most Native Californians did not produce pottery in precontact
times, Indigenous groups in several parts of the region did maintain ceramic
traditions of various forms. The most developed of these centered on the
southern deserts and adjacent coasts, where potters have produced largely
undecorated earthenware ceramics since approximately AD 1000. The Native
inhabitants of the eastern Sierra Nevada region also produced earthenware
vessels, a practice which appears to have spilled across the Sierra Crest and
into the western foothills of the Sierra Nevada range. Despite the lack of
ceramic pots in other areas, Native Californians used fired clay for everything
from figurines to artificial cooking "stones," demonstrating a familiarity with
the basic ideas behind ceramic technology (Dillon and Boxt 2013).

Of course, this focus on stone tools, shell ornaments, and pottery is biased toward the kinds of materials that preserve in the archaeological record. Ethnographic collections, including an amazing set of materials taken by European explorers in the early-to-mid-nineteenth century (e.g., Hudson and Bates 2015), attest to the impressive diversity of material culture items employed by Native Californians as well as the incredible range of objects made from organic materials that are typically missed by archaeologists due to preservation issues. Certainly, the region's elaborate basketry traditions largely obviated the need for ceramic vessels for cooking, storage, or other uses. Baskets also were indispensable for the practice of gathering and processing native plants and they played a central role in many ceremonies and ritual gift exchanges (Bibby 2012; Kroeber 1925; Shanks and Shanks 2006). Taken together, the archaeological and ethnographic data reject the notion of an impoverished material life and instead point toward enduring technological traditions into which Native people incorporated new items during the colonial period.

Ceremonial Life

Given the centrality of religious conversion in the Indigenous experience of missionization, it is also worth considering the role of religion and ceremony among California's precontact peoples. At the broadest level, Native Californians practiced animism, recognizing the spiritual power of landscapes, animals, and plants. Regionally, Native people participated in four major religious systems at the onset of colonialism. From north to south, they include the World Renewal religion of far northern California, the Kuksu complex of north-central California, and the *toloache* religions—Antap and Chinigchinich—of the south-central and southern coasts, respectively. In each area, these religions cut across tribelet and even language boundaries, simultaneously affirming the rights and obligations of individual communities while providing the philosophical and moral foundation of life at a regional scale. The religions involved complex public ceremonies, but initiation into each religions' secret societies was the purview of elite individuals or community leaders. These restrictions on knowledge suggest that the major religions developed from shamanic traditions, which remained important throughout the region, particularly in areas such as Baja California where local people were not incorporated into broader religious networks (Bean and Vane 1978).

The inner workings of the major Native Californian religions defy concise explanation, but an overview of the Kuksu religion serves as an example.

Often referred to as a "cult" because of its highly localized manifestations across north-central California, the Kuksu system consisted of high-status men and some women who led ceremonies involving dancing, singing, and curing that maintained balance and well-being for their people. These practitioners belonged to various secret societies—Kuksu, for which the complex is named, was just one—that conferred high status on their members. During ceremonies, which would typically be held in roundhouses, dancers would impersonate spirits by donning elaborate costumes. The most striking of these were the "Big Head" dancers who wore headgear with feather-tipped sticks that radiated outward in a circular or spherical fashion. The Kuksu religion also incorporated specialists, likely from a specific secret society, who impersonated ghosts and helped initiate young people. Despite the fact that participation in the Kuksu religion was associated with status, its practitioners were not necessarily political leaders and in some cases vied with them for power (Kroeber 1932; Loeb 1932, 1933).

Mourning ceremonies were also a major element of life in Native California. In addition to the mourning of deceased individuals at the time of their death, most groups also held annual mourning ceremonies in honor of all of those who had died in the previous year. Archaeologists have documented such ceremonies throughout southern California, demonstrating the prevalence of the mourning ceremony and its deep antiquity. The physical evidence indicates that ceremony participants destroyed the personal effects of the deceased, often by burning and/or burying them in a large pit located near the center of the village (Hull 2011, 2012; Hull et al. 2013). Early Euro-American observations of mourning ceremonies in central and northern California suggest that mourning ceremonies could last for several days and involved the destruction of shell beads and elaborate baskets. Such events could draw up to three hundred individuals (Gifford 1955; Kroeber 1925; Powers 1877).

Gift exchange was a central component of the four major Native Californian religions as well as local versions of mourning ceremonies practiced throughout the region. Neighboring groups who participated in a given ceremony would both give gifts to and receive materials from the host community. This reciprocity may have helped particular Native communities weather lean years or failed harvests and would have provided an opportunity to publicly affirm alliances between groups. Marriage, too, was a time for the exchange of materials. A prospective husband would offer a gift, typically shell beads, to the parents of his intended wife. If the gift was accepted, it was taken as a sign that the courtship could continue. Just as the giving of goods could forge bonds between two families, as in marriage, gifts could also help ease tensions or hostilities between groups—a fact that structured many early encounters with European newcomers (Bean and Vane 1978; Kroeber 1925). Thus, the long tradition of gift giving set the stage for how Native Californians received European newcomers at the same time that the importance of ceremony for cementing bonds between generations helped them cope with the impacts of colonialism.

Conflict

A final consideration is the role of interpersonal and intergroup violence in Native California. As with political organization and landscape management, scholars have recently revisited the archaeological and ethnographic records in search of a better understanding of the dynamics of violence and warfare in precontact California. The investigation of past conflict among Native Americans can be ethically and politically challenging—in no small part because such research typically relies on the study of human skeletal remains—but the patterns that emerge help to contextualize the sometimes violent resistance Indigenous people put up against the imposition of colonial rule.

Using large-scale databases on Indigenous burials unearthed during archaeological projects in different parts of California, researchers have sought temporal or spatial patterns in the prevalence of different kinds of skeletal trauma. At a general level, these data support the idea that interpersonal violence was associated with resource scarcity and related concepts of territorial ownership (Allen 2012). For example, studies indicate that much of the violence along the Santa Barbara Channel during the period between AD 300 and 1500 was related to drought conditions, with a spike during the Medieval Climatic Anomaly (Jones and Schwitalla 2008). Interestingly, the latter event does not seem to have affected violence in central California, where rates of different forms of skeletal trauma have their own temporal and geographic variation (Pilloud et al. 2014; Schwitalla et al. 2014). Technological changes such as the introduction of the bow and arrow also appear to have impacted the organization of conflict and resultant rates of skeletal trauma across the region.

Within these broad patterns, new laboratory techniques, such as stable isotope analysis, have allowed scholars to tease out the cultural significance of apparent anomalies in the bioarchaeological data. In central California, for example, archaeologists have long noted disarticulated human crania and burials without crania in deposits dating to the Early Period (ca. 2500–500 BC). Originally thought to represent "trophies" taken from enemies during episodes of violent conflict, new isotopic research suggests at least some of these striking examples may actually represent ancestor veneration (Eerkens et al. 2016).

Research in this vein forces scholars to carefully consider the cultural contexts of the bioarchaeological record and not to simply project our current Western understandings of violence and mortuary practices onto past societies.

Taken together, bioarchaeological findings suggest that Native Californians had a capacity for violence equal to that of hunter-gatherers living in other times and places. Yet to say, as many previous researchers have implied, that the region's Native people "lived under the constant shadow of violent death from warfare" (Mathes 2011, 1) contradicts the evidence. Rates of violence ebbed and flowed across time and throughout the region in line with cultural practices and technological changes, often with resource scarcity as an underlying factor. To the participants themselves, it is likely that precontact violence was understood as a necessary part of territorial maintenance, a practice still recalled by elders well into the twentieth century (Bauer 2016b, 74–75). The culturally situated possibilities of violent conflict and its causes, such as trespass, had clear implications for the centuries of interactions between Native Californians and Euro-Americans.

○

This brief overview of life in precontact California sets the backdrop for the more detailed look at Indigenous life in the San Francisco Bay Area and the Sierra Juárez of northern Baja California. The culture histories of these regions fit within the general parameters described previously, but Native people in each area developed their own unique traditions and solutions to life's various challenges. As with the background on Native California as a whole, I focus on the centuries immediately preceding the onset of Euro-American colonialism but with the recognition that the patterns of the late precontact period have important antecedents going back millennia.

Situating Native Life in the San Francisco Bay Area

Surviving oral narratives provide the long-term context for the foundations of Indigenous life in central California. For example, Muwekma Ohlone elder Susana Nichols related a story about the first people to anthropologist John Peabody Harrington in the early twentieth century. She described how Coyote made people from the top of Mount Diablo after the flood, "For now the world was set, and he wanted people." Yet, Coyote thought he had only been dreaming of his children, "and when the people came out, talking, shouting, singing, he got scared. He didn't know where the people had come from, but he made them, he thought them up, they say" (Harrington 1984, reel 71, 517; and see Ortiz 1994, 125–26).

Other Muwekma elders described the creation of several key geographic features of the San Francisco Bay Area. Speaking to Harrington, Angela Colos (María de los Angeles Colos) and José Guzman told how Coyote, in mourning for his son, crashed through bedrock, creating distinctive "natural stone houses" in the Coast Ranges near Mount Diablo (Harrington 1984, reel 37, 502–503). They further related the exploits of Kaknú, a mythical raptor who defeated a man with a body of stone. "The *peñascos* (rock outcroppings) of all the earth are the stones that went from his body when killed" (Harrington 1984, reel 36, 625). Kaknú's deeds also relate to the presence on the landscape of natural salt and red pigment, the latter of which was created by Kaknú's own blood after he was killed by "Doña Vibora," or Rattlesnake Woman (Harrington 1984, reel 36, 625–47; and see Ortiz 1994). Surely only a small sample of what was once a broad corpus of Ohlone oral narratives, these and other tales provided by Nichols, Colos, and Guzman suggest a deep and abiding familiarity with the landscape and the way it came to be.

Archaeologists too have documented long-term connections between Indigenous people and the San Francisco Bay Area. Based on more than a century of painstaking research, they have developed complex cultural-historical schemes to account for the material evidence dating to different periods of precontact life in the region (Milliken et al. 2007, 101–105). To isolate the cultural antecedents of the Indigenous people who first encountered Euro-American colonists in the San Francisco Bay region, we can look to what has been dubbed the "Middle-Late Transition," or MLT. It was during this time, around AD 1000, that many of the hallmarks of what we now consider Ohlone culture—an intensified acorn-based subsistence economy, the florescence of material culture, and characteristic social-political organization—first appear in the archaeological record. Charting these archaeological patterns as they developed across the MLT and Late Period (ca. AD 1000–1770), combined with judicious use of ethnohistorical and ethnographic data, offers the general outlines of social and political life in the late precontact era (Levy 1978; Milliken 2007).

At a broad scale, it seems likely that the region was home to village communities that numbered roughly three hundred people, meaning that these groups included multiple, unrelated kin-based groups under the nominal leadership of a single individual, or "captain." Within this general pattern, marked variation existed across the broader central California region. Some groups were patrilineal, others matrilineal, and still others—particularly groups on the San Francisco peninsula—practiced ambilocal residence

(Milliken 2007, 56–57). Based on the analysis of early European accounts and mission registers, the population density of the core San Francisco Bay Area may have been as high as six persons per square mile (Milliken 1995, 19–21)

Ohlone living in the centuries directly before the onset of Euro-American colonialism fit the model of pyrodiversity collectors. That is, they exploited diverse natural resources from permanent or semi-permanent village settlements, actively managing various resource patches in their home territories. In the San Francisco Bay region, Native people enjoyed easy access to resources within three broadly defined environments: tidal marshlands, grassland prairies, and oak woodlands, each with its own assortment of economically important flora and fauna (Hylkema 2002, 235–36). Along the shores of the bay, ancestral Ohlone and Miwok groups constructed monumental shell mounds, employing waste shell from thousands of meals to raise village sites out of the high tide zone. Tule reed boats, called *balsas*, facilitated fishing and the hunting of shorebirds while anthropogenic fire regimes enhanced the productivity of the nearby grasslands. Oak woodlands were particularly productive, offering the staple acorn harvests that sustained many communities in late precontact times. Connecting these diverse zones, various waterways offered still more resources, such as anadromous and freshwater fish (see Lightfoot and Parrish 2009, 210–50). Thus, although acorns may correctly be considered to have been the cornerstone of the Indigenous diet, archaeological and ethnohistorical evidence suggests that precontact Ohlone used a wide array of plant and animal species including grasses, sea otters, and deer (Hylkema 2002, 252–54).

Technologically, the late-precontact period was a time of major innovation. Native people, for example, widely adopted the bow and arrow, which had far-reaching implications for the organization of obsidian conveyance and manufacturing as well as interpersonal violence (Milliken et al. 2007, 117; Schwitalla et al. 2014). Archaeologists also note the development of new forms of stone mortars and pipes. But perhaps the most striking—and most studied—development is the proliferation of shell beads and ornaments into dozens of discernable types that archaeologists use for the precise cross-dating of particular sites and for insights into trade networks, regional interaction, and social complexity.

In the southern San Francisco Bay Area, for example, sites dating to the MLT have yielded massive quantities of *Olivella* shell beads. During that time, shell beads and other artifacts such as *Haliotis* pendants were distributed relatively evenly among deceased individuals, in one case totaling over thirty-four thousand beads from a single site. In later centuries, beads and other high status burial goods began to be highly concentrated among just a few individuals, a pattern that seems to reflect the concentration of wealth among only certain members of a given village (Bellifemine 1997; Hylkema 2007, 415; Milliken et al. 2007, 111). However, researchers have noted a slow decrease in *total* mortuary wealth, as inferred by shell bead lots, during the Late Period. This may align with Bettinger's (2015) recent suggestion that the tribelet model of political organization was collapsing across the region, resulting in the diminishment of mortuary practices that celebrated individual status (but see Milliken and Bennyhoff 1993). Whatever the cause, the archaeological record suggests that widespread transformations were occurring in the late precontact era, around AD 1500 (Milliken et al. 2007, 117–18).

It is also during this time that ethnographically documented ceremonial systems appear to have formed. For example, at site CA-SCL-690, which dates to the MLT, archaeologists recovered the earliest southern San Francisco Bay examples of distinctive pendants that may be related to the Kuksu religion (Hylkema 2007). Though variations exist throughout the region, these *Haliotis* pendants seem to represent the Kuksu religion's "big head" dancers, with small legs and enormous circular heads (Figure 2) (Bennyhoff 1994; Fredrickson 1994, 100; Gifford 1947:2; Hylkema 2002, 260–61; Leventhal 1993). From its beginnings around AD 1000, the Kuksu religion facilitated

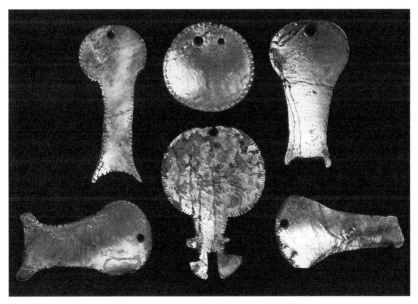

FIGURE 2. Abalone (*Haliotis*) shell pendants from site CA-ALA-329, a shell mound along the southeastern shores of San Francisco Bay. Photo by Joe Cavaretta for the Muwekma Ohlone Tribe. Courtesy of Alan Leventhal and the Muwekma Ohlone Tribal Council.

connections that cut across village communities and language boundaries in the greater San Francisco Bay Area. At its fullest extent in the years before the onset of colonialism, the broad connections offered by the Kuksu complex may have undermined the authority of tribelet chiefs and hastened the disintegration of the already tenuous inter-familial alliances that characterize the classic tribelet model (Bettinger 2015).

Adding to the complicated picture of Indigenous social and political organization in the late precontact period, many archaeologists have posited that San Francisco Bay region was the scene of relatively intense conflict before the arrival of Europeans (Allen 2012, 203). Schwitalla et al. (2014) examined data from nearly seventeen thousand Native American burials excavated in central California, looking for evidence of interpersonal violence such as blunt force trauma or sharp force trauma. During the period between AD 1390 and 1720, roughly 12 percent of individuals suffered some form of major interpersonal violence, with males and females enduring similar rates of blunt force trauma and males being at significantly higher risk for sharp force or projectile trauma (Schwitalla et al. 2014, 75–78). This violence, which represents an increase from previous periods, was likely related to the social and political changes noted in other parts of the archaeological record.

Archaeological evidence for late precontact societies of the San Francisco Bay Area points toward well-defined cultural practices, economic strategies, and religious and political institutions that had developed *in situ* for centuries. Small in absolute size, these communities nevertheless maintained regional connections that tied them together in various ways. The manufacture of diverse and increasingly specialized material culture required access to materials outside of any given community's territory, at the same time that broadly distributed ceremonial practices, such as the Kuksu religion, connected individuals across community boundaries. These connections, however, may have also worked against hierarchical political structures and social inequality. The advent of shell bead money undermined any existing hierarchical relationships based on inherited status, and participation in the Kuksu religion may have allowed individuals to accrue status in ways that sidestepped, and served to erode, the social structure of the traditional California village community, or tribelet. These changes structured many of the encounters of the early colonial period.

Situating Native Life in Northern Baja California

Like the San Francisco Bay Area, the northern region of Baja California has long been at the crossroads of Indigenous interaction. The antecedents of the cultural traditions common to the Paipai and their neighbors are present in developments in the Lower Colorado River Valley starting around AD 500. There, Native people began producing pottery and switched from using the atlatl to the bow and arrow, perhaps representing populations moving west out of the Hohokam culture area in Arizona and Sonora (Shackley 2004; Shaul and Andresen 1989; Shaul and Hill 1998). Scholars have grouped the various peoples who populated the region during this time as the Patayan complex. Over the next few centuries, the use of ceramics and other cultural traditions associated with the Patayan spread to the Peninsular Ranges of southern California and northern Baja California, and the number and size of archaeological sites in the region increased markedly. The period from AD 1500 onward represents the full geographical extent of the Patayan, characterized by well-defined logistical organization, the formation of aggregated settlements, and elaboration of ceramic technology (Hildebrand and Hagstrum 1995, 91; Porcayo Michelini 2018a; Shackley 1998, 631; Warren 1984, 415–20; Waters 1982).

The Patayan complex, however, masks what was a fairly diverse cultural landscape, represented by the various Yuman-speaking groups who occupied the Lower Colorado and neighboring uplands at the time of contact with Europeans. For our purposes, a central question is how the Paipai came to reside in the Sierra Juárez of northern California even though their closest linguistic relatives—the Yavapai, Walapai, and Havasupai—occupy lands in northwestern Arizona. Regional archaeological evidence suggests a divergence sometime shortly after the core attributes of the Patayan archaeological complex first appear in the archaeological record, circa AD 500 (Laylander 2015). In this scenario, the ancestral Pai groups may have resided along the resource-rich Lake Cahuilla, which periodically filled the Salton Trough, only to be driven apart by events such as the drying of the ancient lake circa AD 1200. This model requires further testing but it roughly aligns to Walapai and Yavapai oral traditions that relate how certain groups split off in ancient times (Wilken 1992). Over the intervening centuries, the Paipai rooted themselves in the region and developed close relationships with their neighbors who shared similar cultural traditions despite speaking different languages.

Yet, as in the San Francisco Bay region, language groups obscure still finer social and political distinctions. The major ethnolinguistic groups of twenty-first-century northern Baja California—Paipai, Kumeyaay, Cucapá, and Kiliwa—did not exist as unified polities in precontact times. Before the arrival of Europeans, the basic social unit among the region's Indigenous population was the family band. In this region, extended family groups appear to have mapped into named patrilineal clans, called *shimuls* in the local Indigenous languages (Bendímez Patterson 2008, 21–22; Flores Hernández and Pérez Rivas 2018; Hicks 1963, 43; Laylander 1987, 355–66; Meigs 1939, 16; Owen 1965, 677). While some variations no doubt existed (Shipek 1982), a shimul was typically exogamous and each appears to have maintained its own autonomous homeland (Wilken-Robertson and Laylander 2006, 77). Precontact shimuls contained perhaps as many as one hundred individuals, with varying population densities contingent on the availability of food resources and access to water. The core Paipai homelands of the Sierra Juárez supported perhaps 0.8 to 1.0 persons per square mile (Hicks 1963, 56; Meigs 1935, 140).

Individual shimul territories contained a majority of the group's plant and animal needs and were organized to take advantage of seasonal differences in food resources within a diverse array of ecological zones. Most groups could rely on at least one plant staple—such as agave, mesquite, or acorns—within their core territory, supplementing them with cacti, seeds, fruits, and small game. Potable water was also an important resource, given the arid conditions of the region (Hicks 1963; Hildebrand and Hagstrum 1995; Lightfoot and Parrish 2009, 341–63). Like elsewhere in California, the Native people of the Sierra Juárez actively managed the landscape to enhance productivity, although specific details are lacking for the Paipai. However, there is ample ethnographic evidence that the Kumeyaay used controlled burning for a full suite of landscape management purposes (Shipek 1993), and fire ecology studies point toward late precontact anthropogenic burning in the Sierra San Pedro Mártir, just to the south of the Sierra Juárez (Evett et al. 2007; Stephens et al. 2003).

These patterns are also described by Kiliwa elder Rufino Ochurte in his creation narrative. Following the list of resources created by Earth-Person—the deer, jackrabbits, agave, and chia—described previously, he related:

> With those we maintained ourselves scattered over the mountains. Each one of the bands had its cave. They each owned water holes, and also had possession of mountains and dwelt there. And so further on, others likewise went about living in the same way. Caves they owned and trails; so it was for all the tribes hereabouts. Each water hole was owned; their mountains are there, that's how they did it; further on it went in the same way and on and on [Earth-Person] named them. He filled this land. There were people in these mountains. To the East, to the West here; from here they extended to the South. All the way to Land's End. Nothing but pagans. Indians. There was not a single foreigner. (Mixco 1983, 46–47)

Ochurte's narrative is clearly placed in contemporary times, given the past tense and his use of the term "pagans" (translated from a Kiliwa word meaning "unwashed," or unbaptized). However, the fact that he is speaking about the creation of the world also serves to underscore the antiquity of the cultural patterns he describes: the relatively crowded landscape, the territoriality of each group, and the resources such as water and shelter necessary for survival (and see Gifford and Lowie 1928 for a similar Paipai narrative).

Even though political entities greater than the band or shimul were rare in the region, few clearly defined cultural distinctions can be drawn between named clans or even between larger language groups (Hicks 1963, 44). This broad distribution of cultural practices within and between language families probably has its roots in the exogamous nature of the patrilineal, and usually patrilocal, shimuls. Because women who married into a given clan would often speak a different dialect, language diversity was likely the norm. Children, in this scenario, would have spoken multiple dialects and have been exposed to the cultural traditions of both parents. A further blending can be seen in the presence of lineage names claimed by more than one language group (Field 2012, 563; Owen 1965, 677–79).

Regional ceremonial and economic patterns also played a role in maintaining the broadly shared cultural practices of the Sierra Juárez. Mourning ceremonies, for example, likely served as opportunities for members of different shimuls to interact. These ceremonies have deep roots in the region and, by the colonial period, involved large fiestas given to commemorate those who died over a particular period of time (Hohenthal 2001, 267–71; Meigs 1939, 57–59; Porcayo Michelini and Rojas Chávez 2018; Michelsen and Owen 1967). Members of particular shimuls, moreover, regularly traveled outside their home territories to obtain geographically circumscribed resources, such as piñon (which only occurs at higher elevations) or the marine resources of the Pacific and Gulf of California coasts (Hicks 1963, 201; Meigs 1939, 21).

Archaeological data also suggest that regional networks facilitated the conveyance of highly valued raw materials, such as obsidian, throughout particular ethnolinguistic provinces and possibly farther afield (Flores Hernández and Pérez Rivas 2018; Gay et al. 2017; Panich et al. 2015; Panich et al. 2017). Nevertheless, most late precontact archaeological sites of the southern Sierra Juárez reveal a relatively restricted toolkit, characterized by ceramic vessels, flaked stone tools, and grinding implements and bedrock features (Hicks 1959; McKusick and Gilman 1959; Porcayo Michelini 2018a; Treganza 1942). Pottery is the distinguishing technological tradition, particularly since the Paipai and their neighbors are some of the few Native Californian groups whose ancestors produced ceramic vessels in precontact times (Figure 3). Artisans thinned vessels using the paddle-and-anvil technique and fired them in uncontrolled, low-temperature settings. Decoration is rare, but by the time of contact with

FIGURE 3. Ceramic bowl from a precontact site in Paipai territory. Courtesy of Antonio Porcayo Michelini, Centro INAH Baja California.

Europeans, ceramic forms included vessels for storage, cooking, and serving, as well as various other forms such as pipes and effigies (Van Camp 1979; Panich and Wilken-Robertson 2013; Porcayo Michelini 2013, 2018b; Wilken 1987). Regional data indicate that the prevalence of ceramics rose steadily in the late precontact era, perhaps indicating the growing importance of plant foods that could be stored (Hildebrand and Hagstrum 1995).

Given the limited amount of archaeological work conducted in the Sierra Juárez, little evidence exists for the particulars of conflict in the late precontact period. However, previous researchers have used ethnographic and ethnohistoric information to provide a general overview (e.g., Hicks 1963; Hohenthal 2001). Intergroup violence was relatively rare, but as recalled by Paipai elder Benito Peralta, "In those days the Indians would fight for different reasons, sometimes over wild foods" (Wilken-Robertson 2000, 3). Thus, motivations included access to resources and territorial infringement but also murder, marital infidelities, or witchcraft. Men were the primary combatants, armed with the wooden war club or bow and arrow. Some vengeance killings apparently escalated into long-running feuds between particular shimuls and may have led to the formation of some military, if not political, alliances between members of multiple lineages. Overall, however, intergroup violence appears to have resulted in only isolated deaths and sustained hostilities were probably rare.

As elsewhere in the Americas, Native people lived in northern Baja California for millennia prior to the arrival of Euro-Americans. Several lines of evidence suggest that Paipai-speaking people arrived in the region relatively recently though they quickly became integrated into the broader social landscape. At the heart of this sociocultural network was the shimul around which life and identity was organized. Due to the practice of exogamous marriage, members of particular shimuls could be found throughout the region, leading to a common set of cultural trappings despite differences in language. Further connecting the region's small polities were widely distributed economic networks that moved resources such as shell beads and obsidian across great distances. Communal economic pursuits like piñon harvesting brought together members of multiple groups as did ceremonial obligations such as those required for mourning. Like Native people throughout California, the Indigenous inhabitants of the Sierra Juárez developed non-hierarchical social and political institutions that nonetheless allowed for a notable degree of regional integration. These patterns helped determine how they dealt with the first waves of European newcomers.

Summary

The preceding discussion is meant to provide a general understanding of the broad contours of Native California in the centuries prior to the onset of colonialism and to illustrate how the groups that eventually became known as the Ohlone and Paipai fit within them. These sketches, however, should not be understood as static baselines against which the subsequent changes in each area can be measured. Instead, we can examine how the late precontact political and economic contexts of each area structured Native people's negotiations of the early colonial impositions that were to follow (Lightfoot et al. 2013b). In other words, not only were the patterns evident for the late precontact period structured by what came before but they also structured what came next. As we move forward in time to the next chapter, what are the major implications for how Native life in late precontact California structured the initial colonial encounters?

For the regions of interest, it seems likely that political organization was subsumed in social organization. In the Bay Area, the village community, consisting of multiple extended family units, was probably the norm. However, the sharp decline in mortuary wealth in the years just before contact suggests that Native polities there may have been undergoing the same decentralizing shifts as other parts of the region (Bettinger 2015). In the Sierra Juárez, social organization was the extended family, with the shimul system similar in form to the ethnographically documented family band of the Great Basin (Owen 1965). Thus, the importance of specific individuals or families in the context of Bay Area village communities and the prominence of family bands in the Sierra Juárez suggests that Native Californians were predisposed to deal with outsiders in ways that favored the interests of particular individuals or their kin and not necessarily the broader community or ethnolinguistic group. In other words, the existing patterns of social-political organization in the Bay Area and the Sierra Juárez would lead us to expect that Native people approached early colonial encounters in heterogeneous ways.

The evidence also suggests that Native people in both regions were intimately tied to place. As demonstrated by both archaeology and oral narratives, the ancestors of the Ohlone and Paipai were advanced students of the landscape. They relied on their territory to sustain them year in and year out, kept close track of the seasonal availability of key food and raw material resources, and imbued the landscape with meaning. Sustained Euro-American colonialism had profound ecological effects across California, but Native Californians may have drawn on their knowledge of local landscapes to adapt more quickly than previously acknowledged to environmental change. Further, the closely packed cultural landscapes likely meant that flight was not a viable option during the early colonial period, though this equation changed with time and demographic shifts. The relatively high rates of violence evident in the archaeological record for central California likely relate to the propensity of Indigenous people to defend their territories against encroachment by outsiders.

Yet, social relationships were broader than the "extraordinary localism" applied to Native Californians by previous researchers (Heizer and Elsasser 1980). In the Bay Area, the Kuksu religion connected people far and wide, while in Baja California, Native people frequently left their lineage territories to visit the coasts, harvest piñon, or attend mourning ceremonies. In both regions, moreover, widespread economic networks enabled the flow of materials such as shell beads and obsidian across ethnolinguistic and community boundaries. As with the general contours of political organization, these connections suggest that some Native Californians would have been cautiously open to the new ideas and materials brought to the region by outsiders. This openness, however, did not flow from the inherent superiority of Euro-American technology or beliefs but from the relatively cosmopolitan nature of Native California. Despite having small populations in well-defined territories, particular Indigenous groups regularly maintained connections with their neighbors and more distant communities. Each group, moreover, had a long history during which it dealt with outsiders, faced adversity, and weathered the unpredictable. It was this dynamic context into which the first European explorers arrived in the sixteenth century.

2

Native Worlds and European Arrivals

IN THE SPRING OF 1769, Paipai-speaking families watched cautiously as two parties of foreigners passed through their territories. These outsiders included Franciscan missionaries and Spanish colonial soldiers who were moving northward to colonize Alta California. Though the expeditions incorporated Native people recruited from missions farther south on the Baja California peninsula, direct verbal communication was nearly impossible, making the situation particularly tense. The Paipai observers were probably relieved to see that the foreigners, who also brought with them large numbers of animals and supplies, appeared to be passing through on their way to some other place. Stories of similar visitors who had long been a presence across the Colorado River to the east and others who had periodically appeared along the Pacific Coast, underscored the unpredictable nature of such incursions. Most of the outsiders, the Paipai knew, came bearing gifts but they had also proven themselves quick to attack at the slightest sign of resistance. Still others appeared to be suffering from unusual maladies. The arrival of the Spanish in 1769, then, was not necessarily surprising—indeed, news of their northward advance was disseminated faster than the slow pack trains could travel—but the local Paipai knew to keep a watchful eye on them.

When the second group appeared, one man decided to approach the visitors. His real name is unknown, but Franciscan missionary Junípero Serra called him El Baylón, or The Dancer. In keeping with common practice, the Spanish offered this man food but initially he refused. Serra writes that the man danced around the food to make it edible, a request that the Spanish allowed with much amusement. The Dancer motioned to the newcomers that they should include more and more items to the pile around which he was dancing before he eventually changed course and proceeded to dance around the entirety of the Spanish provisions. Dancing complete, the man apparently relaxed and agreed to eat. He communicated that the other Spanish party had passed through the same area previously and estimated that Serra and his group had four and a half days travel between them and their destination in San Diego. Yet, just as Serra began daydreaming of the future moment when he could baptize The Dancer, the man grabbed his stick and rattle—the paraphernalia of a ceremonial leader—and returned to the hills (Serra 1955, 91).

Perhaps the man sensed the implications of Serra's intent and decided to retreat before the missionary could initiate him into the unknowns of a foreign religion and a radically different social order. Or perhaps Serra misunderstood what he had witnessed. It is unlikely that the man merely wanted something to eat, particularly since Native Californians did not take quickly to Euro-American foods. Rather, viewed from the perspective of local Indigenous groups, it is more plausible that the man whom Serra called El Baylón was hoping to shield his kin from the interlopers who seemed intent on cutting across tightly guarded tribal territories and whose predecessors had already shown violent intent toward local residents. The dances he performed were not for the amusement of the Spanish but may instead have been intended to harm them in some way (Beebe and Senkewicz 2015, 188). The study of the first contacts between Europeans and Indigenous people—written largely from the outsiders' perspective—is hindered by such misunderstandings. In this chapter, I attempt to piece together how such events may have been perceived by Native Californians.

First Contacts

Early Coastal Encounters, 1540–1603

Despite the cultural diversity of its Indigenous peoples, for over two centuries, Europeans thought of California as a single geographical entity. This land extended from the southernmost tip of the Baja California peninsula at Cabo San Lucas to the northern *frontera*, a line that crept steadily northward into the region that came to be known as Alta California. The initial exploration of the peninsula occurred just years after the fall of Tehnochtitlán during a time when conquistadors were the main colonial ambassadors of the Crown. Explorations of the northwest coast of Mexico began in 1523, and within a decade a Spanish ship, the *Concepción*, had made landfall in the Bay of La Paz in Baja California Sur. Local Pericues were openly hostile to the newcomers, apparently killing some twenty crew members and quickly forcing the rest back to sea. Nevertheless, reports of pearls and other riches from the shore party resonated with Spanish explorers, driving further investigation of the region including a short-lived colony founded by Hernán Cortés in 1535 (Crosby 1994, 4; Engstrand 1997, 80–81).

Other voyages soon followed, intended to provide the Spanish Crown with a clearer understanding of California's geography. These included Francisco de Ulloa's exploration of the Baja California peninsula in 1539–1540; the voyage of Juan Rodríguez Cabrillo in 1542, during which his ships may have ventured as far north as what is today Oregon; and the expedition led by Sebastian Vizcaíno that explored most of the coast along Alta and Baja California in 1602–1603. The noted Englishman Francis Drake sailed along the California coast in 1579, stopping for more than a month somewhere near Point Reyes, just north of San Francisco, to secure supplies and repair his ship. Though isolated, these encounters involved large multiethnic crews comprised of between 100 and 250 individuals and members of various Native Californian groups (Engstrand 1997; Lightfoot and Simmons 1998; Wagner 1929).

As the Spanish expanded their presence in the Pacific to the Philippines in the mid-sixteenth century, colonial officials became interested in establishing a California port to service the Manila galleons on their long homeward journeys. The first known stopover of a ship sailing from Manila took place in 1587, when a vessel under the command of Pedro de Unamuno landed near what is today Morro Bay, California. Less than a decade later, Sebastian Rodríguez Cermeño made landfall near Point Reyes while exploring the coast on the return trip from the Philippines. His ship, the *San Agustín*, sank there during a storm. The crew made the return trip to Mexico in a small launch but the loss of the cargo incited royal officials to prohibit further exploration of the California coast by Manila galleons (Engstrand 1997, 90; Lightfoot and Simmons 1998, 141–42). For the following two centuries, most galleon crews steered their vessels southward to their home port of Acapulco once the first signs of land were spotted (Brown 2001, 19–21).

No other vessels are known to have landed in California as part of the Manila trade, and the Vizcaíno voyage of 1602–1603 was the last documented maritime exploration that reached the Alta California coast for more than 165 years. However, other early contacts may have occurred between Euro-Americans and Native Californians. Given that one or two galleons plied the California coast annually from the 1560s through the 1810s, it is possible—even likely—that there were other, undocumented landfalls prior to the establishment of permanent colonies (Erlandson et al. 2001, 14–15). After the months-long journey across the Pacific, Manila galleon crews would have been weary and in need of firewood and fresh water. Given the prohibitions, captains may have simply not recorded clandestine stops in California. Though historians have compiled some tantalizing clues (Brown 2001, 29), such encounters are lost to time barring a future archaeological or archival discovery. For the others described previously, varying levels of documentation exist, providing some insight into the implications of early contacts for California's Indigenous societies (Lightfoot and Simmons 1998).

Establishing a Colonial Presence, 1697–1773

The Spanish missions of California are today the most visible remnants of the region's colonial past, but like Native Californian societies, their histories represent complex intersections between local and global phenomena. It is worth mentioning from the outset that the very form of colonialism in California was a reaction to the existing political economies of its Indigenous inhabitants. The mission institution, as manifested in California, was refined over decades of work by various religious orders and their royal sponsors intent on bringing Indigenous people under colonial control. Hunting and gathering peoples, like Native Californians, proved to be the most resistant to these efforts, effectively bending the will of empire to meet them, at least partially, on their own terms (Jackson and Castillo 1995; Thomas 2014; Wade 2008). The full implications of the missions for Native Californians will be explored in the following chapter; here, I offer a brief overview of how the mission system was established in Alta and Baja California.

In October 1697, Jesuit missionary Juan María de Salvatierra founded the first permanent colony in California, Mission Nuestra Señora de Loreto (Figure 4). This establishment, in the southern portion of the Baja California peninsula, followed more than a century and a half of failed attempts to establish colonial outposts in that region. Over the course of the next seventy years, the Jesuits established nearly twenty missions and a large number of *visitas*, outlying chapels occasionally visited by the padres. These hinterland outstations were designed in part to familiarize Native peoples with the Christian faith and European lifeways so that they might one day join the flocks at one of the central missions. There were also practical reasons for the Jesuit reliance on visitas—the missions could not support large populations due to poor conditions for agriculture. During the Jesuit period, then, the majority of Baja Californians continued to live in their Native *rancherías*, or villages, where they maintained their cultural practices and traditional modes of subsistence (Aschmann 1959, 234).

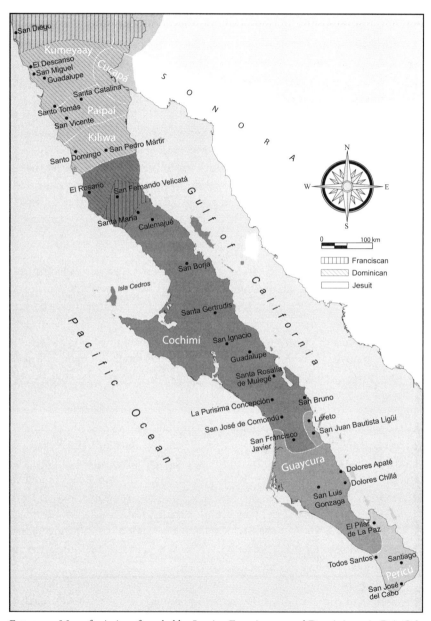

FIGURE 4. Map of missions founded by Jesuits, Franciscans, and Dominicans in Baja California with approximate ethnolinguistic boundaries (after Laylander 1997 and Meigs 1935).

King Carlos III expelled the Jesuits from all of their holdings in New Spain in June 1767, following a broader pattern of suppression aimed at limiting their influence. In the Californias, the Native people of the southern and central portions of the Baja California peninsula had felt the Jesuit presence most keenly. Beyond the loss of territory, the Indigenous population fell dramatically during the Jesuit period due to the synergistic effects of disease and structural violence (Jackson 1981). The Jesuits also sent expeditions northward, including those led by Eusebio Kino, Fernando Consag, and Wenceslao Linck, all of which explored the upper reaches of the Gulf of California (Crosby 1994; Hohenthal 2001, 4–6). The effects, if any, of those expeditions for Native people living beyond the reach of the missions are unknown. By as late as 1767, many Indigenous groups, the Ohlone and Paipai among them, had witnessed few direct impacts of colonialism, despite 250 years of contact between Native Californians and Europeans. The next 250 years, however, proved to be much different.

With the expulsion of the Jesuits, the Franciscan order was called to advance the mission field and to secure California against competing colonial interests. Under the leadership of Junípero Serra, the Franciscans quickly began to undertake their task of pushing the frontera northward to San Diego and beyond. To do so, they built their first and only mission in Baja California, San Fernando de Velicatá, near the 30th parallel (Rojas Chávez and Porcayo Michelini 2015; Sauer and Meigs 1927). However, Serra and the Franciscans did not linger in Baja California and instead leapfrogged the northern peninsula to concentrate their efforts in the vast, largely uncharted territory of Alta California. In 1769, a pair of ships and two overland parties moved northward to San Diego (Hackel 2013, 150–51). After leaving the familiar environs of Cochimí territory in the central peninsula, the expeditions passed through the lands of Kiliwa, Paipai, and Kumeyaay groups. The Franciscans founded their first Alta California mission in San Diego, among the Kumeyaay, in July 1769. In the following years, they explored coastal California as far north as the Ohlone homelands of the San Francisco Bay region, establishing more missions and coming into contact with Native people who had likely never seen Europeans before (Figure 5).

During the time that Serra and his Franciscans were making a name for themselves in Alta California, Dominican missionaries quietly took over the mission field in Baja California. Though their arrival on the peninsula was delayed by hardships, including a shipwreck and the death of their leader, the Dominicans were ready to begin missionary work by early 1773. They were responsible for continuing the overland trail system, the Camino Real,

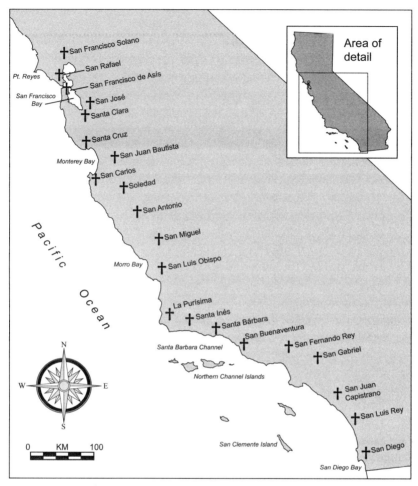

FIGURE 5. Map of the Franciscan missions of Alta California and other places mentioned in text.

north from San Fernando Velicatá to the southernmost Alta California mission at San Diego, filling in all the necessary missions and colonial outposts in between (Meigs 1935; Neiser 1960). The overland trail was important to both religious orders because expeditions from the eastern colonies of New Spain were increasingly threatened by Native peoples involved in the Yuma Uprising along the Colorado River and because the sea route took many months and was seldom reliable (May 1973, 49). This work brought them into contact with many groups who, like the Paipai, had hitherto escaped sustained contact with outsiders.

Indigenous Negotiations

The preceding historical overview subsumes the long period of exploration of
the Pacific Coast of North America up to the founding of the initial Spanish
missions in Alta California and northern Baja California. It is, for the most
part, well-trodden territory. How Indigenous people made sense of these early
encounters, which were in many cases fleeting and separated by long intervals,
is poorly understood by comparison. In examining the five aspects of Native
life introduced in the previous chapter—political organization, subsistence
economies, technology, ceremonial life, and conflict—we can turn to the
documentary and archaeological records for evidence of how Native people
experienced the earliest contacts with Europeans.

Social-Political Organization

Initial European observations of Native Californian communities generally
align with the expectations drawn from precontact archaeology regarding
population, settlement distribution, and political organization. Of course, regional differences were apparent, with early explorers reporting larger groups
living on the Channel Islands and nearby coastal areas and smaller groups
living to the south (Lightfoot and Simmons 1998). Writing in 1770, Serra
described the Santa Barbara Channel as "a country dotted with a great number of well-organized pueblos" (1955, 173), while Dominican missionary
Luis Sales, in contrast, suggested that the Native people of northern Baja
California "have no government" besides a captain, "but he has no jurisdiction, nor do they obey him" (1956, 26–29). Despite the obvious biases of the
missionaries captured by these statements, the documentary record suggests
no major social or political disjunctures between late precontact times, the
sixteenth-century voyages, and the first overland expeditions.

Nevertheless, it is possible that Native Californians had suffered from epidemic diseases transmitted during early contacts, which may in turn have caused
social and political reorganization prior to permanent colonization (Preston
1996). Research on the Northern Channel Islands—where Cabrillo and his
crew, numbering some 250 men, overwintered in 1542–1543—highlights
the potential demographic impacts of early maritime contacts. In one study,
analysis of 215 calibrated radiocarbon dates from Chumash sites suggests
demographic shifts immediately following the Cabrillo voyage, indicative
of significant population reduction or village coalescence (Erlandson et al.
2001; and see Erlandson and Bartoy 1995). Recent scholarship, however, has

stressed the contingent and uneven nature of early epidemics (Jones 2015). Other parts of California that hosted sixteenth-century visitors—such as the Point Reyes area of western Marin County—do not exhibit dramatic changes in the contemporaneous radiocarbon record nor do archaeological patterns from the interior Central Valley reflect introduced disease in the sixteenth or seventeenth centuries (Engel 2019; Kealhofer 1996). Instead, the nature of possible pathogens, combined with the geographic parameters of early contacts and political organization of Native California, would have likely limited the geographic and temporal impact of any precolonial epidemics (Lightfoot and Simmons 1998, 163–64).

Despite the small size of precontact polities, the documentary record demonstrates the existence of robust regional interaction spheres that cross-cut sociopolitical divisions. For example, Native people at several distinct locations intimated to members of the Cabrillo and Vizcaíno expeditions that other Europeans were present in the interior of the continent. Cabrillo even sent letters with Indigenous messengers to deliver to his compatriots who were apparently exploring farther inland. In the case of the Vizcaíno voyage, which slowly tacked northward against the prevailing winds, news of the ships' arrival spread far ahead of the expedition (Aschmann 1974, 179; Lightfoot and Simmons 1998, 147). More than a century and a half later, similar communication networks remained intact. In June 1769, in Paipai territory, Serra received news from a Native individual regarding the activities of the Spanish parties who had already arrived in San Diego, demonstrating the existence of broadly distributed regional connections (Beebe and Senkewicz 2015, 186–87).

Subsistence Economies

Early encounters between Europeans and diverse groups of Native Californians often involved food. Some Native individuals, such as The Dancer described previously, broke bread with the newcomers during their early encounters, but the available evidence suggests that most Indigenous people were initially skeptical of European foods. Writing of his encounters with Kumeyaay people near what is today Ensenada in 1769, Serra noted, "If we tried to present them with something to eat, their answer was that for such things they did not care" (1955, 145). In the same year, missionary Juan Crespí reported a similar reaction to European food just to the south. There, a Native man "was given a griddle cake and meat but would not eat it" (Crespí 2001, 215). Among the Tongva of the Los Angeles Basin and nearby Channel

Islands, the aversion to European cuisine was particularly strong. According to Kroeber, they believed that to eat foreign foods would invite sickness so "they politely accepted every gift, but every scrap of food was held in such abhorrence as to be buried secretly" (1925, 631).

While it is probably safe to say that Native Californians almost universally preferred to maintain their hunting and gathering practices despite the increasingly frequent opportunities to acquire European foods, the extent to which early contacts may have precipitated environmental changes that affected Indigenous hunting, gathering, or fishing practices remains a topic of ongoing research. William Preston (1997), for example, suggests that widespread environmental changes almost certainly occurred in Alta California before 1769. This scenario is still being debated but there is no doubt that some invasive weeds were in Alta California prior to the onset of missionization as evidenced by their presence in adobe bricks from early mission structures (Hendry 1931; Hendry and Kelly 1925). Once permanent European settlement began in the 1760s and 1770s, a whole host of introduced plants and animals was unleashed on the region. Their spread, however, was gradual during this period, as herds had to be brought overland from the Baja California peninsula and the mission agricultural regime was slow to take hold.

Technology and Material Culture

The first 250 years of contact between Native Californians and Europeans consisted of short, isolated events, most of which were mediated by gifting or other exchanges of material culture. For example, nearly all of the earliest maritime explorers and initial overland expeditions from Baja California and New Spain used gifts to engender peaceful relations (O'Neil 1992). In many cases, Native people reciprocated, which is not surprising given the importance of gift exchange in Native Californian cultures. Between 1540 and 1603, items that passed from European to Indigenous hands included cloth, beads, ribbons, and other small objects. In return, Native people gifted the explorers with necessities—primarily food, water, and wood—and more esoteric items such as bundles of feathers and herbs in certain times and places (Lacson 2015; Lightfoot and Simmons 1998, 153–54). These exchanges, and the materials that made them possible, were all imbued with cultural significance.

One common thread connecting many of the early encounters—both direct and indirect—is that Native Californians actively incorporated foreign things and people into existing practices and worldviews. Analysis of grave goods collected from Santa Catalina Island, off the Los Angeles coast, revealed foreign objects acquired and deposited in keeping with local understandings of hospitality and mourning. These goods likely originated from interactions with the Cabrillo and Vizcaíno voyages and perhaps during an unreported landfall of a Manila galleon or other vessel (Ringelstein 2016; and see Heizer 1941, 324). In Baja California, Cochimí people mined the beach-strewn wreckage of a sixteenth-century Manila galleon—likely the *San Juanillo*, lost in 1578—recovering coins, a metal candlestick, wax, and many pieces of Chinese porcelain (Von der Porten 2019). Local Cochimí used the porcelain to fashion arrow points and flaked tools while other objects remained in use some 180 years later at the time of the first encounters with Jesuit missionaries (Barco 1973, 252–53; Ritter 2014). Farther north, Coast Miwok similarly recycled items taken from the wreckage of Cermeño's *San Agustín*, lost near Point Reyes in 1595. Some porcelain fragments in particular were modified into items that mirrored Indigenous forms such as clamshell beads and abalone ornaments (Russell 2011).

The kinds of gift exchanges recorded during the early explorations of the California coast also took place during the initial overland explorations beginning in the late 1760s. The expeditions of 1769, for example, purposefully brought supplies of glass beads to distribute to Native people they encountered along their way (O'Neil 1992). Crespí's journal provides details about the frequent exchanges between the Spanish and Native Californians; in one series of encounters near San Diego, for example, local Kumeyaay accepted gifts of beads and ribbons, reciprocating with food, arrows, and nets (2001, 239–43). In addition to beads, Indigenous people also quickly learned that the Spanish were a useful source of tobacco. During his travels scouting locations for future mission sites in Alta California, Serra reported that unbaptized Indians were eager to acquire tobacco, with some even greeting him with the imploring salutation, "Tabaco, Padre!" (1956, 141, 146–47). Far from mere trifles, both beads and tobacco were important components of Native Californian life, and Indigenous people likely saw the newcomers as sources of potentially potent variants of items that were already highly valued and symbolically charged (Panich 2014; Cuthrell et al. 2016).

Ceremonial Life

Just as Native people incorporated new material goods into existing traditions, so too did they make sense of Euro-American individuals within existing cosmologies. The best documented example comes from the landfall of Francis Drake in June 1579. Given the lack of geographical specificity in the surviving documents, the exact location of the encounter is unknown, but most scholars agree that it probably took place in Coast Miwok territory north of San Francisco Bay. There, Drake and his men spent thirty-six days among local people, who engaged in a series of performances that included the "crowning" of Drake himself. The idea that Indigenous people worldwide mistook Europeans for gods is a common trope, but the constellation of practices recorded during Drake's visit—orations, gifts of feathers, processions, costumes, women wailing and grieving, and the destruction of property— suggests that the Coast Miwok perceived Drake and his crew not as gods but rather as visitors who specifically sought to partake of seasonal mourning or Kuksu ceremonies (Heizer 1947; Kroeber 1925, 277; Lightfoot and Simmons 1998). In this interpretation, the timing of Drake's landing provided the crucial context for his reception, which differed dramatically from that of Cermeño, who landed to no such fanfare in what may be the same harbor only sixteen years later.

For their part, Europeans consistently celebrated public masses and held elaborate ceremonies of possession during landfalls on the early voyages (Lightfoot and Simmons 1998, 148). Many decades later, a similar attention to the ritual requirements of colonization characterized the overland journeys that brought the Franciscans up the peninsula to Alta California and their subsequent sojourns throughout the region (Beebe and Senckewicz 2015; Thomas 2014). How did Native people respond? In some cases they may have been drawn in by these displays but they likely also considered them carefully, perhaps viewing missionaries as competitors to the ceremonial specialists within their own tribal groups. Describing the reaction of the Kumeyaay to their first encounters with the Spanish, Richard Carrico notes, "As worldly as the Kumeyaay were, the Spaniards did not represent the resurrection of some lost deity nor were they seen as immortal. In spite of the efforts of the Spaniards to secretly bury their dead, the Kumeyaay took note not only of the deceased, but of the sickly composure of the living. The tired, scurvy ridden sailors and dusty, threadbare men of the overland march from Loreto in 1769 did not engender awe or evoke a mood of spiritualism in the Kumeyaay" (1997, 154). The same was no doubt true for other Native Californians who encountered early European explorers.

Conflict

Conflict between Natives and newcomers marked the earliest voyages to California, as witnessed by the first Europeans to make landfall in the southern

Baja California peninsula. Farther north, Francisco de Ulloa reported hostile reaction from the Indigenous residents of Isla Cedros, off the west coast of Baja California in 1540. Firsthand accounts relate that islanders used physical force to discourage the Spanish from landing (Des Lauriers 2014). The Vizcaíno expedition, which visited the island in 1602, reported the same reception. According to a missionary on the voyage, "On [Isla Cedros] there were some wild and warlike Indians who did not wish us to be where we were, and who threatened us and by signs gave us to know that we should leave the locality" (Aschmann 1974, 178). Similar animosities were almost immediately rekindled after the long hiatus in Spanish activity north of central Baja California: just weeks after the founding of Mission San Diego in 1769, local Kumeyaay attacked the outpost, wounding several of the newcomers (Hackel 2013, 167). Indeed, friction between outsiders and Native Californians was a common element of initial encounters, many of which stemmed directly from Indigenous understandings of trespass and resource ownership.

Other early interactions unfolded much differently. In the sixteenth and seventeenth centuries, some Native Californians greeted explorers and their crews enthusiastically (Lightfoot and Simmons 1998, 145–47). Later, Franciscans Junípero Serra and Juan Crespí wrote glowingly of the positive receptions they received in many villages on their early journeys through the region (e.g., Crespí 2001, 261; Serra 1955, 135). As noted above, these friendlier encounters often relied on both sides recognizing the importance of gift giving practices. In Payómkawichum (Luiseño) territory, Native scholar Pablo Tac surmised that the local captain was initially suspicious of the first missionary he encountered—declaring, "What is it that you seek here? Leave our country!"—but eventually welcomed the Franciscan after an exchange of gifts (Haas 2011, 171). When gifting expectations were not met, however, tensions could quickly rise. During Unamuno's 1587 landfall in Chumash territory, local residents attacked the crew, killing two. According to historian Albert Lacson (2015, 9–10), this fatal incident may have been set off by the newcomers' misunderstanding of how to effectively signal their peaceful intentions during a gift exchange initiated by local Chumash people.

The archaeological record can also inform us about interpersonal violence during the time of the earliest contacts between Native Californians and Europeans. In their analysis of bioarchaeological data for central California, Al Schwitalla and colleagues (2014) note that interpersonal violence reached its highest levels after AD 1720. The authors attribute this violence to a "rippling effect" of early conflicts between Indigenous people and Euro-Americans in the American Southwest that sent shockwaves through the broader region. California and the Southwest were connected in many important ways during precontact times (Smith and Fauvelle 2015), but the dates used by the study actually correspond more closely to the early years of contact in California itself. Placed in its proper chronological context, the marked increase in interpersonal violence documented by Schwitalla and colleagues corresponds to similar patterns of violence spurred by Euro-American colonialism across the Americas (Ferguson and Whitehead 1992).

O

Native negotiations of the earliest coastal encounters and later terrestrial expeditions share certain commonalities. In many cases, gift exchanges set the tone for intergroup relationships, a practice with deep roots in regional traditions. Native Californians readily accepted Euro-American beads, cloth, and other items, integrating them into existing systems of value. Similarly, specific individuals or groups of Euro-Americans were occasionally incorporated into Indigenous ceremonial life, as suggested by the reception Drake received among the Coast Miwok in 1579. Tensions flared when Native Californians interpreted—often correctly—the Euro-American interlopers as trespassers intent on violating the sanctity of tightly guarded territorial boundaries and the resources within them. While each encounter played out in its own contingent way, all were structured not just by European agency but also by the expectations and cultural knowledge of Native people into whose territories the newcomers arrived.

Early Encounters in the San Francisco Bay Area

Ohlone people were likely aware of Europeans by the late sixteenth century, having heard of the landfalls of Cermeño and Drake in Coast Miwok territory in what is today Marin County. A few years later, in the winter of 1602–1603, Vizcaíno and his party landed in Monterey Bay and met closely related Rumsen and/or Esselen people. A Carmelite friar among their group noted the "affable Indians, good Natives and well disposed, who like to give what they have" (Broadbent 1972, 47). News of this encounter likely reached village communities in the San Francisco Bay Area, but Europeans remained ignorant of the bay itself for more than two centuries after the Cabrillo expedition first passed outside of the Golden Gate.

The first direct contacts between the Ohlone people of the San Francisco Bay Area and Europeans took place in 1769 as the Spanish reconnoitered the region in connection with their planned settlement at Monterey. This initial incursion encountered various Native groups living on the San Francisco peninsula and along the southern reaches of the bay. Specific village communities reacted in different ways. Some groups offered food or other goods to the newcomers, whom they tried to entice into their villages. At a community near the Pacific Coast, Crespí remarked, "These heathens here made a present of a great many large black and white pies: the white pies were made of acorns . . . They brought two or three pouches of the sort of tobacco that they use, and our people took whatever they wanted of it" (2001, 577). Others, however, were not as welcoming. In an area that anthropologist Randall Milliken (1995, 34–35) identifies as being in the territory of the Puichon Ohlone on the eastern side of the bay, local residents refused gifts from the Spanish scouts. Crespí observed, "If they tried to give them anything, either they would not take it or if they did would throw it away" (2001, 609).

If the Ohlone initially wondered why the Spanish were crisscrossing the region, it soon became clear that the newcomers intended to establish a permanent presence. Just to the southwest of San Francisco Bay, the Spanish established the Presidio of Monterey and Mission San Carlos Borromeo in 1770, news of which would have certainly made its way to the homelands of Ohlone groups living to the north. The Spanish returned to the San Francisco Bay Area later that year, though they noted few details regarding their interactions with Native people. From the available evidence, it appears that relations were amicable. For example, after receiving beads from the Spanish, Ohlone people living near the future site of Mission San José offered feathers and a goose decoy to the foreign party (Milliken 1995, 36). Such interactions continued for several years as Spanish expeditions continued to probe the area's cultural and physical geography.

Colonial accounts of the next major expedition to the Bay Area, in 1772, offer a cross section of interactions with various Native groups between Monterey and the Carquinez Straits (Brown 1994). In the Santa Clara Valley, Ohlone people refused to greet the Spanish, and their neighbors to the north met the Spanish well-armed, with their bodies painted and in a state of agitation. As the Spanish moved northward into the East Bay, they passed several villages of seven to ten houses each. The inhabitants watched from a distance and only occasionally called out to the group of newcomers. It seems likely that these Ohlone communities were intentionally avoiding contact, but the Spanish read the situation differently. Crespí interpreted their reticence as evidence that they were "very good well-behaved heathens," and his companion Fages suggested that they were "shouting as though from joy at seeing us" (Brown 1994, 13–14). North of what is today Berkeley, Ohlone residents at one village were more welcoming, offering food, feathers, and two goose decoys in exchange for glass beads. After passing through Bay Miwok territory along Suisun Bay, the Spanish party turned south through the Diablo Valley, where members of local Ohlone communities seem to have followed the intruders' progress in order to alert their neighbors along the route. The Spanish then crossed back to plains of the eastern San Francisco Bay near the future site of Mission San José, noting several large villages before returning to Monterey.

In 1775, a Spanish ship anchored near Angel Island in San Francisco Bay for several days, during which Coast Miwok people from the Marin peninsula and Ohlone people from the eastern side of the bay visited and exchanged gifts with the newcomers (Santa María 1971, 57–69). Though Coast Miwok groups controlled Angel Island itself, an episode there offers a telling example of how the Spanish viewed the people whose territories they were entering. The account comes from Franciscan missionary Vicente Santa María, a passenger aboard the ship, who discovered a Native shrine on the island. He described three shafts topped with feathers, bearing some resemblance to a starburst, positioned in the cleft of a rock. All around this display were arrows stuck into the ground "as if symbolizing abasement." He went on, "This last exhibit gave me the unhappy suspicion that those bunches of feathers representing the image of the sun (which in their language they call *gismen*) must be objects of the Indians' heathenish veneration; and if this was true—as was not an unreasonable conjecture—these objects suffered a merited penalty in being thrown on the fire" (Santa María 1971, 47).

The Spanish clearly abhorred Indigenous beliefs, but they typically approached their initial face-to-face interactions with Native people very differently. These were facilitated by gift exchanges that served as potent social lubricants among people of widely divergent worldviews. Like Native Californians throughout the region, Ohlone people often presented the Spanish with gifts of food and gladly received foreign objects in return—particularly glass beads and cloth that the Spanish purposefully brought along for just these kinds of occasions (O'Neil 1992; Lacson 2015). There is little doubt the Spanish viewed these exchanges through an ethnocentric lens. For example, the same Santa María who destroyed the Coast Miwok shrine on Angel Island recalled "the brief pleasure of handing out to them the glass beads and other little gifts I had had the foresight to carry in my sleeves" (Santa María 1971, 47). But to Ohlone people, cloth and to a larger extent glass beads were easily incorporated into existing notions of adornment, wealth, and personal status (Panich 2014).

Despite the prevalence of gift exchanges and the generally friendly relations between the Spanish and Ohlone groups through the mid-1770s, relations were beginning to sour. While exploring the San Francisco peninsula in 1774, Captain Fernando Rivera y Moncada described his group's encounters with Ohlone residents along the route, some of whom initiated gift exchanges. Writing of one such interaction, Rivera y Moncada stated, "They gave me two gluey batches of atole-gruel (for which I made a suitable return), that would have been appreciated another time; this time, as soon as I was out of their sight, I ordered it thrown into the woods" (Stanger and Brown 1969, 138). Perhaps offended by the actions of the Spanish, Ohlone men farther along the trail conspicuously kept the Spanish on their left-hand side, offering a slight advantage if they needed to draw their bows should more serious trouble arise. After spotting an expedition led by Juan Bautista de Anza crossing the Santa Clara Valley two years later, Matalan Ohlone people ran alongside the Spanish party, gesturing for them to stop their forward advance. As suggested by Shoup and Milliken, "The Matalans may have been tired of the foreigners wandering through their lands without even stopping to acknowledge them, let alone exchange gifts and receive formal permission to cross through" (1999, 21).

Tensions boiled over in the summer of 1776, when the Spanish sent a party from Monterey to establish a presidio and mission near the tip of the San Francisco peninsula. The local Yelamu Ohlone apparently welcomed the settlements at first, resulting in several weeks of frequent and friendly interaction. This peace was shattered in August as Ssalson Ohlone from the south attacked the Yelamu, successfully driving them from their villages after a deadly engagement. Though the exact motives for the attack are unknown, it is likely that the Ssalson did not want their enemies, the Yelamu, to gain new and powerful allies in the form of the Spanish (Milliken 1995, 63; Newell 2009, 108–109). Yelamu men returned to their lands over the course of the fall, watching the Spanish as they constructed Mission San Francisco de Asís. According to missionary Francisco Palóu, these men started to "disgrace themselves" by engaging in petty thefts and threatening behavior toward Spanish soldiers and Native people from Mission San Carlos who had accompanied the Franciscans. After the Spanish arrested and whipped one man, a skirmish ensued in which colonial soldiers shot two local men, one of whom died of his wounds. Two survivors were whipped and threatened with death should they continue to resist the Spanish (Palóu 1926, 136–38).

A similar incident followed a few months later as the Spanish sought to establish themselves near the southern edge of San Francisco Bay, in the territory of the Tamien Ohlone. Mission Santa Clara de Asís was founded there in January of 1777, complete with a range of domesticated animals. Local people quickly availed themselves of mules that belonged to the soldiers stationed at the fledgling mission. The local guard requested assistance from the Presidio of San Francisco, and with the arrival of the reinforcements, the soldiers went searching for their mules. They found them being roasted by Native people, whom they immediately attacked. Encountering resistance, the colonial guard killed three Ohlone individuals as an example and carried off the surviving leaders to the mission where they were whipped (Palóu 1926, 161). It is perhaps not surprising that the Franciscans had to wait several months before they were able to baptize the first Ohlone individuals of the southern San Francisco Bay Area, as local communities no doubt kept their distance for as long as they could.

The years between the initial encounters in 1769 and the establishment of Spanish settlements along San Francisco Bay in 1776 and 1777 highlight the region's political diversity and the variety of approaches taken by Ohlone groups to deal with the sudden arrival of outsiders. Well-documented expeditions, such as the foray up the eastern side of the bay chronicled by Crespí and Fages in 1772 (Brown 1994), offer important detail about the placement and size of Native settlements. But they also point toward highly localized strategies employed by Ohlone communities. Gift exchanges facilitated many early encounters, something that both sides likely knew from the centuries-long history of meetings along the California coast. Yet, not all Ohlone wished to participate in such exchanges, and individuals on both sides seem to have willingly violated the social implications of gift-giving practices by throwing away the materials they received. If the earliest engagements were relatively friendly, many Ohlone people appear to have grown increasingly resentful of the Spanish presence as the years passed and the frequency of Spanish expeditions across Ohlone homelands intensified. By the founding of first missions along the shores of San Francisco Bay, some Ohlone people remained open to the benefits of allying themselves with the Spanish while many others had seen the duplicity of the colonial approach and wanted nothing more to do with it. Whether they could maintain that stance indefinitely, however, was an open question.

Early Encounters in the Sierra Juárez

Spanish explorers traveled to northern Baja California on an intermittent basis in the early years of colonization, recording a number of interactions with local Native peoples on the periphery of the Paipai world (Hohenthal 2001, 4–7). The effects of these events are unknown, but it is possible that the interactions between local residents and several different expeditions—among them those led by Cabrillo, Ulloa, Vizcaíno, Consag, Kino, and Linck—could have affected Paipai communities in ways we are yet to fully understand. In neighboring San Diego County, the archaeological record exhibits a sharp decline in the number of radiocarbon dates directly after the Cabrillo expedition landed in San Diego Bay in 1542. These data, which are a rough proxy for the density of Native settlement, may represent the spread of disease or simply the reorganization of local communities in the wake of Cabrillo's visit. In either case, previous settlement densities resumed by the time of the founding of Mission San Diego (Scharlotta 2015, 222–24).

The first confirmed encounters between the Spanish and Paipai-speaking people took place in 1769, during the two overland expeditions that brought the Franciscans to Alta California. On April 16 of that year, the initial party, led by Rivera y Moncada, met a small group of people by a spring in the southwestern portion of the Paipai ethnolinguistic province. These individuals included a man who sported colored bands—white, yellow, and red—across his face. Crespí lamented the fact that communication proved impossible, but after the group was gifted beads and other items of personal adornment, he stated that "they left well pleased" (2001, 212–13). A separate account, however, indicates that Spanish soldiers had abducted an elderly man prior to the arrival of the entire colonial party. They surmised the man was an "old witch doctor" based on his actions. Later that day, the expedition's scouts brought to the camp a small group of Native people. The single adult male in the group was visibly angry, displaying "the same fury as in the old man," which may have prompted the giving of gifts described by Crespí (Cañizares et al. 1952, 268–69). The exact details of the accounts are difficult to reconcile, but it is hard to believe that the Native participants would have been "pleased" to have been captured and interrogated in a foreign tongue (Beebe and Senkewicz 2015, 188).

Adding to the intrigue surrounding this inauspicious beginning is the fact that Serra met The Dancer at the same spot nearly two months later. Whether The Dancer was one of the men detained during the first expedition, we will never know. His accoutrements—a rattle and stick—generally correspond to the kit of a ceremonial specialist, which can be compared to the earlier party's descriptions of a "witch doctor" and a man with a painted face. In either event, the man Serra called El Baylón was likely aware of the previous encounter and hoped to forestall further abductions. Local people's feelings toward the Spanish were made clearer a few days after the episode with The Dancer. On June 15, 1769, Serra wrote, "From on top of the hill facing us, a number of Indians fully armed sprang up; and one of them began to shout unintelligible words with great violence. From his gestures we gathered that he wanted us to turn back" (1955, 99). The following day, in view of the Pacific, a group of Spanish soldiers came upon what was likely a campsite that Native people had quickly abandoned in advance of the soldiers' arrival. Serra noted that the colonial soldiers recovered "a large, flat bowl, with designs in the clay, wickerwork woven together firm and strong, and other pieces of pottery of fine, intricate workmanship" (1955, 101). While Serra may have been impressed with the material culture of the coastal Paipai, they were not always receptive to his sudden appearance in their lands.

As it turned out, the Franciscans did not linger in Paipai territory, as they ceded control of the peninsula not long after Serra and Crespí made their way north to Alta California. Taking up the mantle of missionization in Baja California in 1773, the Dominicans sought to extend the Spanish colonial frontier and the Camino Real, its main thoroughfare, northward along the Pacific Coast toward San Diego. During their brief stay in Baja California, the Franciscans had reconnoitered this frontier region during the two overland expeditions of 1769 and in other poorly documented trips that were made between the incipient mission field of Alta California and the established colonial centers of the peninsula. This route directly intersected the east-west-trending zone of Paipai-speaking groups, and soon Paipai families were contending with a growing Spanish presence in their homelands. Though the Paipai today occupy upland enclaves, the Pacific Coast was a populous area in precontact times. Passing along the coastal region between San Diego and Velicatá, one colonial soldier reported nineteen rancherías with an estimated population of two thousand individuals (Meigs 1935, 13).

Like the Franciscans in Alta California, the initial phase of the Dominican project saw the establishment of key coastal mission locations and the later infilling of gaps in that chain. Mission San Vicente de Ferrer, the first mission squarely within Paipai territory, was founded in 1780. It was strategically located at the terminus of the main arroyo leading west out of the mountains where the "wild Indians" still maintained total autonomy in the area around Santa Catarina (Nieser 1960, 150). Unbaptized Native people constantly tormented the fledgling mission, in what Sales referred to as "many sudden assaults on the part of the heathen, since they are arrogant, and always inclined to do evil" (1956, 166). Mission Santo Tomás was founded in 1791 on the northern edge of the Paipai ethnolinguistic province. Both missions were oriented to the Pacific, leaving the Sierra Juárez as a refuge for Native people avoiding or escaping the missions.

As the missionary presence began to ripple across the region, Yuman groups along the Colorado River destroyed two Franciscan outposts in 1781, effectively closing the overland trail between California and the rest of New

Spain. Despite this setback, the allure of reopening an overland route from Sonora to California continued to intrigue the Spanish (Mason 1978) and perhaps played a role in the establishment of Mission San Pedro Mártir, in the mountain range of the same name, in 1794. With this mission, called *'aqá'alqák pajlíwá* (or "casa de los frailes") by the local Kiliwa (Harrington 1985, reel 171, 36), the Dominicans gained a foothold in the interior mountain ranges of the northern peninsula. From there, the Spanish hoped to establish a Dominican mission near a mountain pass called El Portezuelo, which leads through the Sierra Juárez and on to the Colorado Delta.

It was around this time that the Native groups living near the site of the modern-day community of Santa Catarina began hosting European visitors. Though others likely scouted the area somewhat earlier, the first documented encounter occurred in 1794 (Mason 1978, 277). Indigenous residents led the Spanish expedition to permanent water, relaying that they knew the spot as *Jaca-tobojol*, or "where the water runs over the rocks" (Meigs 1935, 31; and see Bendímez Patterson 1989, 19). A second expedition to the area in 1795 left San Vicente and reached the future site of Mission Santa Catalina by way of the arroyo system that would become the scene of many important events over the course of the next fifty years. This group, led by Ensign Ildefonso Bernal, provided a detailed account of the region, which praised Santa Catalina in particular for its ready supply of water and Indigenous people. The area was said to include five rancherías numbering between five hundred and six hundred individuals in all (Meigs 1935, 32–34; Nieser 1960, 269–71). The activities of the Spanish, however, likely confirmed the worst suspicions of local residents, when Bernal and his men arrested two women who had escaped from Mission Santo Tomás. To force the surrender of the fugitives, Bernal captured and bound the local chief and the husband of one of the women (Hohenthal 2001, 9; Mason 1978, 283).

In 1796, José Joaquín Arrillaga—then lieutenant governor of California—personally visited the area around Santa Catalina during several expeditions to the mountains of northern Baja California to evaluate potential mission sites. The account of his travels provides a detailed look at the physical and cultural geography of northern Baja California (Arrillaga 1969). For our purposes, several items stand out from his observations and those of the two previous expeditions discussed above. First, Arrillaga noted several different rancherías and their leaders, suggesting that multiple discrete communities lived in the general vicinity of the future mission. He also described a large harvest fiesta near Santa Catalina that brought together people from many different groups, and in other places, he noted the movements of Native people between the Sierra Juárez and the eastern deserts for both ceremonial and economic purposes (Arrillaga 1969, 59–61, 73). These observations confirm archaeological interpretations of a relatively crowded, well-connected region. Second, it is clear that the Native people of the Sierra Juárez were already adapting to the presence of colonial establishments to the west and east. Arrillaga, for example, noted that in 1796 a Paipai captain living near Santa Catalina was called "Capitán de la Yegua" (Captain Mare) due to the fact that he owned a mount that he had received from Indigenous groups living along the Colorado River (1969, 30). In Cucapá territory, near the Colorado Delta, Arrillaga encountered many people riding horseback and growing crops (1969, 79, 87). In all his travels through the Sierra Juárez, however, he did not note the use of introduced foodstuffs in autonomous Indigenous villages. Instead, he remarked on the wild foods that they ate, such as agave, prickly pear, and piñon (e.g., Arrillaga 1969, 34).

His account also gives us insight into the developing attitudes of the Paipai toward the Spanish. During some encounters, both sides participated in what was becoming a common exchange of gifts. Arrillaga, for example, almost always presented Native people with tobacco. And some Paipai, Capitán de la Yegua among them, appeared to have welcomed the Spanish, aiding them as interpreters and guides. Yet, the Spanish had little tolerance for what they saw as illicit activity, and Arrillaga, as lieutenant governor, may have wanted to set a particularly strong example. After leaving Santa Catalina in July, he visited El Valle de la Trinidad, where he seized a young girl—a fugitive from Mission San Vicente—during a harvest fiesta. He also learned of other individuals who had fled Mission San Pedro Mártir and were being sheltered in a nearby ranchería (Arrillaga 1969, 30–31). As he continued his travels throughout the region, he was constantly on the lookout for runaways. Returning to Santa Catalina in September, he convinced the inhabitants of a local ranchería to give up a fugitive and a stolen mule (Arrillaga 1969, 61–62). Some Paipai may have resisted these aggressive tactics by refusing to engage with the Spanish. As summer turned to fall, Arrillaga noted more frequently that Native people in the Sierra Juárez fled their villages as soon as his advance was known, leaving only traces of their presence. After catching up with one such group, Arrillaga was told that they feared the soldiers in particular (Arrillaga 1969, 55–59, 73).

A generation after Crespí and Serra first passed through Paipai lands, the Sierra Juárez remained Native ground. Dozens of independent rancherías occupied the region around Santa Catalina, with particular groups adopting differing tactics for dealing with the newcomers. Some may have seen the Spanish as potential allies or as sources of goods, but the Spanish noted that the Indigenous population around Santa Catalina was as a whole reluctant to leave their homelands for the coastal missions (Mason 1978, 280). In many cases, Native people avoided contact altogether, perhaps because their communities harbored individuals fleeing the region's newly established missions. Despite the proximity of the Dominican outposts, few direct impacts can be detected from the archival record. Indigenous people may have incorporated horses into their understanding of status and mobility but they did not see the value in Euro-American foods, which in many cases they flatly rejected (Meigs 1935, 20). Taken as a whole, the evidence from these early encounters suggests that the eventual Native refugium of the Sierra Juárez had its roots in the earliest years of colonization.

Summary

Prior to the 1770s, most Native Californians living north of the 30th parallel (about three-quarters of the way up the Baja California peninsula) had experienced only intermittent interactions with Europeans. Ohlone- and Paipai-speaking people—separated by some five hundred miles—first encountered Europeans during roughly the same period, in the late 1760s. They watched as colonial expeditions cut through the territories of their village communities, only occasionally stopping to pay proper respect. And these communities kept a careful eye on the Franciscan and Dominican missionaries who began to establish mission settlements in their respective homelands over the course of the next decade. Native people in the San Francisco Bay Area and the Sierra Juárez, like their neighbors across the region, initially treated the missionaries and soldiers who accompanied them with a mix of cautious hospitality and unmistakable defiance. As the permanent nature of the missions became clear, Indigenous people throughout the Californias had to make increasingly difficult choices about how to deal with the ever-expanding colonial presence.

Yet, from the perspective of lived experience, the imposition of colonial rule proceeded slowly and uncertainly across several decades, as will be explored in the following chapter. From earliest interactions through the late 1760s, then, colonization was still in the process of becoming, despite the ceremonies of possession performed by the newcomers. The Spanish foothold on the Pacific Coast of California—as in other regions of the Americas—was, at this early phase of colonialism, precarious at best (Buscaglia 2017). Colonial explorers, missionaries, and soldiers operated with limited supplies, had tenuous lines of communication with their compatriots, and were unfamiliar with local physical and cultural geography. The interactions that unfolded between Native Californians and Europeans were in many ways directed by

Native action, particularly in the earliest maritime encounters. As the European presence took on a more permanent, colonial character in the 1760s, local residents' ability to fully manage the presence of the outsiders was restricted but not altogether lost.

The differential actions of Native people during early meetings—including both maritime and overland expeditions—throughout the region reveal something of the social and political terrain of Native California. As previously demonstrated, Ohlone and Paipai people varied widely in how, or whether, they received the first groups of Europeans to enter their territories, patterns that mirrored those of the diverse range of groups in between. This variation suggests that a fundamental structuring principle was at play, one of Indigenous autonomy (cf. Reid 2015, 26). Rather than a monolithic Native response to foreign intrusion, we can see that specific communities and individuals within them made pragmatic choices about how and when to engage the Euro-American newcomers. Examining this continuum of choices, in turn, reinforces the ethnographic and archaeological models positing a diverse sociopolitical landscape, populated by groups who in many cases were accustomed to decentralized authority and decision-making practices. Yet, this point is missed in much scholarship that is focused solely on the interactions between "Europeans" and "Indians" (Rizzo 2016). Instead, it is worth considering that the archival and archaeological records reflect the concerns and strategies of particular individuals, families, and village communities. Native negotiations of early encounters framed their later dealings with more enduring colonial institutions, such as the Spanish mission system.

3

Making Choices in the Early Mission Period

ON JUNE 6, 1777, SAUNIM and Tomolinquis, an Ohlone couple, watched Fr. Tomás de la Peña enter their village somewhere along the Guadalupe River near what is today downtown San Jose. For the previous six months, Peña and other outsiders had been working to establish Mission Santa Clara de Asís just a little farther downstream, and like many of their neighbors, Saunim and Tomolinquis had kept their distance. But this day was different. Their six-month-old daughter had fallen gravely ill. So had many other children in their village and in neighboring communities. It was clear that something terrible was happening, and Saunim and Tomolinquis must have been desperate. Through an interpreter, Peña stated that he could save their daughter. Despite the growing unease that local Ohlone felt about the newcomers, their livestock, and their buildings, Saunim and Tomolinquis assented. In a brief ceremony, Peña baptized the young girl and another from the same village. He then left. Visiting three separate villages, he baptized twenty ailing children that day, returning to the mission to record them in a book of baptisms that eventually grew to include over eleven thousand Native individuals. The first—the daughter of Saunim and Tomolinquis—he named Clara, in honor of the patron saint of the fledgling mission. Much to the relief of her parents, Clara survived, though one-third of the children baptized that day succumbed to their illnesses in the following weeks.

It is unclear whether the adults who witnessed these baptisms made any connection between the priest's actions and the survival or death of their children. There is no doubt, however, that by 1777, the Indigenous communities of the San Francisco Bay Area faced a quandary: what to do about the Europeans who had begun to establish permanent outposts along the bay the previous year. In addition to the outbreak of strange illnesses that accompanied their arrival, the outsiders had proven themselves to be lethally duplicitous. In their initial encounters, the Europeans offered gifts of beads and food while their priests made gestures of friendship. Yet, when Ohlone people availed themselves of the goods and beasts that were left unattended, they were cruelly punished and several were gunned down in what were likely intentional shows of force (see Milliken 1995, 64–67). This pattern was not entirely foreign to Native people, who themselves had complex gift-giving practices and for whom trespass was a major source of conflict; in many ways, the newcomers were behaving in a manner not unlike local village communities. The questions, then, were: Why had the Europeans come? And what did they intend to do once they had fully entrenched themselves in the local sociopolitical landscape? The answers came in rapid succession with the founding of Mission San Francisco de Asís in June of 1776 and Mission Santa Clara de Asís in January 1777. It was up to Ohlone families to choose their next steps.

Encountering the Mission System, 1769–1810

The Spanish colonial strategy encountered by Native Californians from 1769 to 1810 was rooted in three distinct institutions: military garrisons called presidios, secular civilian pueblos or towns, and religious missions. Native people—in particular, their labor—were critical to the operation of all three types of settlements, but only the missions were explicitly designed to bring Indigenous families and individuals into the colonial fold. The mission, as an institution, was adapted to achieve a diverse but interrelated set of goals. From the point of view of the missionaries who ran the establishments, the primary objective was religious conversion to Roman Catholic Christianity, with baptized Indigenous people taking on the social position of neophytes.* Military commanders and civil authorities were suspicious of the power wielded by the religious orders (recall that the Jesuits were expelled from New Spain in 1767) but they nevertheless recognized that missions represented a cost-effective way of securing the frontier. From the perspective of the military, then, the missions helped to pacify the territory by congregating California Indians in a small number of settlements where they could be closely monitored. Politically, the missions offered a framework through

---

* Many contemporary Native Californians find the term "neophyte" offensive, and I have limited its use accordingly.

which the relatively egalitarian communities of California could be governed. And through rigidly enforced daily routines, the material culture and subsistence practices of California's Indigenous populations could be remade to be more legible to Europeans and their ethnocentric expectations. The missions were a manifestation of many, sometimes contradictory, colonial objectives, but most of those involved in their operation hoped that they could successfully remake Native Californians in the mold of the European peasantry.

The founding of particular missions was planned well in advance, with the missionaries and other colonial officials making careful consideration of local supplies of water, arable land, wood, and potential converts (Aviles and Hoover 1997). With time, the missions were intended to leverage Indian labor to become the agricultural backbone of the colony. Mission herds started off relatively small—all animals had to be brought from New Spain or existing missions in Baja California—but within a generation consisted of tens of thousands of cattle, horses, and sheep. Principal crops included wheat, barley, and maize. The missions themselves followed a basic spatial template: a central quadrangle contained the church, priests' quarters, storerooms, and workshops. Native families at each mission occupied their own neighborhood, often referred to as the ranchería, though the priests typically segregated unmarried girls and boys into their own dormitories as they approached adolescence. Farther out were the fields, orchards, and pastures that supported the missions' agricultural enterprise (Costello and Hornbeck 1989; and see Haas 2011, 175–79 for a description of a typical mission compound from the perspective of nineteenth-century Native scholar Pablo Tac). These lands were ostensibly held in trust for Indigenous people, who would return to them as smallholders after the successful period of missionization, originally thought to be a decade or so.

In California, as elsewhere, the missions employed a strategy of *reducción* and *congregación* in which the multitude of autonomous Indigenous polities would be literally reduced and their members congregated at a handful of head mission establishments. Recruitment began with the communities closest to the new mission and slowly radiated outward from there. In the early years, then, the missions were home to members of several villages that spoke similar dialects and shared many cultural practices. In short, the first generation or so of most missions often shared the same ethnolinguistic background. The tragic reality, however, was that these mission communities were not self-sustaining. Given the strict social controls and heavy labor demands that were integral to the process of missionization, Native populations living at the Franciscan outposts were particularly susceptible to introduced diseases. Deaths outnumbered births annually at most missions, and few children born in the missions lived to see adulthood (Cook 1976; Jackson 1994). To grow their establishments, missionaries cast ever wider nets for potential converts, often from the outset. For Native Californians and the missionaries alike, two largely unintended consequences became apparent during the first few decades of missionization. The process of reducción and congregación was grimly facilitated by the poor health of the missions' populations but the continual addition of newly baptized people to those same mission communities stymied colonial efforts at enculturation by ensuring a constant influx of Indigenous people born and raised in autonomous villages (Jackson and Castillo 1995, 7).

Native Negotiations

The prevailing scholarly view of the early mission period in Alta California, ca. 1769–1810, depicts it as "a time of little choice" for Native Californians. This phrase comes from the title of Milliken's (1995) ethnohistorical study of the Native groups of the San Francisco Bay region, and his primary thesis has been generally accepted throughout the Californias. Milliken's basic premise is that the synergistic effects of introduced diseases, ecological disruptions, and political and military domination made the missions the only viable alternative for Native Californians, who faced a complete breakdown of their traditional way of life in the period between 1769 and 1810. This approach intersects the deeply ingrained assumption that missions were carceral, or prison-like, institutions from which individuals could not leave once they had accepted the sacrament of baptism (Madley 2019). Together, these positions leave little room for Indigenous agency or autonomy in the mission period. While there is no doubt that the growing colonial presence in the region posed major constraints for Native people throughout Alta and Baja California, a new generation of scholars is investigating the various choices made by the region's Indigenous residents.

One important observation is that Native Californians did not passively accept missionization. There is ample evidence, particularly from archaeology, that Indigenous people chose to maintain or rearticulate many aspects of their precontact lifeways inside the mission estate in ways that can be understood as "noncooperation" (Jackson and Castillo 1995, 73–80). As explored below, Native Californians refused mission enculturation programs and political domination on a massive scale, sometimes with the tacit approval of missionaries and other colonial officials. To understand this phenomenon, one must recognize that the missions were, at a demographic level, fundamentally

Native places (Panich and Schneider 2015; Schneider and Panich 2014). For example, most Alta California missions eventually housed between one thousand and fifteen hundred Native individuals in their peak years, compared to only two missionaries and a handful of colonial soldiers. The Indigenous populations of contemporaneous Dominican missions were often much smaller—between two hundred and three hundred individuals for the frontier missions of northern Baja California—but Native populations there similarly dwarfed those of colonial descent.

There is also growing awareness that baptized individuals could and did leave the missions. Although many people simply chose to leave without permission (e.g., Bernard and Robinson 2018), Native Californians continually demanded to be allowed to return to their homelands periodically. Colonial authorities acquiesced as early as 1783, when they devised a system of passes, called *paseo*, to help identify neophytes on approved leaves (Milliken 1995, 95). Under this practice, mission residents were granted permission to return to their homelands for one or two weeks at a time, totaling up to ten weeks per year in some cases (Sandos 2004, 199). Paseo was common up and down the mission chain, providing the opportunity to revisit homelands, maintain social connections, continue ceremonial obligations, and obtain outside materials for use in the mission rancherías (Arkush 2011, 83; Duggan 2018, 246–47; Hackel 2005, 84–85; Lightfoot 2005, 62–65; Schneider 2015a, 514; Schneider and Panich 2014, 17–18). It also signaled that missionary control was not absolute. As missionary Fermín Francisco de Lasuén wrote of Native peoples' desire to occasionally leave the missions: "The majority of our neophytes are so attached to the mountains that if there were an unqualified prohibition against going there, there would be danger of a riot" (1965b, 215).

Taken together, these interrelated developments in California mission historiography—the recognition of missions as both Native and relatively porous places—offers investigative keys that can unlock further insights into how Native Californians maintained the ability to choose their own life courses despite the constraints of missionary colonialism.

Social-Political Organization

An enduring question centers on the extent to which precontact social and political organization persisted in the mission period. To the colonists, Indigenous people were collectively viewed as *Indios*. This designation placed them at the bottom of a racialized *casta*, or caste, system that separated them from non-Native individuals, who were considered *gente de razón* (literally, "people with reason"). The major difference within the category of Indio was baptismal status: those who had been baptized were called *neofitos* while those who had not were referred to as gentiles. That these terms for Native people—Indios, neofitos, gentiles—masked important ethnolinguistic and political diversity was in many ways intentional. For the missionaries, in particular, the creation of a racialized class of Indian neophytes allowed them to institute a political economy that might be thought of as forced communalism in which precontact divisions were minimized and new forms of collective identity were encouraged (Haas 2014; Lightfoot 2005; Voss 2008).

Native people, however, resisted such flattening of social and political organization, sometimes using colonial institutions to their advantage. Particular individuals, for instance, chose to actively retain affiliation with their ancestral villages in order to be eligible for leadership positions within the mission estate. As early as 1778, Indigenous communities at certain missions elected their own leaders—*alcaldes* and *regidores*—who often represented the most prevalent Native groups within a given mission's population. These men, for they were always male, typically represented families that had enjoyed high status outside of the mission and perpetuated many of traditional trappings of tribal leadership (Hackel 1997, 363–64; Skowronek 1998, 687–88). In other cases, such as at Mission El Rosario in Baja California, it appears that local Native leaders chose to forge alliances with the missionaries early on, perhaps to guard against the erosion of their own standing (Moore and Norton 1992). Of course, many Native Californians held out against the missions for decades (Byrd et al. 2018), but the decision about whether or not to enter the mission seems to have often hinged on the ability to maximize the fortunes of one's own family and not necessarily the welfare of the entire village community (Thomas 2015).

Marriage also offered opportunities to remake longstanding alliances within the mission system. Many early marriages mirrored precolonial patterns, but with the poor health of mission populations, Native Californians had to look farther afield for potential partners over time (Peelo 2010). Still, the practice of marrying outside of one's own village community was often a hallmark of precontact marriage strategies intended to forge alliances, particularly between elite families (Newell 2009; Pérez 2018). In this way, intergroup marriages can be seen as the rearticulation of existing practices to maintain community stability in the face of demographic change. Though the composition of many Native groups became more diverse during this period, this shift was internally driven and born of a concern for community persistence (Hull 2015).

Subsistence Economies

In addition to the sorrows wrought by high mortality rates, Native people also had to contend with the ecological effects of invasive plants and animals which, in time, radically transformed the ecology of coastal California. These ecological changes are often seen to have driven mission recruitment (Allen 2010; Coombs and Plog 1977; Larson et al. 1994), a situation that was only exacerbated when Spanish officials outlawed the practice of burning as part of Indigenous landscape management in 1793 in order to avoid endangering their growing herds of livestock (Farris 2014, 144–46). As summarized by historian Steven Hackel, "The awful, if accidental, genius of Spanish colonization in California, then, was not just in creating a subsistence crisis among Indian communities through introduced diseases, plants, and animals; it was in offering what appeared to be a solution in the form of food Indians raised at the mission" (2005, 72).

This scenario, however, rests on the relative timing of environmental changes and the baptism of local Native groups at particular missions. In two of the most detailed studies of this issue—at Missions Santa Cruz and San Antonio de Padua—researchers found that baptisms of nearby Indigenous communities mainly occurred *prior to* the establishment of large livestock herds, local environmental modifications, and other ecological disruptions at the missions (Curry 2018; Peelo 2009). These groundbreaking studies offer a counterpoint to the "ecological hypothesis" in two disparate locales and support an emerging perspective that the immediate ecological impact of introduced plants and animals, particularly cattle, has been overstated (Fischer 2015, 44–55).

We must also recognize that Native Californians had complex subsistence practices that were designed to buffer short-term environmental fluctuations. Many Indigenous people—both within and outside the missions—continued to hunt and gather during this period. In some instances, the Franciscans even encouraged people to return to the homelands to harvest wild resources as the mission agricultural programs were initially unstable (Farris 2014; Hackel 2005). These excursions are evident in the archaeological record as in deposits from the Native ranchería at Mission San Luis Obispo that demonstrate mission residents' continued use of grasslands, chaparral, and oak woodlands during the period between 1800 and 1810 (Popper 2016). At a large Native village near Santa Monica that was occupied from precontact times into the 1810s, analysis of plant remains indicates that Indigenous residents favored wild plants, primarily grasses, over introduced cultigens at a nine-to-one ratio, even though cattle are known to have been in the area as early as 1787

(Reddy 2015). These examples, along with evidence from throughout the region, demonstrate that local resources remained important to many groups despite the growing presence of introduced species.

Material Culture

As a reflection of daily practices—such as labor, leisure, worship, diet, and more—the material culture of Native Californians living in mission settings has been an important topic of research, particularly in archaeology. Many foundational studies explicitly examined the assumed acculturation of Native people as revealed through the relative proportion of materials deemed to be "Indian" or "European" from particular archaeological deposits (Deetz 1963; Hoover 1989). This research seemed to support the idea that Native people rapidly abandoned material practices, such as stone tools or house forms, for the supposedly superior technologies imported by the Spanish and other colonizers. To be sure, missionaries and military officials in California brought all manner of items from Mexico, many of which were given to Native Californians. Items such as clothing and beads were particularly important as social lubricants during the tense years of the late eighteenth and early nineteenth centuries (Duggan 2004, 2016; Lacson 2015). Most recent archaeological research, however, contradicts the very premise of earlier acculturation models. Instead, the evidence indicates that Native Californians incorporated new objects into existing understandings of value and utility at the same time that they rearticulated many material practices to fit new colonial circumstances.

Research in the homelands of Chumash and Tongva people in southern California illustrates this point. There, several sites have revealed evidence that individuals acquired glass beads, horse tack, and other materials through their labor at early ranchos (Douglass et al. 2018; Reddy and Douglass 2018). At the Chumash settlement of Humaliwo, for example, archaeologists excavated an early colonial period cemetery where Native people left offerings such as shell beads and plank canoe components, perhaps as markers of inherited status, as well as thousands of glass beads and a range of metal objects (Bickford 1982; Gamble 2008). These finds suggest that rancho labor offered novel pathways to social prominence and simultaneously provided an alternative to the missions. Native people who did join area missions may have maintained their own distinct material practices, as suggested by an analysis of soapstone vessels from sites across the Chumash region including both mission sites and autonomous villages; in both cases, however, individuals used existing technological practices to navigate local social circumstances (Brown 2018).

And evidence from a traditional-style dwelling from the Tongva neighborhood at Mission San Gabriel suggests strong continuities in the organization and use of domestic space within the missions (Gibson et al. 2018). As these studies demonstrate, Native Californians in diverse settings used new forms of material culture in ways that meshed with existing technological practices.

Ceremonial Life

There is also growing scholarly consensus that Native Californians did not readily accept Roman Catholic Christianity. Though missionaries in California and later scholars have tended to treat baptism and conversion as synonymous, the realities of colonization meant that many Native Californians were baptized without a full understanding of Christianity or the implications of mission life (Hackel 2005, 139–43). As noted by Sandos, "Accepting the ritual of Baptism after eight to thirty days of rote recitation of Christian prayers did not mean Indians expelled other beliefs from their hearts and heads" (2004, xv). This recognition requires a rethinking of the apparent success of the California missions in spreading Christianity to Indigenous people. Previous writers have touted the many thousands of individuals who were baptized during the mission period in Alta and Baja California, but a recent analysis suggests that fewer than 5 to 8 percent of those who received the sacrament truly embraced Christianity (Cordero 2017).

Archaeologically, there is good evidence for the perpetuation of Indigenous religions during the early mission period. For example, Native people throughout the colony used artistic expression as a way to encode mission structures with Indigenous symbolism, as was the case with Kumeyaay artisans who etched designs similar to precontact rock art motifs on tiles used at colonial sites in San Diego (Carrico 2018; and see Chavez 2017; Haas 2014; Robinson 2013). Mission residents also continued communal mourning ceremonies, which played an important part in Native Californian community integration going back thousands of years. The remnants of such ceremonies have been found at Mission Santa Clara (discussed later in this chapter) and at Mission San Gabriel, suggesting that baptized individuals mourned their dead in culturally appropriate ways, perhaps in a clandestine manner to avoid punishment (Dietler et al. 2018). Outside the missions, Native people throughout southern California likewise held mourning ceremonies into the early nineteenth century (Douglass et al. 2018; Hull 2012; Reddy and Douglass 2018). In the same region, the mission period intersected with the spread of the Chinigchinich religion during the 1790s. Its exact origins are unclear, but archaeological and ethnohistorical evidence for the importance of the religion is robust. This includes archaeological deposits on San Clemente Island, far from the nearest Spanish mission, where Indigenous people may have actively avoided the incorporation of Spanish goods, such as glass beads, in their ritual practices (Johnson 2006; Lepowski 2004; Rareshide 2016).

Conflict

Conflict during the early mission years took on a variety of forms. In some cases, Native people fought each other, a common pattern along the edges of expanding states worldwide (Ferguson and Whitehead 1992). In other cases, Native Californians physically resisted missionization. Initial conflicts with the newcomers largely mirrored Indigenous response to trespassing or other crimes against particular village communities (Jackson and Castillo 1995, 73). Yet, new circumstances also called for new tactics. Arson seems to have been a useful tool in the early period before tile roofs became ubiquitous at the Alta California missions. Chumash people set fire to Mission San Luis Obispo three times in the period from 1776 to 1782. Whereas unbaptized Native Californians ignited the first of those blazes with flaming arrows, arson also offered plausible deniability in an era of candle light, open fire cooking, and highly flammable building materials. A devastating fire at Mission San Miguel in 1806 may have been the result of local Salinan people hoping to inflict damage on the Franciscan institution without drawing attention (Sandos 2004, 163).

Other Native people banded together to protect themselves. For example, one of the most successful uprisings occurred at Mission San Diego in 1775. There, Kumeyaay people from allied villages attacked the mission, killing Franciscan Luis Jayme as well as a blacksmith and carpenter. The insurgents burned the church and looted religious paraphernalia. As demonstrated by Carrico (1997), the specific actions of the revolt represented a reasoned response to the growing Spanish presence, which brought with it the rape of women by colonial soldiers, active undermining of Indigenous spiritual leaders, the threat of forced labor, and the spread of introduced diseases. A decade later, at Mission San Gabriel, a spiritual leader named Toypurina worked with Native people living at the mission to organize a coordinated attack that likewise drew support from multiple village communities. As with the earlier uprising at San Diego, Indigenous accounts demonstrate that specific grievances, like disruptions to the existing sociopolitical landscape, motivated its leaders (Hackel 2003).

○

There is no doubt that the Indigenous groups of Alta California and northern Baja California faced enormous challenges during the first 40 years of missionization. Particular communities grappled with ever-shifting combinations of obstacles, not limited to violence, forced labor, social controls, disease, and ecological changes. It is important to recognize the horrors that colonialism unleashed—as captured by several generations of scholars—but a growing body of evidence also points to the localized ways that Native people met these challenges to give their communities a fighting chance. While each group has its own story, the bigger picture is one of contingent persistence: Native Californians made intelligent choices that allowed them to weather the impositions of colonialism as best they could.

Making Choices in the San Francisco Bay Area

The negative implications of missionization would have been immediately clear to Ohlone people. The founding of the first two missions in the San Francisco Bay Area were both marred by violence: Spanish soldiers unleashed lethal force against local Ohlone people just days after the founding of Mission San Francisco in 1776 and Mission Santa Clara in 1777 (Milliken 1995, 64–67). Such acts must have deterred potential converts, and the missions grew slowly in their first few years. Mission Santa Clara, for example, did not immediately attract a resident Native population as attested by the initial baptisms of Clara and other children in their natal villages. This arrangement was likely the result of mutual accommodation between Native people and colonizers. For local Ohlone families, offering their children for baptism may have been a way to forge political alliances with the newcomers without accepting changes in lifestyle; for the Franciscans, it offered a foothold in an unfamiliar region until mission infrastructure was completed.

At the same time that the Franciscans were founding their initial missions, secular colonists established the pueblo of San José de Guadalupe in 1777 (Figure 6). Just a short distance from Mission Santa Clara, the pueblo offered local Ohlone people an alternative to life under the mission bell. By the late 1780s, for example, Franciscans complained that the pueblo's secular colonists allowed Native Californians to "live in their old freedom and gentile customs" resulting in their refusal "to submit to the bond of the gospel and the laws of Christianity" (Skowronek 2006, 133). Some Native people also saw the pueblo as a potential source of goods and animals. In 1783, local Ohlone appropriated

mares from the Pueblo of San José, though colonists murdered two Ohlone in
the resulting punitive expedition. Other Ohlone people who killed Spanish
livestock risked imprisonment at the Presidio of San Francisco, where they
suffered daily lashings (Shoup and Milliken 1999, 28).

Native people quickly acquired familiarity with European animals and
domesticated plants, but large-scale ecological changes only slowly rippled
outward from missions and other colonial establishments. In 1786, missionaries at Santa Clara offered their Ohlone population the option of returning to
their homelands so that the mission's remaining food supplies could be sold
to the military who had run low on provisions. In a telling window in the
internal politics of the mission, the Ohlone chose "life in the open" without
lengthy deliberation (Hackel 2005, 244–45; Shoup and Milliken 1999, 30).
Still, there is evidence that even unbaptized people were experimenting with
agriculture as suggested by the fact that local families were already growing
maize near the site of Mission San José in 1795, two years prior to its founding (Brown 1994, 28–29). And Arrillaga's decree in 1793 against prescribed
burning must have greatly affected the Ohlone villages of the broad plains

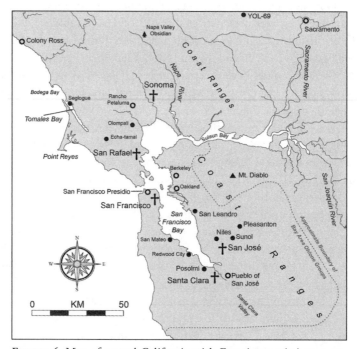

FIGURE 6. Map of central California with Franciscan missions, post-
mission Ohlone communities, and other places mentioned in text.

of the eastern and southern San Francisco Bay Area who up to that point had largely resisted resettlement at the missions. These people's increasing interest in European foods may be linked to changes in local hunting and gathering conditions.

With the growing Spanish presence, the Ohlone groups of the San Francisco Bay Area had to make increasingly difficult choices. At Mission Santa Clara, 586 Ohlone individuals—most of them adults—joined the mission community in autumn 1794. During this major wave of baptisms, which extended all the way until the April of the following year, the mission's Indigenous population increased dramatically, reaching 1,541 at the end of 1795 (Shoup and Milliken 1999, 42). Native people, primarily from Ohlone groups in the East Bay, also joined Mission San Francisco in large numbers during this time, with the population almost doubling between October 1794 and May 1795 (Duggan 2016, 26; Milliken 1995, 129–34). The reasons for these massive movements remain unknown. With participation in the mission system, however, the overall health of the region's Native population declined dramatically. An epidemic struck Mission San Francisco in late 1795 and the number of deaths at Mission Santa Clara steadily rose during the second half of the 1790s (Milliken et al. 2009, 103; Skowronek 2006, 164–81).

Archaeology gives us insight into how the Ohlone people negotiated this tumultuous period, which included large numbers of both baptisms and burials. Excavations within an early portion of the Santa Clara mission cemetery in use between ca. 1781 and 1825 indicate accommodation in the realm of mortuary practices. Despite being laid to rest in the *campo santo*, Ohlone individuals were buried with a range of grave goods—including glass beads, shell beads, abalone pendants, and mission tiles—all of which were prohibited by Catholic doctrine of the time (Hylkema 1995; Leventhal et al. 2011; Panich 2015). Roughly 20 percent of beads recovered from the early cemetery were glass, suggesting that introduced objects were quickly incorporated into Native traditions. In fact, Ohlone preferences directly influenced the purchasing patterns of the Franciscans as indicated by a trend toward white glass beads—the preferred bead color of Native people throughout the greater San Francisco Bay region—in the missions' account books during the period of 1777 to 1808 (Panich 2014). Further evidence that Ohlone people mourned their dead in culturally specific ways comes from the Native ranchería, where the remains of an apparent mourning ceremony were documented archaeologically (Figure 7). Dating to approximately 1805, this intentionally filled pit (Feature 63) contained over two thousand burned shell beads as well as other high-value items that were interred together in keeping with local Indigenous mourning practices (Panich 2015; Panich et al. 2018d).

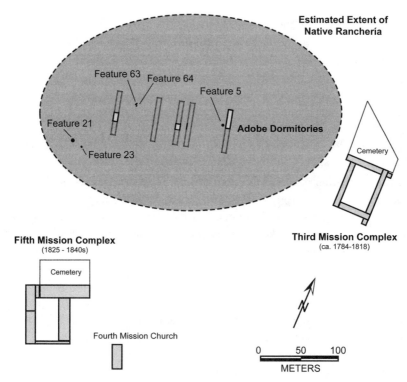

FIGURE 7. General layout of Mission Santa Clara with features mentioned in text.

If the evidence suggests a balance between baptism and noncooperation among Indigenous people at Mission Santa Clara, their compatriots at Mission San Francisco seem to have had enough. Statistics compiled by Cook (1976, 60) suggest that over eight hundred people fled Mission San Francisco between the years 1793 and 1807, representing roughly half of all the fugitives reported in the entire colony during that period. After the large influx of Native people in 1794–95, some two hundred Huchuin Ohlone abandoned Mission San Francisco for their homelands in the East Bay, where they violently rebuffed attempts to bring them back (Milliken 1995, 157–62). Other colonial observers warned that the use of force against Native Californians would result in further uprisings. For example, in 1794, officials discussed the overzealous tactics used by one of the Franciscans at Mission Santa Clara, who regularly whipped Native people who spoke against the missions and threatened to burn down the villages of those who refused baptism. In response, local Ohlone groups were said to be planning a general uprising against the Pueblo of San José and Mission Santa Clara (Shoup and Milliken 1999, 43–44).

The mid-1790s also saw the founding of Mission San José, an event that can be seen as a concession on the part of the Spanish (Duggan 2018, 241). Established in 1797, the mission was close to the homelands of Huchuin Ohlone who had fled Mission San Francisco in 1795 and to the countless others who had hitherto avoided the missions altogether out of a desire to remain in their homelands. Cognizant of neophytes' fondness for their ancestral territories, the Franciscans also allowed some seventy Ohlone people from Mission Santa Clara to transfer to Mission San José, acting as a seed population at the time of its founding. Nearly all of that group were originally from the area around the eventual site of Mission San José, what the priests at Santa Clara dubbed the district of Santa Agueda (Milliken 2008, 36; Peelo et al. 2018b, 172). Like the apparent compromise on the part of Native people to accept baptism as long as the mission was within or near their ancestral homeland, this type of transfer of individuals from one mission to another can be seen act of accommodation. Writing in 1790, Lasuén noted of such movements, "It has been found by experience that they like this; and in no other way can they be kept quiet and induced to continue their education" (1965a, 212).

By the early 1800s, few additional people from the immediate environs accepted baptism at the Bay Area missions, a turning point that some researchers have interpreted as evidence for a landscape wiped clean of its Indigenous population (Milliken 1995; Milliken et al. 2009). However, there are several hints that Native Californians in the San Francisco Bay Area retained strong ties to their ancestral villages, some of which may have served as sites of refuge for those fleeing or resisting the mission system (Byrd et al. 2018; Schneider 2015b). One example is the practice of paseo, which previous scholars have argued was the connecting thread that allowed Ohlone people to maintain cultural continuity in the Bay Area missions (Arkush 2011; Newell 2009). Lasuén noted of the Ohlone residents of Mission Santa Clara in 1802, "For one who has not seen it, it is impossible to form an idea of the attachment of these poor creatures for the forest . . . Those who are attached to the mission are few" (1965b, 284). Native people on paseo commonly opted to remain in their homelands rather than return at the end of their furlough. Others simply left the missions without official permission (Cook 1976, 57–64). These observations suggest that Ohlone people, like Native Californians throughout the province, rejected the notion that baptism tied them eternally to the mission community.

Few documents exist that explicitly discuss the practice of paseo in the region but its prevalence can be assessed through a careful reading of mission death records. At Mission San Francisco, for instance, roughly 300 individuals died in their ancestral homelands over the course of the Spanish period, indicating that Native people manipulated the paseo system to ensure that they could die and be mourned in culturally appropriate ways (Newell 2009, 151–52). Similarly strong patterns exist for Mission Santa Clara (Panich 2015; Peelo et al. 2018b). My analysis using the Early California Population Project database (Huntington Library 2006) shows that 421 Ohlone deaths at Mission Santa Clara were recorded as occurring outside the mission in the years 1777 to 1810.* The first group of entries represents the 23 children who died shortly after they were baptized in their home villages by Fr. Peña in 1777 and another 50 or so represent accidental deaths or those of the group who left to aid in the founding of Mission San José. Still, 342 Ohlone individuals appear to have died, and in many cases were buried, in their home villages prior to 1811—in stark contrast to the idea of the mission as a rigidly bounded community. For many of these people, their deaths were noted as having taken place *"afuera en sus respectivas rancherías de gentiles"* though only isolated deaths were explicitly linked to paseo (e.g., SCL Death 3760).† At Mission San José, 80 individuals were listed as dying outside the mission between its founding in 1797 and the end of 1810, a time when Ohlone people made up the vast majority of the mission's Native population. Of those, 71 were listed either as dying in Native villages or elsewhere in the hinterlands (e.g., *"en el monte"*). These include Hodorica, who died in July 1804 *"en su tierra donde estaba de paseo"* (SJS Death 455).

Marriage was also an important mechanism by which Ohlone people maintained social and political connections. At Mission San Francisco, for example, sacramental records suggest that Ohlone individuals used marriage to forge common community and ease hostilities between particular village groups (Newell 2009). During Mission San Francisco's early years, social reconstructions demonstrate that local Ohlone elites continued the traditional use of marriage as a way to forge social and political alliances with members of prominent families or from particular ancestral villages (Cordero 2015). Native people may also have used this strategy at Mission Santa Clara where roughly two-thirds of marriages were between members of different ancestral communities from 1777 to 1809, a period when the mission's Indigenous population was almost strictly Ohlone (Peelo et al. 2018b). At Mission San José, it seems that Native people maintained existing social organization, even if that meant segregation between groups living at the same site. Based on

---

* This includes fourteen individuals who appear to have died in this period but whose deaths were not entered into the register until 1811–1812.

† Unless otherwise noted, all entries from Alta California sacramental records are from the Huntington Library's Early Califonria Population Project database. Specific entries will be referenced by their ECPP mission code, sacrament type, and sequential number.

FIGURE 8. Native dancers observed by Langsdorff during his visit to Mission San José in 1806. Robert B. Honeyman, Jr. collection of early Californian and Western American pictorial material, BANC PIC 1963.002:1023-FR. Courtesy of The Bancroft Library, University of California, Berkeley.

observations in 1806, the German naturalist Georg Heinrich von Langsdorff noted, "These neighboring tribes formerly lived at great mutual enmity . . . As an instance of this, the misioneros cannot induce them to intermarry. They will unite themselves with only those of their own tribe, and it is an exception that they mingle or associate with members of any tribe other than their own" (1814, 104) (Figure 8).

Archaeology can also inform our understanding of the enduring connections between missionized Ohlone people and their homelands. One example comes from a village in the southern Santa Clara Valley where archaeologists recovered a burial dating to 1795–1805 that was adorned with over three hundred glass beads as well as some twenty-eight hundred shell beads and ornaments identical to those found at contemporaneous mission sites (Hildebrandt et al. 1991) (Figure 9). This individual, a man in his twenties, may very well have been one of the mission residents who died while on paseo. At the missions themselves, archaeological deposits conclusively dating to this time have been difficult to identify, but three pit features from the ranchería

at Mission Santa Clara (Features 21, 23, and 63) date to the first decade of the
nineteenth century. These materials offer a rare glimpse into a period during
which nearly all Native people there were of Ohlone descent (Allen et al.
2010; Panich et al. 2018d; and see Peelo et al. 2018a). For example, obsidian
from these deposits originated far from the mission itself. Most came from
the Napa Valley source area in the North Coast Ranges but some originated
as far away as the eastern Sierra Nevada. Large numbers of shell beads were
also recovered, particularly from Feature 63, the remnant of the mourning
ceremony. Interestingly, these assemblages all include clamshell disk beads, a
type of bead that was not used by Ohlone people in the southern San Francisco
Bay region prior to the colonial period. Mission burials predating 1811 and
the extramural burial mentioned above also contained clamshell disk beads,
suggesting that Ohlone people acquired new sources of beads—both shell and
glass—while in residence at the mission (Panich 2014; Panich et al. 2018d).
Features 21 and 63, moreover, also produced relatively large quantities of
acorn, hazelnut, goosefoot, tarweed, and other native plant foods (Allen et
al. 2010, 139–46), indicating that Native people both had access to such
resources and used them as part of their diet at the mission.

Materials that likely belonged to a Native *vaquero*, or cowboy, including a
portion of a horse bit and boot spur, were recovered from Feature 63, which
dates to circa 1805. Indigenous vaqueros enjoyed relatively high status within
the mission hierarchy and were able to more freely move about the landscape
during a time when colonial officials actively restricted Native Californians'
ability to obtain and ride horses (Panich 2017). Nevertheless, Franciscans at

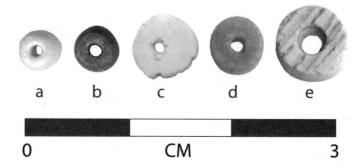

FIGURE 9. Common glass and shell beads found at San Francisco Bay Area missions and autonomous Native villages. From left to right: (a) white compound
glass bead; (b) red-on-green compound glass bead; (c) Class H *Olivella* disk bead;
(d) *Haliotis rufescens* disk bead; (e) clamshell disk bead.

Mission Santa Clara ordered dozens of horse bits and more than one hundred pairs of spurs to be shipped from Mexico in the years prior to 1811 (Skowronek et al. n.d.). The records suggest that numerous Ohlone men learned to ride horses and likely served as vaqueros. Their identities are limited to isolated appearances in the sacramental registers: four Ohlone vaqueros served as godparents prior to 1811 and one Ohlone vaquero, Cosme, died after falling from his horse in 1808 (SCL Death 3848). That vaquero gear was found in association with an Indigenous mourning ceremony dating to precisely that time may allow us to put at least one name to the individuals whose deaths were commemorated in the privacy of the mission ranchería.

Yet, not all deaths during this time were accidental in nature. Luecha Ohlone people of the eastern Coast Ranges attacked a Spanish party in 1805, killing the *mayordomo* of Mission San José and three Indian auxiliaries. A Franciscan missionary, Pedro de la Cueva, was shot in the eye with an arrow but survived. The Spanish reprisal was brutal. According to the official report, soldiers and settlers from the Pueblo of San José attacked the Luecha village "with swords drawn," resulting in the death of ten Native men and one "little girl struck by accident." They also kidnapped twenty-five women and children to be used as leverage. Not long after, some Luecha were baptized at Missions San José and Santa Clara (Milliken 1995, 185–98). The following year, a measles outbreak—first noted at Mission El Rosario in Baja California—swept up the coast into the Bay Area, striking Missions San José, Santa Clara, and San Francisco over the course of the late winter and early spring. At Mission San José alone, some 140 individuals (representing 16 percent of the total population) perished in the epidemic (Jackson 1984; Milliken 2008, 45).

There is no doubt that the period between the mid-1770s and 1810 marked a major transformation of the social worlds of the San Francisco Bay Area as Native people were buffeted by the growing strength of Spanish colonial rule as well as the sinister combination of introduced diseases and the harsh conditions of colonialism. Not only had the Spanish established themselves in all corners of Ohlone territory, more than eighty-two hundred individuals—most of them of Ohlone descent—had died at Missions San Francisco, Santa Clara, and San José by the end of 1810 (Huntington Library 2006). But the question remains: were local Ohlone groups defeated—militarily, socially, and psychologically—as previous scholars have argued? The review of the available evidence presented here paints a different picture: one of Native groups who were struggling but who nevertheless chose to maintain their communities and sense of self against strong opposition.

Making Choices in the Sierra Juárez

Despite the presence of Dominican missions on the Pacific margins of the Paipai region as early as the 1770s, the first and only mission in the Paipai homelands of the Sierra Juárez was Mission Santa Catalina, founded in 1797 (Figure 10). Roughly two dozen Native people from other missions were sent to Santa Catalina to help with construction and these individuals made up the majority of the population for the first few months. Local Paipai were slow to join the mission, and like Mission Santa Clara in Alta California, the majority of Mission Santa Catalina's early baptisms were of children (Nieser 1960, 272–73). As recounted by Rufino Ochurte, a Kiliwa resident of Santa Catarina, at first "[t]here weren't many who came to the mission. They'd come around very little. While the friar was about his things, they'd watch and comment. They slowly began to draw closer. Yet, though they approached, they really didn't hang about very much. They'd say 'It's alien! It's evil!' 'You never know,' they'd say. They'd remain yonder at a distance. By proselytizing he kept the people away" (Mixco 1983, 221).

The mission's strong military presence is another indicator of the cool reception the Dominicans received among local people. Letters between Spanish officials in 1796 and 1797, for example, speak of the need to send extra soldiers and artillery to secure Mission Santa Catalina during its founding (Arrillaga 1797a, 1797b; and see León Velazco 2001, 112). The mission continued to house an unusually large contingent of colonial soldiers, ranging from fourteen to twenty-one, during its early years. Despite these precautions, Native people were raiding the mission's herds as early as 1799 (Ruiz 1799a). A large adobe wall eventually surrounded the mission complex with a tower or bastion on the northwest corner; the mission was also well armed with small cannons and associated supplies. These facts, in combination with its role in the ill-fated reopening of an overland route through the Colorado River Valley, have led to the idea that Santa Catalina was a "fortress mission" (Mason 1978, 278–79).

Although our understanding of how the Dominicans treated Native people is hindered by the lack of surviving primary documents or oral narratives, some general observations can be made. Like their Franciscan neighbors to the north, the Dominicans hoped to employ the policy of reducción despite northern Baja California's arid landscape (Meigs 1935, 29). Sales, for example, related that "the heathen Indians, once instructed and baptized, remain inhabitants of the newly founded settlement although they may have lived forty leagues away" (1956, 165). Once at the mission, Native people endured a strict enculturation program. Rules set forth in the 1780s sought to limit

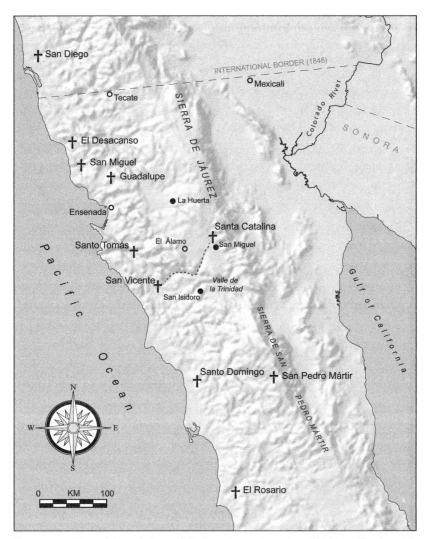

FIGURE 10. Map of the missions of the Dominican Frontier of Baja California, with selected Native settlements and settler towns.

hunting and forbade the continuation of Native people's "pagan dances, fights and wrestling, drinking, and painting themselves" (Nieser 1960, 179). In describing a typical day at a Dominican mission, Sales plainly states that "continual vigilance is necessary to see that the men do not get together with the women" and that after supper "faults are reprehended, and they are beaten with whips" (1956, 160).

Major epidemics swept through northern Baja California in the late eigh-teenth and early nineteenth centuries, no doubt affecting Paipai-speaking people at the coastal missions. For example, an outbreak of typhus or ty-phoid fever struck Mission Santo Domingo in 1800–1801. Measles hit the same mission in 1805–1806 and also killed at least thirty-four individuals at Mission San Vicente (Jackson 1981, 333; Meigs 1935, 136; Nieser 1960, 314). Save for a letter from 1799, stating that *"han terminado las enfermedades"* at Mission Santa Catalina (Ruiz 1799b), burial records and population totals suggest that Paipai living there were largely spared the worst of these out-breaks (Panich 2010a). Other clues into the relative health of Native people at Santa Catalina are the facts that the mission was consistently home to more women than men, and had a relatively high percentage of children, during the first decade of its existence (Panich 2010a, 240–46). Elsewhere, gender imbalances favoring men and small family size have been identified as factors that hindered the demographic viability of mission communities (e.g., Hackel 2005, 108–11; Jackson 1981, 301–11).

Given the combination of challenges to health and freedom at the missions, it is not surprising that Native people varied in their response to the Domini-cans' recruitment efforts. As noted by Sales, missionaries in northern Baja Cal-ifornia searched out would-be converts in their villages, bringing them "some little gifts" to entice them into the missions (1956, 164). According to geogra-pher Peveril Meigs, Native people in the 1920s recounted how the Dominicans even used gifts to attract groups who had made it clear they were not interested in joining the missions, "Where the Indians were wild and inapproachable, food was left along trails known to be frequented by them, in the hope of gathering them in. At first the Indians would not eat the unfamiliar forms of food, saying of the corn, 'It is human teeth,' and of the beef (quite different from the accus-tomed venison), 'It is human flesh'" (1935, 20).

From the onset, the Native people of northern Baja California employed variable strategies for dealing with the Dominican newcomers. Some, as de-scribed by Sales, "receive the proposal gladly, others, even though they take note of the advantages they can obtain for body and soul, when the missionary has rested from talking to them answer: *Quien sabe, Padre?*" (1956, 164–65). Still others, he noted, simply fled. In a separate letter, he admitted that even after baptism, many Native people chose to return to their home villages. This, of course, was not acceptable to the missionaries. "If they run away from the church and the troops they are hunted down, taken from their forests and beaten. And though they are caught a hundred times and well beaten, still they run away, and they are always found at the same spots" (Sales 1956, 41). Punishment also extended to gentiles, as noted by a letter stating that if unbaptized individuals were caught "tormenting the Christians, they will be punished with fifty lashes in the presence of all the Indians of the mission" (Ruiz 1797).

These abuses notwithstanding, some Paipai chose to align themselves with the Dominicans. Within a year of its founding, Mission Santa Catalina counted 100 inhabitants—34 adults and 66 children—and by 1808, 261 Native people were attached to the mission (Panich 2010a, 242). Unlike the San Francisco Bay region, where baptismal records can be tied to specific village communities, we have little information about Mission Santa Catalina's Native population during this time. Given that recruitment typically proceeded geographically, we can tentatively assume that most of them were Paipai. Available archaeological data are similarly limited in that they do not lend themselves to tight chronological separation (and therefore will be discussed in more detail in the following chapter), but it is worth noting here that apparent Native residential areas at the mission yielded very few goods introduced by the Dominicans. Instead, excavations revealed thousands upon thousands of fragments of locally made pottery, wares that differ but little from those that had been made in the region prior to colonization (Panich and Wilken-Robertson 2013). The everyday toolkit of mission residents also appears to match that commonly used in precontact times, consisting of locally available lithic raw materials, obsidian obtained from geological deposits some distance from the mission site, and even a deer antler pressure flaker (Panich 2011b) (Figure 11).

FIGURE 11. Notched deer antler pressure flaker, used to make projectile points and other stone tools, found during excavations in the Native ranchería at Mission Santa Catalina in 2006.

The material evidence suggests a marked porosity of the mission community, and there is some indication that the Dominicans adopted a modified policy of reducción—similar to that employed by the Franciscans at Missions San Luis Rey and San Diego—in which alternating groups of Native people were allowed to return to el monte (Garduño 1994, 94). Details on how this may have worked in Baja California, including a variant of the paseo system, come from regulations set forth in 1781 by the president of the Dominican missions. He stated that Native people should be allowed to return to their homelands prior to baptism since cutting them off completely would negatively affect their attitudes toward the mission. Though they were bound to the mission community after baptism, they could apply for a "leave of absence" to travel outside of the mission provided they were "accompanied by a good and intelligent Christian Indian, to pray the Rosary with them, to recite the Doctrine, and to counsel them in the best way" (Nieser 1960, 255). Whether this latter stipulation was rigorously enforced is unclear. For example, when among the Cucapá in 1796, Arrillaga met a "Christian Indian of San Vicente who, with permission of the Father in charge, came to his ranchería for his health. His ranchería is near Santa Catalina in the Sierra. He had come to the river for recreation" (Arrillaga 1969, 79). This account clearly demonstrates how the Paipai, like other Indigenous people throughout the Californians, manipulated the practice of paseo to suit their own purposes.

The continued affinity of the Paipai for their homelands suggests that many baptized Native people likely chose to keep hunting and gathering during the early mission years. Documentary evidence regarding agricultural production at Mission Santa Catalina is limited, but figures from 1800 and 1801 indicate that the mission had the smallest herd sizes (cattle, sheep, horses, and goats) and crop yields (wheat and corn only) for any mission in the Dominican frontier (Meigs 1935, 167). This situation led Meigs to surmise, "The Indians must have continued to eat wild plants even after the establishment of the mission" (1935, 121). His guess is borne out by archaeological data indicating the consumption of several wild plant species alongside corn, wheat, beans, and peaches (Panich 2009, 254–60). However, scholars have noted a thirty-year hiatus in the fire history of the Sierra San Pedro Mártir that coincides with the founding of the Dominican mission there (Evett et al. 2007; Stephens et al. 2003). This seems to indicate a temporary disruption to local landscape management practices, perhaps due to Arrillaga's province-wide prohibition on Native burning and/or other effects of missionization.

Religious conversion proceeded slowly, if at all. The Dominicans were instructed to teach Catholic doctrine in Native languages except for Wednesday, Friday, and Sunday, when "it must be recited in Spanish" (Nieser 1960,

179). However, it is unclear whether missionaries mastered local languages or if Native people fully understood what they were reciting in Spanish. As suggested by Ochurte's oral narrative, recorded in 1969, "They say we didn't speak Spanish too fluently. They'd understand one or two words at first . . . He [the missionary] could have taught them to read, but he obviously didn't. If he had, all these people would be educated. But he didn't, he'd just baptize them. He really mocked them, it would seem" (Mixco 1983, 222). Outside of the missions, Indigenous fiestas and mourning ceremonies continued even as missionaries and soldiers broke up and discouraged such gatherings (Sales 1956, 47–51). Dominican observers blamed the reluctance of local residents to convert to Catholicism on the continuing influence of the Native *hechiceros*, or traditional healers. According to Sales, the teachings of these men, whom he categorized as liars and manipulators, "are believed by those unfortunates [the local Indigenous people] more firmly than what the friars tell them" (Sales 1956, 38–41). One oral narrative from Santa Catarina relates how a missionary sought a meeting with a local hechicero. Though they talked much of the day, the Paipai healer refused to enter the mission with the priest, saying, "No, my custom is different" (Mixco 1977, 224–25).

Others adopted a more aggressive posture toward the Dominicans. In 1803, Native people killed two missionaries at Mission Santo Tomás, due west of Mission Santa Catalina. The first assassination, of Fr. Miguel López, apparently went undetected by colonial authorities and was only investigated after a second missionary at Santo Tomás, Fr. Eudaldo Surroca, was killed four months later. The official investigation of these deaths leaves many unanswered questions, but the killings and the events that followed involved people from several Paipai-speaking communities (Englehardt 1929, 626–27; León Velazco 2007: Reyes 2004; Reyes 2009, 78–86; Zárate Loperena 1995). Among those accused of the second death was Bárbara Gandiaga, a neophyte woman originally from Mission San Fernando Velicatá, a Cochimí mission. While primary documents dating to the time leave little indication of her motive (Reyes 2009), a later and somewhat contradictory account suggests that Bárbara and two male neophytes committed the murder to put an end to a pattern of sexual abuse perpetrated by the missionary (Rojo 2000, 85–87).

Shortly after the murders, a regional uprising engulfed northern Baja California. This broader insurrection may have been instigated when Indigenous residents fled Mission Santo Tomás fearing retribution for the deaths of Fathers López and Surroca. Certain people from that mission apparently allied with distant groups like the Cucapá, threatening a "general insurrection." Colonial officials were forced to suspend their investigation of the killings so that the troops could capture the fugitives and reconsolidate colonial control of the region, a process that reportedly took two months to achieve (Reyes 2009, 85). Once tensions had cooled, some of the fugitives returned to Santo Tomás, though many of the women did so with husbands other than those who were chosen for them by the missionaries (Rojo 1972, 23–29).

The troubles did not stop after the return of the Tomaseños in 1803. Documents from 1804 mention that Native people carried out killings in the dangerous arroyo between Mission Santa Catalina and Mission San Vicente during the spring and that a group of Indigenous prisoners escaped in the early summer, killing two soldiers near Santa Catalina in the process (Arrillaga 1804a, 1804b; Ruiz 1804). Perhaps in retribution, colonial officials launched a campaign against the unmissionized people living near Mission Santa Catalina later in 1804. One soldier was killed in action against the "rebellious gentiles." Spanish soldiers and Indian auxiliaries pursued the perpetrators to the mission, where they had taken shelter with those who had killed the two soldiers earlier in the year. A battle at Santa Catalina left one Native man dead and four others mortally wounded. For their part, the insurgents managed to lodge a stone-tipped weapon in the head of the Spanish sergeant leading the expedition. Two soldiers and two Indian auxiliaries were also injured in the action (Arrillaga 1804c, 1804d).

Given this unrest, the parallel investigations of the assassinations at Santo Tomás dragged on for several years. The inquiry into Surroca's murder concluded first in December 1805. Bárbara Gandiaga and two Native men from Santo Tomás—Alexandro de la Cruz and Lázaro Rosales—were sentenced to death, and the heads and right hands of the accused were to be severed and publicly displayed at the mission (Nieser 1960, 243; Reyes 2009, 85–86). The sentence was carried out in August 1806. The colonial authorities forced Native representatives from most of the frontier missions, including Santa Catalina, to witness the executions. As historian Bárbara Reyes points out, these ruthless acts "were meant to send a message to the region's Indigenous population, thwart any plans of retaliation against the missionaries, and preclude any future insurrections" (2009, 86).

If the Native residents of the region were at all swayed by the executions, the ensuing peace did not last long. Just two years later, in 1808, another major rebellion swept across the Dominican frontier. This uprising likewise involved Indigenous people from many different backgrounds, consisting of baptized people and gentiles alike and cutting across many ethnolinguistic divisions. Among those who rose up against the Spanish were Native people from the mountain missions of Santa Catalina and San Pedro Mártir as well as several gentile rancherías ranging from the Pacific Coast in the west to Cucapá territory in the east. The rallying cry was purported to be, "We do not want padres and missions, because the missionaries capture our wives and our daughters, baptize them by force, separate them from us, and give them to other men who do not love them and whom they do not love" (Rojo 2000, 88). According to one Native witness, rebels attacking the military guard, or *escolta*, stationed at Mission Santa Catalina screamed, "We do not want padres! We do not want missions! Death to them all!" (Rojo 2000, 90).

Clearly, the Native inhabitants of the Sierra Juárez retained the capacity to choose their own pathways during the early years of Dominican missionization. Some Paipai individuals and their neighbors accepted baptism although many found that mission life conflicted mightily with Indigenous traditions regarding individual autonomy and marriage patterns. Archaeological evidence clearly associated with the early years is minimal, but the broad patterns indicate the maintenance of many important cultural traditions such as pottery and stone tool manufacture. The historical record also illuminates how the Spanish presence inadvertently facilitated regional alliances in spite of the decentralized nature of local social and political organization. At the outset of missionization, colonial observers claimed that local Native people "recognize no ruler" (Sales 1956, 47), a statement in keeping with the autonomous family bands thought to have been the basic social unit in the region (Owen 1965). Yet, the rebellions that cut across so many internal divisions in the region, uniting neophytes and gentiles as well as people from Kumeyaay, Paipai, Kiliwa, and Cucapá rancherías, attest to the broad connections between the region's lineages.

Summary

Ohlone and Paipai people faced similar challenges in the four decades between 1769 and 1810. Catholic missionaries sought to convert California Indians both spiritually and culturally at the same time that colonial soldiers attempted to secure the Pacific Coast for Spain. In both regions, no small number of Native people became associated with the missions, but the available evidence suggests that they actively chose to maintain existing political hierarchies, marriage patterns, religious ceremonies, material culture, and some subsistence practices. These forms of noncooperation reflect the situational autonomy of Native Californians despite the growing constraints of Spanish colonialism. Others openly resisted the mission system by fleeing, manipulating paseo, or engaging in armed uprisings. These tactics are important reminders that the missions were established within existing Indigenous landscapes—homelands that remained central to Native people's lives and that provided them with the material and psychological resources necessary for persistence.

The evidence also points toward some regional differences in how Native people dealt with the imposition of colonialism. Though the intended missionary programs themselves differed little save for the details (Aviles and Hoover 1997), existing Indigenous political economies in many ways structured how the early years of missionization played out in each region. In the fecund and densely populated coastal plains and inland valleys of the greater San Francisco Bay Area, colonists established several settlements—missions, presidios, and pueblos—throughout the Ohlone world. The growing colonial presence on the landscape limited the options of people hoping to avoid the missions while remaining in their ancestral homelands. Colonists and their livestock also intensified the transmission of diseases to Indigenous populations and the ecological changes wrought by introduced species. In this milieu, Native people likely saw the missions as one possible option for maintaining community connections in the face of changes sweeping across the region. By the time large numbers of non-Ohlone people joined the Bay Area missions, starting around 1810, many Ohlones were using the colonial institutions to support their own interests even as they chafed against the social controls and enculturation programs.

The arid interior of northern Baja California, in contrast, had neither the population density nor the agricultural potential to support more than two mission establishments. Though many Paipai-speaking people did enter the coastal missions, the Sierra Juárez remained a refuge zone for nearly a generation after the arrival of the Dominicans. This equation changed with the founding of Mission Santa Catalina in 1797, at the crossroads of Native resistance to Spanish colonialism in the region and near the homelands of Paipai groups and their Kumeyaay, Kiliwa, and Cucapá neighbors. That these groups (with the possible exception of the Kiliwa) frequently intermarried in precontact times likely gave people a range of options for coping with the expansion of the colonial frontier into the sierra. Some joined Mission Santa Catalina, potentially as a way to secure a new and powerful ally in the form of the Spanish. Others, however, banded together in a broad-based and near constant resistance that flourished in the relatively fluid social landscape of the peninsula's interior. As with the Ohlone of the San Francisco Bay Area, Paipai-speaking people made strategic choices—based on the interests of their own families and communities—that helped shape the contours of the early mission period. In the years that followed, both groups continued to maintain their communities despite the impacts of missionization.

4

Native Persistence and the Collapse of the Missions

NEAR THE END OF 1834, the Dominican missionary Félix Caballero set off from the newly founded mission of Nuestra Señora de Guadalupe del Norte along a little-used interior trail toward Mission Santa Catalina Virgen y Mártir. Besides being more direct, this route avoided the well-trodden but dangerous arroyo between San Vicente and Santa Catalina that had long served as a thoroughfare for Indigenous rebels from the Sierra Juárez and the Colorado Delta. Indeed, Native warriors had swarmed out of the mountains only months before, attacking Mission San Vicente and other settlements. Warily, Caballero climbed into the mountains, passing the important Kumeyaay rancherías of San Antonio and La Huerta, eventually crossing into Paipai territory after reaching the Álamo Plain. Despite the decision of some local people to relocate to the missions, many villages in the area maintained significant populations. The autonomy of these latter groups may have troubled Caballero, but after working the Dominican frontier for twenty years, he knew that additional voluntary baptisms were unlikely. Even the founding of Mission Guadalupe, the latest mission in all of the Californias, was predicated on an agreement with the local Indigenous leader, Jatñil, not to proselytize among his tribe. In northern Baja California, Native people had essentially forced a stalemate. The power of the Dominicans was so diminished by this point that Caballero was one of just two missionaries stationed in the entire region, a reflection of the realities of life in the frontera and the secularization decrees pushed by politicians in distant Mexico City.

Perhaps Caballero mulled these thoughts as he followed the winding trail into the Sierra Juárez, known then as the Sierra de Santa Catalina for the mission of the same name. There, a small but stable group of Native people had persevered for over a generation. They lived without a permanent missionary presence, produced inconsistent agricultural returns, and retained a strong preference for doing things in the old ways. Still, Caballero must have felt this was better than the alternative. Once at Santa Catalina, he called the people before him to make his annual census. He recorded 239 individuals consisting of married couples, their children, widows and widowers, single individuals, and those who had died since his previous enumeration. As he conducted his census, the mission's inhabitants offered their Spanish name, given at baptism, but also frequently included the name of their shimul, which the missionary recorded as a surname. Caballero transliterated these into Spanish as best he could though the slight differences in regional dialects undermined his goal for consistent renderings. Satisfied that all was in order—Santa Catalina was, ironically, one of the most populous missions in the region at this late date—Caballero conferred with the captain of the escolta, then left the way he had come.

Among the married couples he recorded that day were Agueda Jamsulchi and Isidoro Colojuat and their son José. This small family was in many ways representative of Native life at the mission. Agueda, a member of the Jamsulch shimul, was born near the infamous arroyo connecting Missions Santa Catalina and San Vicente. Her husband, Isidoro, was part of the Kwal-xwat shimul from the eastern slopes of the Sierra Juárez. Despite the fact that they were from opposite sides of the Paipai world, they spoke the same language and represented two of the four most prominent shimuls living at Santa Catalina in 1834. That they married each other, rather than individuals from their own shimul, was not surprising. Shimuls in this region mapped onto extended family bands which practiced exogamous marriages; in fact, no two spouses listed on the 1834 census hailed from the same shimul. Though it is easy to conjure an image of them insisting that Caballero record their shimul affiliations—their true social identities, rather than just their Spanish names—their motives for residing at the mission are lost to time. It is only through judicious interpretation of the historical, ethnographic, and archaeological records that we can begin to understand how Agueda and Isidoro, like thousands of other Native Californians, endured the pressures of missionary colonialism in California, from its peak around 1810 through its gradual decline during the 1830s and 1840s.

Changing Colonial Circumstances, 1810–1840s

If the first forty years of missionization in Alta California and northern Baja California presented a fairly uniform set of challenges for Indigenous people, Native Californians spent the following four decades navigating the fragmentation of the colonial order in highly localized ways. This unraveling had its roots in political developments in Europe that rippled across the Americas during the early years of the nineteenth century. In 1810, the onset of the Mexican War of Independence effectively prevented royal funding and material supplies from reaching California. Isolation from the colonial government affected the missions in two ways. They lost both their own direct subsidies and additional income from the military, which had previously used a portion of its now-defunct government funding to purchase mission goods and hire Native labor. The military's needs did not disappear after 1810, straining an already tense relationship with the missionaries and their Native charges. Without imperial restrictions on foreign trade, moreover, the export market for mission-produced products, in particular hides and tallow, expanded rapidly. For Native people living at mission establishments, these changes resulted in increased labor demands and growing hostilities with missionaries and other colonial officials (Archibald 1978; Duggan 2016; Farnsworth 1989).

Widespread economic changes occurred simultaneously with major demographic shifts, particularly at missions along the central coast of Alta California. Over time, fewer and fewer individuals from groups immediately surrounding the missions were baptized, and those who did enter the mission system suffered greatly from the combined effects of disease, labor requirements, and social disruption (Cook 1976; Jackson and Castillo 1995). Partly to ensure a steady supply of labor to meet the new demands of the 1810s, the Franciscans at these missions began active proselytization among the numerous Indigenous groups living near the San Joaquin River and other parts of the great Central Valley. This pattern ensured a steady stream of new arrivals, born and raised outside of the mission system, at exactly the same time that the mission system was under even greater pressure to produce economic surpluses. It is not exactly clear how these challenges played out farther south, particularly in Baja California, but evidence from the Central Coast indicates that the Franciscan enculturation programs gave way to more urgent economic concerns (Farnsworth 1989). Farther north, the Russian-American Company operated Colony Ross on the Sonoma Coast between 1812 and 1841. The Russian enterprise, based largely on the hunting of sea otters and fur seals, was yet another thorn in the side of the missions as it effectively halted their northward expansion and served as competition for California Indian labor (Lightfoot 2005).

Mexico won its independence from Spain in 1821, a victory that spelled the end of the California mission system. In the late 1820s, missions in Alta California began freeing select Native individuals in accordance with the Decree of Emancipation in Favor of the Neophytes. In 1833, the Mexican government passed a law secularizing the California missions, and regulations concerning its implementation in Alta California were added the following year (Haas 1995, 2014; Hackel 2005; Jackson and Castillo 1995). By this time, the Dominicans had already shuttered many of the former Jesuit missions on the Baja California peninsula but they fought to keep the missions of the frontier region open despite the secularization decree (Meigs 1935, 156). They were only partially successful and most of the Dominican establishments were abandoned or destroyed by the early 1840s. In Alta California, the missions limped along after secularization but were hobbled as private settlers appropriated mission lands and supplies. In this milieu, large numbers of Native people across the Californias abandoned the missions and, beginning in the 1830s, returned to their homelands for good.

Native Negotiations

Native Californians coped with the second and final phase of the mission period in much the same ways as they did the first. The key patterns noted in the previous chapter—that the missions were fundamentally Native places and that they were more porous than previously thought—continued to offer Indigenous people some autonomy despite the ever-present threats of punishment, sickness, and death. Even four decades after the establishment of the first Alta California missions, Franciscans noted mixed success in their program of cultural conversion, citing both the poor demographic health of the mission populations and the resistance of those in the hinterlands. For example, missionaries at San Buenaventura wrote in 1815, "The son counts eighteen years as a Christian but the father is an obstinate savage still enamored of his brutal liberty and perpetual idleness. The granddaughter is a Christian but the grandmother is a pagan. Two brothers may be Christians but the sister stays in the mountains . . . Such is the situation" (Geiger and Meighan 1976, 61–62). This observation speaks both to the variable strategies Native people adopted to refuse missionization and to the myriad connections they maintained with people and places outside of colonial control.

Social-Political Organization

Over the course of the early nineteenth century, the general contours of Indigenous social organization inside the missions underwent important structural changes. Whereas some communities successfully reasserted precontact roles in the early years of the mission system (e.g., Cordero 2015), demographic shifts caused by poor health and the expansion of mission recruitment meant that Native people were forced to contend with increasingly complex social worlds as the colonial period wore on. Previous research has identified two broad patterns in Alta California. Indigenous groups at the southern missions maintained precontact polities and social structure due in part to the Franciscans' inability to fully implement the policy of reducción in the most arid portions of the province. In the northern region of Alta California, people of diverse tribal backgrounds bonded together based on the shared experience of living and working at particular mission establishments (Haas 2014; Lightfoot 2005; Peelo 2011). Through this pattern of coalescence, mission-based Native populations typically acquired generalized identities associated with the missions themselves (e.g., Clareño, Gabrielino, etc.) but it is likely that these externally applied ethnonyms masked considerable internal divisions (Panich et al. 2014; Panich et al. 2018d).

Time was an important variable affecting the nature of mission communities. Indigenous people who were baptized in the early years had, for better or for worse, adapted certain aspects of their precontact polities and lifeways to the constraints of the mission system (Haas 2014). These people—whom colonists dubbed *Cristianos Viejos*, or "Old Christians"—may not have truly embraced Christianity nor were they particularly loyal to the colonial order but they nonetheless saw some advantages to aligning themselves with Euro-Americans, who by now were clearly here to stay. Newly baptized individuals, in contrast, grew up beyond the reach of the Spanish Empire. They were certainly aware of the presence of the mission system—from interactions with colonial expeditions, fugitives from the missions, or perhaps even their own relatives who had accepted baptism—but by and large the missions themselves and the Native people already living there were totally foreign to these *Cristianos Nuevos* (Milliken et al. 2009; Sandos and Sandos 2014). Whereas the constant influx of new arrivals provided the missions' Indigenous populations continual access to outside materials and people versed in traditional practices, the amount of social integration likely varied. Those who had been in the missions for a generation or more used colonial structures to support group persistence at the same time that new arrivals likely looked more to their ancestral communities for backing and guidance.

Subsistence Economies

By 1810, more than a generation after the founding of the first missions in Alta California and northern Baja California, Native people throughout the region continued to engage in some hunting and gathering practices. Perhaps one of the most detailed windows into the lives of Native Californians living at the Alta California missions comes from an *interrogatorio*, or questionnaire, circulated between 1813 and 1815 (Geiger and Meighan 1976). In response to questions about foodways and subsistence, Franciscans at all eighteen missions for which there were responses included details about Indigenous hunting and gathering practices. In some cases, the missionaries were no doubt describing activities that California Indians enjoyed "in their pagan state" but fifteen out of the eighteen responses included information regarding the continuation of hunting and/or gathering among the Native populations living at particular missions (Table 1). In practice, Native foods remained an integral component of the diet at many missions, where Indigenous people were given leave to collect wild foods such as seeds and acorns (Farris 2014; Popper 2016). Hunting forays, for example, were part of daily life for men living at Mission San Luis Rey, according to Pablo Tac (Haas 2011, 149–51). Data from outside the missions are fewer, but archaeological reports, such as one on the excavation of a village site (CA-YOL-69) near the Sacramento River Valley, show little evidence of the use of introduced plants or animals as late as the 1830s (Wiberg 2005).

Table 1. Summary of Franciscan responses detailing Native hunting and gathering practices from the interrogatorio of 1813–1815.

Mission	Hunting/Fishing	Gathering (Subsistence)	Gathering (Non-Dietary)
San Diego	X	(X)	
San Luis Rey	(X)	(X)	X
San Juan Capistrano	(X)		(X)
San Gabriel			X
San Fernando	(X)	X	X
San Buenaventura	X	X	X
Santa Bárbara	X	X	
Santa Inés		X	X
San Luis Obispo		X	X
San Miguel		X	X
San Antonio		X	X
Soledad			X
San Carlos	X		X
San Juan Bautista	X	X	X
Santa Cruz	X		
Santa Clara			(X)
San José			(X)
San Francisco	X	X	

X = described for Native residents of mission; (X) = described but context unclear. *Source*: Geiger and Meighan 1976. Responses explicitly relating to unbaptized people are not included (but see Schneider et al. 2018, 54).

At the same time, however, many Native people had acquired import-ant agricultural skills and had become familiar with Euro-American crops, animals, and cuisine. Based on historical and archaeological evidence, we know that the missions produced a wide array of fruits, vegetables, and live-stock, but the degree to which mission residents were able to partake of the full variety of foods—beyond the mission staples of beef, corn, wheat, and barley—is unclear (Graham and Skowronek 2015). The reliance on beef, and the growing importance of the hide and tallow trade after 1810, pro-vided Native people with the option of working on mission ranches, which proliferated across the region, some with their own chapels and associated rancherías (Webb 1952, 92–95). The mission herds increased in tandem with raiding as groups of Native Californians—many of them from the Central Valley—depleted the livestock of coastal missions and other colonial set-tlements. Though little archaeological evidence exists, historical accounts indicate that raiders particularly valued horses, both for their mobility and as food (Broadbent 1974; Panich 2017). The overall picture, then, is one of a gradual accretion of introduced species into existing subsistence practices and foodways, a process which was likely tied to the intensity of ecological change in any given locality.

Technology and Material Culture

Despite the enculturation programs employed by Franciscan and Dominican missionaries, Native Californians maintained a host of distinctive technolog-ical and material practices, many of which they rearticulated to accommodate new items introduced by colonists. Beyond the margins of colonial Califor-nia, for example, Native people living at CA-YOL-69 and other sites in the Central Valley buried their dead with thousands of glass beads and other Euro-American goods along with distinctive *Olivella* shell beads that date to the late mission period (Bennyhoff 1977; Schenck and Dawson 1929; Wiberg 2005). These items circulated through multiple networks, connecting gen-tiles, mission fugitives, colonial expeditions, and American fur-trapping par-ties. Mission residents likely maintained privileged access to Euro-American goods which they could use to trade for wild foods, obsidian, and shell beads (Arkush 1993; Panich and Schneider 2015). In this way, the steady move-ment of goods throughout the region served to break down rigid distinctions between "European" and "Indian" materials as well as social identities such as gentile or neophyte.

Within the missions themselves, there is evidence that Native people took advantage of easing acculturative pressures by continuing various technological practices, among them the production and use of stone tools, gaming pieces, and shell beads (Dietler et al. 2015; Dylla 2017; Farnsworth 1989; Panich et al. 2018c; Peelo et al. 2018a). The constant arrival of newly baptized individuals, born and raised outside of the missions, also created a social context that favored the perpetuation of broadly defined Indigenous practices, often within the relative privacy of the mission rancherías (Figure 12). Archaeologically, it has proven difficult to securely associate particular deposits with either existing mission populations or new arrivals. Yet, the excavation of adobe structures—used to house long-tenured and/or high-status Native families—and nearby features at several mission sites indicates that Cristianos Viejos maintained various technological practices rooted in precontact times (Allen 1998; Farris 1991; Hoover and Costello 1985; Panich et al. 2014, 2018a; Peelo et al. 2018a). Established mission residents also developed new technological traditions such as pottery making or horse handling which, though novel, may have offered ways to forge social connections among other mission residents during a time of challenging demographic shifts (Peelo 2011; Panich 2017).

FIGURE 12. Native gaming at Mission San Francisco, circa 1816. Depicted by Louis Choris, a German-Russian artist who accompanied Otto von Kotzebue during his expedition to the West Coast of North America. Courtesy of the Library of Congress.

Ceremonial Life

Native Californians, particularly those who entered the mission system as adults, maintained a strong attachment to traditional beliefs into the second half of the mission period. For example, Franciscans responding to the interrogatorio of 1813–1815 expressed dismay at the propensity for California Indians to deposit beads and other materials with the deceased (Geiger and Meighan 1976). This practice has been documented archaeologically at mission cemeteries throughout Alta California (Panich 2018). Yet, as noted by historians Robert H. Jackson and Edward Castillo, the interrogatorio also reveals a deep ignorance on the part of the missionaries regarding Indigenous religious beliefs, suggesting that Native Californians had ample opportunities to perpetuate aspects of traditional ceremonies without detection (1995, 35). This position is certainly supported by archaeological investigations of Native residential areas at Alta California missions. There, archaeologists have recovered charmstones, bird bone whistles and tubes, tobacco seeds, and the remnants of mourning ceremonies, all of which point toward the clandestine practice of Indigenous ceremonies and rituals out of sight of the padres (Arkush 2011; Cuthrell et al. 2016; Dietler et al. 2018; Greenwood 1976; Panich et al. 2018a).

Native Californians also found ways to openly continue aspects of their ceremonial lives in the missions, often in ways that blended existing practices with Christian teachings. Visual culture was particularly important in this regard as Native people inserted themselves, via the incorporation of Indigenous design elements, into the very fabric of mission spaces (Chavez 2017, 126–60; Haas 2014, 83–115; Kryder-Reid 2016, 55–69; Robinson 2013, 310–14). Dancing, likewise, allowed people to transmit important cultural knowledge while ostensibly celebrating feast days or other mission holidays (Haas 2014, 72–80; Skowronek 1998, 684). Pablo Tac, for example, suggests that mourning dances continued at Mission San Luis Rey (Haas 2011, 143–45). And statistics regarding the administration of important Catholic sacraments like annual communion and viaticum (final communion) suggest that many rejected such public affirmations of religious faith. Analysis from the period between 1814 and 1819, for example, indicates that large majorities of Native residents of missions up and down Alta California failed to take annual communion. Viaticum was administered to only about one-third of baptized individuals who died during that period (Hackel 2005, 170–81). Clearly, conversion was much more tenuous than baptismal figures alone would suggest.

Conflict

Conflict increased after 1810. One major source of friction was fugitivism
and associated punishments as Native Californians continued to flee the
missions in substantial numbers (Cook 1976). Among those individuals returning to their homelands were men with specialized knowledge of horses
and other livestock, which they effectively deployed against the colonial order. Raiding became common by the 1820s, with mounted parties sweeping
through the missions and other colonial settlements from their protected
enclaves in the region's interior (Panich 2017; Phillips 1993; Zappia 2014).
The expansion of raiding and the constant flight from the missions took
place at the same time that the nature of the colonial project in California
was being undermined by lack of direct funding and oversight. Rather than
enticing Native people to embrace mission life with ornate church interi-
ors, musical instruments, and clothing, the Franciscans increasingly used
physical coercion to maintain control of Indigenous populations (Duggan
2016). Soldiers pursued fugitives into the interior, often using such expeditions as an opportunity to capture not just runaways—who were brutally
punished—but also unbaptized individuals, typically women, who could
be used as bait to attract their families to the missions (Skowronek 1998,
682–83). Indian auxiliaries played important roles in many punitive expeditions, as well as other conflicts, suggesting that some Native people used
colonial institutions as ways to settle old scores or to maximize their benefits
vis-à-vis other Indigenous groups.

Large-scale rebellions continued to occur as well. One of the most notable was the Chumash Revolt of 1824, which began at Mission Sana Inés
before spreading to La Purísima and Santa Bárbara. At the latter, the conflict
took several lives and resulted in the burning of multiple mission structures. Unlike some earlier uprisings, however, the leaders came from within
the mission communities themselves, including an alcalde, Andrés, from
Mission Santa Bárbara (Sandos 1985). Several other uprisings, centering
on missions in the San Francisco Bay Area and northern Baja California,
followed similar patterns and will be discussed in more detail later. On
the whole, the rebellions of the second half of the mission period were led
by individuals who had spent considerable time in the missions or were in
other ways familiar with the colonial regime. This pattern contrasts with
that of the early mission period when many conflicts were led by the leaders
of particular Native villages and centered on grievances, such as trespass
and concern for territorial resources, that were common in precontact times
(Jackson and Castillo 1995).

O

The second four decades of the mission period were markedly different than the first. The unraveling of the colonial project meant that Native people associated with particular missions devised unique strategies for perpetuating community cohesion. At some missions, this likely meant the coalescence of previously autonomous communities, whereas in others, divisions remained strong between those who entered the missions at different points in time. A unifying theme linking Indigenous people at all missions was the constant contact with new arrivals who carried with them direct knowledge of life outside of colonial control. Based on archaeological and documentary evidence—and contrary to common assumptions about the success of the missionary enculturation program—it is clear that nearly all mission-based Native Californians maintained various cultural traditions in the relative privacy of the mission rancherías. For those who grew up in the missions, however, the realities of precontact California were no longer the sole structuring forces in their lives. Instead, the mission estate offered a scaffolding that Native people could lean on as they actively rearticulated aspects of material practice and group identity.

Enduring Colonialism in the San Francisco Bay Region

The political and economic changes that swept across the colony after 1810 transpired alongside dramatic demographic shifts among the Native populations living at the missions of the San Francisco Bay region. By the 1800s, fewer and fewer Ohlone people were entering the mission system and the ranks of those who had were continually being thinned by contagious diseases and the exacerbating effects of social controls and labor demands. As the original Ohlone populations grew smaller in the opening decade of the nineteenth century, the Franciscans sought new converts farther from the original mission territories. At Mission Santa Clara, for example, Fathers Catalá and Viader observed in 1814, "There are no more Indians in the area to conquer except toward the east" (Geiger and Meighan 1976, 17). Through the meticulous analysis of mission baptismal and death records, we know that the process proceeded unevenly but eventually Ohlone-speaking people found themselves a minority at all of the San Francisco Bay missions.

This transition occurred first at Mission San Francisco, which had incorporated Bay Miwok and Coast Miwok people relatively early on; together, they outnumbered Ohlone people by 1805 (Milliken et al. 2009, 108). The Native populations of Missions Santa Clara and San José remained predominantly

Ohlone through 1810, when Yokuts-speaking people and others from along the San Joaquin River and adjacent areas of the Central Valley began moving to both missions in large numbers. At Mission San José, for example, the proportion of the mission population drawn from Ohlone communities plummeted from 77 percent in 1810 to just 13 percent a decade later (Milliken 2008, 4). Despite the hundreds of Yokuts people who joined Mission Santa Clara after 1810, Ohlone people there continued to be in the majority until the 1820s (Milliken 2002, 60–61; Shoup and Milliken 1999, 82).

Mission San Francisco offers a compelling look at the structural changes of individual mission populations. There, the year 1814 marked a major demographic milestone: the death of Biridiana, the last adult Yelamu Ohlone to have witnessed the founding of the mission in her homeland (SFD Death 3516; and see Milliken et al. 2009, 117). By that time, the mission, once home to hundreds of Ohlone people, also included large numbers of people speaking Bay Miwok, Coast Miwok, and Patwin languages and representing a dizzying array of ancestral village communities. Yet, with the founding of Mission San Rafael in 1817, many Coast Miwok people accepted transfers to be closer to their Marin-peninsula homelands. Afterward, a new wave of Patwin speakers arrived at Mission San Francisco, though they too returned home via inter-mission transfer with the founding of Mission San Francisco Solano, in present-day Sonoma, in 1823 (Milliken et al. 2009, 121–28).

Missions Santa Clara and San José were similarly diverse. Many Ohlone residents of these mission rearticulated traditional marriage practices by aligning with groups whose ancestral homelands were in close proximity to their own. After 1810, for example, only 16 percent of Ohlone marriages at Mission Santa Clara were between people from the same ancestral ranchería or district. Instead, members of many village communities, the Tayssen and Luecha among them, married individuals from neighboring Ohlone groups. Marriages between Ohlone and Yokuts people were rare but are represented in the records, particularly between members of elite lineages, which may represent intentional alliance-building strategies (Peelo et al. 2018b). The vast majority of marriage records at Mission San José lack information about the participants' ethnolinguistic background (Huntington Library 2006), but previous research indicates that Ohlone people there sought traditionally acceptable marriage partners at the same time that they used marriage as a way to forge alliances with more distantly related groups (Field et al. 1992, 424). Ironically, these connections forged in the missions facilitated the spread of Native religions, as evidenced by the recollections of Coast Miwok elder Maria Copa in the early twentieth century: "Did they dance kuksui [Kuksu] at San José? I should say so. My grandmother said that the people here had to buy kuksui Dance from the San José people" (Collier and Thalman 1991,

235). Similar patterns are evident among Ohlone people living in Mission San Francisco in its later years, from 1824 to 1833. Some, primarily from the San Francisco peninsula, married members of different ethnolinguistic groups, even as others, especially those from the East Bay, continued to marry Ohlone individuals from different ancestral villages (Milliken et al. 2009, 131–32).

A central question regarding the mission demographic shifts of the early nineteenth century is whether or not all living Ohlone people had joined mission communities by 1810. This is the argument made by previous researchers, notably Milliken who interprets the end of baptisms from specific village communities as evidence that those particular communities ceased to exist (1995; 2002; Milliken et al. 2009). Yet, there is emerging evidence to the contrary. Archaeologically, the prevalence of obsidian and shell beads at Missions Santa Clara and San José attest to the presence of autonomous Native populations and the persistence of certain regional exchange networks (Panich 2014, 2016b; Panich et al. 2018b). The documentary record also sheds light on the broader Indigenous landscape during the second half of the mission period. The Mission Santa Clara death records, for example, reveal a steady stream of Bay Area Ohlone people and their mission-born children who died outside the missions during the 1810s and into the 1820s (Huntington Library 2006). As late as the autumn of 1822, an Ohlone man named Vigilio, originally from the district of San Carlos in the southern Santa Clara Valley, died while on paseo (SCL Death 5543).

Similar accounts exist from across the region, suggesting that there must have been people and places that mission residents wished to visit during paseo or as fugitives. A visitor to San Francisco Bay in 1816 was struck by the joy that the opportunity to leave the missions instilled in Native people: "Twice in the year they receive permission to return to their native homes. This short time is the happiest period of their existence; and I myself have seen them going home in crowds, with loud rejoicings . . . Every time some of those who have the permission, run away; and they would probably all do it, were they not deterred by their fears of the soldiers, who catch them and bring them back to the Mission as criminals" (Kotzebue 1821, 283–84). Of course, the missionaries themselves took a somewhat dimmer view of the practice. At Mission San Francisco, the Franciscans described mission residents who ventured to "the countryside where they have been with the pagans such as their parents who hold on to the old practices." This observation dates to 1814, a time when the mission was home to about three hundred Bay Area Ohlone people (Geiger and Meighan 1976, 51; Milliken 2009, 108). Taken together, these sources point toward the continued existence of a populated and meaningful landscape beyond the mission walls.

Ohlone people also found ways to use the missions to support their own interests. At Mission Santa Clara, for example, analysis of the sacramental registers reveals that Ohlone individuals kept important positions such as alcalde and vaquero well into the second half of the mission period (Huntington Library 2006). For example, out of the nine Native men who are listed as alcalde in the sacramental registers after 1810, six were Ohlone (Table 2). Three of these men were from the Tayssen group, serving between 1817 and 1840, suggesting that particular ancestral communities remained important throughout the mission period (Peelo et al. 2018b). Ohlone people also maintained a tight grip on important positions within the increasingly multiethnic populations at other missions. At Mission San José, renowned for the musical ability of its Native population, some 70 percent of all the *musicos* listed in mission records through the 1820s were of Ohlone descent (Sandos and Sandos 2014, 622). These data suggest that Ohlone people used positions within the mission system to maintain social status, either as specific village communities or together as Cristianos Viejos.

Table 2. Documented Native Californian alcaldes at Mission Santa Clara.

Spanish Name	Active Year(s)	Baptism #	Death #	Stated Origin	Ethnolinguistic Affiliation
Miguel Antonio	1783, 1785	195	346	San Francisco (ranchería)	Bay Area Ohlone
Manuel Donulo	1784	145	2765	San Francisco Solano (ranchería)	Bay Area Ohlone
Julian Altamirano	1786	170	2996	San Francisco Solano (ranchería)	Bay Area Ohlone
Buenaventura	1787	746	905	San Bernardino (district)	Bay Area Ohlone
Luis Antonio*	1799	52	4355	San Bernardino (district)	Bay Area Ohlone
Jacinto*	1799, 1801	397	4001	San Carlos (district)	Bay Area Ohlone
Benjamin	1825	3047	7297	San Carlos (district)	Bay Area Ohlone
Miguel	1826	498?	6973	Santa Ysabel (ranchería)	Bay Area Ohlone
Neofito	1827	4760	6297	Tayssenes (group)	Bay Area Ohlone
Pio	1835, 1842	4805	7976	Tayssenes (group)	Bay Area Ohlone
Esperidion	1840	5437?		Tayssenes? (group)	Bay Area Ohlone
Silvano	1840	6814	7920	Apelames (group)	Yokuts
Jubenco	1841	?	?	?	?
Quadrato	1842	6034	7872	Mission-born	Bay Area Ohlone parents
Restituto	1843	6641	8052	Janalames (group)	Yokuts

Source: Early California Population Project database (Huntington Library 2006). Few documents record individual Native alcaldes who served in the Bay Area missions. Most of these men were identified as alcaldes in baptismal records in which they are listed godparents or witnesses. It is unclear why Inigo, who is the best-known Native alcalde from Mission Santa Clara, does not appear in the records. Those marked with * were mentioned in a letter concerning elections at Mission Santa Clara (Viader 1799).

Archaeological evidence also illuminates the lives of mission-based Ohlone after 1810. At Mission Santa Clara, for example, archaeologists have investigated two features—labeled Feature 5 and Feature 64—that appear to represent the perpetuation of mourning ceremonies into the late 1810s or early 1820s (Panich 2015; Panich et al. 2018d). Both features are deep pits closely associated with adobe dormitories that were likely occupied by long-tenured Ohlone during that time (see Figure 7). These features contained hundreds of shell beads and other important objects that speak to the high status of the individuals represented by the assemblages. Vaquero gear was also recovered from both pits, a fact that correlates with data from the mission's sacramental registers suggesting that most Santa Clara vaqueros were of Ohlone descent, at least through 1820 (Huntington Library 2006). Feature 64 was adjacent to Feature 63, which contained an almost identical assemblage but appears to have been filled some fifteen years earlier. This pattern may indicate that particular high-status Ohlone people maintained relatively stable rights to portions of the Native ranchería at Mission Santa Clara (Panich et al. 2018d). Feature 5, moreover, contained hundreds of preserved tobacco seeds representing both native and domesticated species of the plant, suggesting that Ohlone people incorporated some introduced species into existing ceremonial rites at the same time that hunting and gathering continued to provide important wild resources (Cuthrell et al. 2016).

Archaeological deposits at Missions San Francisco and San José are more difficult to associate with individuals from specific ethnolinguistic backgrounds but mirror the evidence for the persistence of Native Californian cultural practices at Mission Santa Clara (Figure 13). At San José, for example, archaeologists found the remnants of what appears to be a sweat lodge, or *te-mescal*, in which twenty abalone pendants had been deposited (Thompson and Galvan 2007). Beyond these and the shell beads and obsidian noted above, excavations at both missions attest to the importance of local food sources, which likely offered respite from the monotonous diets of grain and beef provided by the missions (Graham and Skowronek 2015). While the small faunal assemblage from Mission San Francisco included rabbits, fish, and shellfish, materials from multiple projects at Mission San José demonstrate the continued importance of deer for mission residents, representing some 7 percent of identified faunal specimens (Ambro 2003; Panich 2018a). These archaeological patterns confirm historical observations about the importance of Native foods. In 1814, missionaries at San Francisco noted that the Indigenous people there, who included several hundred Ohlone, "supplement our food with their seeds, the produce of the sea and the hunt" (Geiger and Meighan 1976, 88). A British visitor to the Bay Area missions noted as late

FIGURE 13. Stockton series projectile points collected during recent archaeological projects in the Native rancherías at Mission San José (left) and Mission Santa Clara (right). Both were manufactured with obsidian from the Napa Valley source area.

as 1826 that Native people at San Francisco were "grinding baked acorns to make into cakes, *which constitute a large portion of their food*" (Beechey 1831, 20; emphasis mine).

During the 1810s, Native residents of the San Francisco Bay region decided to take action to rid themselves of certain Franciscans. The most successful effort was at Mission Santa Cruz, home to some Ohlones from the San Francisco Bay Area and many related people. In 1812, a coalition that included at least two individuals baptized at Mission Santa Clara assassinated Padre Andrés Quintana, who was known for his cruel punishments of Native people who ran afoul of the colonial order. This act, which the conspirators managed to conceal for the better part of a year, may have stemmed from the Indigenous practice of removing spiritual leaders who did not fulfill their responsibilities to the community (Asisara 1989; Rizzo 2016). Two years later, at Mission Santa Clara, there is some indication that two Ohlone men who had achieved high status within the mission hierarchy—Marcelo and Inigo—attacked José Viader, a long-serving Franciscan at that mission (Skowronek 2006, 204). Viader, who oversaw mission labor requirements, survived the attack, but these events indicate that the Cristianos Viejos, far from being docile converts, carefully policed the limits of colonial power over their communities.

Colonial expeditions to California's interior were becoming more common during this time, heightening the tensions between long-serving or mission-born people of Ohlone descent and those belonging to autonomous groups to the east. Indeed, colonial expeditions—likely incorporating Ohlone auxiliaries from the Bay Area missions—resulted in the deaths of dozens of Yokuts and interior Miwok people during the 1810s and 1820s; many others were captured and brought to the missions (Cook 1976, 245–47). Given the deteriorating relationship between the missions and interior groups, it is perhaps no surprise that some four hundred Yokuts people fled Mission San José in 1827. The presence of American Jedediah Smith and his party of trappers in the Yokuts' Central Valley homelands may have encouraged their departure, as some accounts suggest that the Americans vowed to shield Native people from the missions. Whatever the cause, the resulting testimony of California Indians revealed barely concealed animosity between newcomers to the mission and the established Ohlone population (Sandos and Sandos 2014). Visitors' accounts also suggest that Native people maintained social distance at Mission San José during this time, as in Alfred Robinson's description of two distinct dance parties during the celebration of the feast day of St. Joseph in 1832 (1851, 97–98).

Regional tensions flared again in the late 1820s. Led by Estanislao and Cipriano, established residents of Missions San José and Santa Clara, respectively, hundreds of Yokuts people fled from those two missions in 1828 promising a regional rebellion. Again, colonial officials used the antagonisms between Ohlone people and those of the Central Valley to their advantage, as dozens of Indian auxiliaries joined presidio soldiers and angry settlers as they tried to put down the insurrection over the course of the next year (Phillips 1993, 78–82). A virulent malaria epidemic that swept through the Central Valley in 1833 may have slowed organized insurgency originating in the hinterlands but apparently did little to stop horse raiding by interior groups (Cook 1960, 188–89; Hurtado 1988, 46–47). In 1839, a new uprising shook the Bay Area missions, this time led by a Native rebel named Yozcolo, who may have fought alongside Estanislao a decade earlier (Berger 1948, 330). Though his tribal background and anti-mission exploits are not well documented, Yozcolo's final stand took place in the hills near present-day Los Gatos, at the southern end of the San Francisco Bay region. There, Yozcolo and his forces were defeated by Indian auxiliaries (who may have had their own motivations for participating in the conflict), and colonial authorities displayed his severed head outside Mission Santa Clara as a warning against further rebellion (Flores Santis 2014, 71–72; Phillips 1993, 112–13).

In addition to the troubles posed by autonomous Native groups, the Bay Area missions were secularized in the mid-1830s. Mission San Francisco, by then the smallest in the area, was officially secularized in 1834–1835, with Missions Santa Clara and San José following suit between 1836 and 1837. Many Ohlone continued to live near mission sites for at least another decade, but the overall impact of missionization was immense. Of the thousands of Bay Area Ohlone who were baptized at Missions San Francisco, Santa Clara, and San José over the course of the colonial period, just 600 Ohlone or their mixed-heritage offspring remained attached to those missions in 1834. This number includes 103 individuals at Mission San Francisco, roughly 360 at Mission Santa Clara, and 139 at Mission San José (Milliken et al. 2009, 108, 136, 151). Of course, these numbers exclude Ohlone people who never joined the missions and don't fully account for those individuals who had already abandoned the mission system, but there is no denying the fact that the missions resulted in a catastrophic loss of Native life in the region.

Those Ohlones who remained in the Bay Area missions in many ways coopted the colonial system as a foundation for the continuation of their communities. At Mission San Francisco, for example, they remained associated with the mission after many others left for Mission San Rafael in 1817 and Mission San Francisco Solano in 1823. Indeed, Ohlone individuals made up approximately one-half of the Native population there throughout the remainder of its existence (Milliken et al. 2009, 121–28). At Mission Santa Clara, a similar pattern prevailed, with Ohlone remaining a relatively large proportion of the overall mission population throughout the later years. Though they comprised some 31 percent of the baptized population in 1836, this number is probably too low given that most Central Valley people left the mission immediately after secularization (Milliken 2002, 60–61; Shoup and Milliken 1999, 94–95). Similarly, Ohlone individuals made up a minority of Mission San José's Native population thought to be still living in the 1830s and 1840s. These figures are bolstered by the influx of hundreds of Central Valley people who joined Mission San José to escape the malaria epidemic of the early 1830s (Milliken 2008, 70–71) but they don't fully account for the equally large number of Yokuts, Patwin, and interior Miwok people who began to abandon the mission as early as the Estanislao-Cipriano Rebellion of the late 1820s. Taken together, then, Ohlone influence on mission communities during the 1830s and 1840s is probably greater than suggested by the sacramental registers alone.

The gradual disintegration of the mission communities played out over the course of the late 1830s and the 1840s. From 1839 to 1840, William Hartnell, *visitador general* of the Alta California missions, surveyed the remnants of the region's Franciscan establishments. At Mission Santa Clara, he enumerated 291 individuals while at San Francisco and noted, "Within the mission proper there is no Indian community but at San Mateo where all the plantings are, there are 90 souls" (Hartnell 2004, 82, 89). He further indicated that the Native people of Missions San Francisco and Santa Clara had been ill served by the administrators appointed after secularization and that most wished for their freedom. Hartnell was more optimistic about Mission San José, noting 589 individuals there, even if the Franciscan in charge lamented that most of the people had left to rejoin the gentiles or were working for ranches or other missions (Berger 1948, 332; Jackson and Castillo 1995, 94). As colonial elites profited from the secularization of the missions, Native labor was still in high demand. Between 1843 and 1844, for example, several orders required that California Indians who had not been legally emancipated return to Missions Santa Clara and San José, where they could be put to work (Shoup and Milliken 1999, 116). Despite these seeming reversals, a final law regarding secularization passed in Alta California in 1845, effectively shuttering the region's missions.

The second half of the mission period presented many challenges for Ohlone people. Colonial expansion increasingly alienated them from their homelands, family members continued to be lost to the combination of disease and the hardships of mission life, and an influx of Native people from the Central Valley left them outnumbered in the San Francisco Bay missions. Tensions with the new arrivals seem to have been a near constant as Ohlone people used their positions within the colonial order to retain status and community cohesion. Still, by the late 1830s, some of these social pressures may have begun to ease. With secularization, the Franciscan project was in ruins, and the Cristianos Nuevos returned to their homelands in California's interior in large numbers, leaving the missions in the hands of the Ohlone and those who had married into their longstanding communities.

Enduring Colonialism in the Sierra Juárez

Following the chaotic events of the first decade of the nineteenth century, the Indigenous groups of the Sierra Juárez and neighboring regions seem to have won the grudging respect of the Dominican missionaries and colonial soldiers. For example, it was probably during this time that the Dominicans abandoned the mountain mission of San Pedro Mártir (Meigs 1935, 148). Though Native people continued to reside at Mission Santa Catalina, they did so without the presence of a full-time missionary. From 1819 onward, the missionary in charge of Santa Catalina, Félix Caballero, shared his duties with Mission San Miguel. Two other missions, Guadalupe and Descanso, were added to his charge in the 1830s, suggesting only minimal missionary involvement in the day-to-day operations of Santa Catalina for most of this period (Engelhardt 1929, 631; Nieser 1960, 280).

Despite the dwindling presence of the Dominicans, Native people living in the missions of northern Baja California were subject to rigid social controls. Manuel Clemente Rojo, a prominent early observer originally from Peru, described a typical day in the Dominican missions, summarizing that "[t]he Indians on the mission settlements of the Frontier lived without liberty, deprived of all of life's pleasures, and obliged by force to work without recompense. One hour before dawn each new day, they got them up, in winter and in summer, and took them to the church to sing some praises and to say some devout prayers, words of which they learned to repeat without most of them understanding their meaning" (1972, 28). This account is typical of many contemporary observers' perspectives of the Californian mission system, which may incorporate their own specific biases (Reyes 2004), but nonetheless underscores the fact that the Dominicans were no less stringent than their Franciscan neighbors.

Indigenous oral narratives support this notion. Perhaps the first recorded insider account of the missions of northern Baja California comes from Jatñil, a noted Kumeyaay leader from the Nejí Mountains, whose recollections were archived by his friend Rojo in the second half of the nineteenth century (Rojo 1972, 2000; and see Zarate 1993). In one narrative, Jatñil recalled how he was abducted from a Pacific Coast beach while gathering clams. After being imprisoned at Mission San Miguel, he was baptized against his will: "One day they threw water on my head and gave me salt to eat, and with this the interpreter told me that now I was a Christian and that my name was Jesús; I didn't know anything about this" (Rojo 1972, 29–32). A century later, Rufino Ochurte related a Kiliwa narrative that stated, "They would dunk people to baptize them: 'This is a good thing I am doing!' he'd declare when he'd finished. 'You might tell the others,' he would say. They'd come and tell about it: 'This man is going to do that to us!' 'No indeed! One never knows what might happen!' they'd answer" (Mixco 1983, 220). In Santa Catarina, oral narratives collected during my research (Panich 2009, 127–31) and in previous studies (e.g., Bendímez Patterson 1989, 22–23; Garduño 1994, 111–13) reveal that Paipai people still remember the heavy labor demands and social controls of the mission period.

Yet, aside from these testimonies and the historical glosses offered by Rojo, few firsthand accounts exist for the Sierra Juárez during the 1810s or 1820s. An isolated population figure for Mission Santa Catalina from 1812 notes 279 individuals—100 men, 110 women, 25 boys, and 44 girls—the largest generally accepted population estimate from the entire colonial era (Nieser 1960, 276). Still, there is evidence that the mission remained unpopular with neighboring groups. In 1823, for example, Fr. Caballero journeyed from Santa Catalina to Tucson, in what is today Arizona, bringing thirty cattle and a dozen horses to offer as gifts to Cucapá groups near the Colorado River. These people received the livestock gladly but the whole encounter seems to have been a setup. On their return trip, the Cucapá again greeted Caballero and his party warmly but robbed them during a river crossing the following day. The group of colonists was sent downstream "naked and barefoot" while the Cucapá made off with their mounts and supplies (Bean and Mason 1962, 11–12, 20–21). Five years later, a party of American fur traders led by James Ohio Pattie met many Native people from Mission Santa Catalina in the same general area; at least one was a fugitive and others may have been on paseo. Upon reaching Santa Catalina, the Americans noted the absence of missionaries and cattle alike, the latter having been plundered by "the free, wild Indians of the desert" (Pattie 1930, 250, 264–68).

The crumbling of the Spanish Empire seems to have left the Dominican missions in relative obscurity. The Dominicans themselves, however, were reluctant to abandon their endeavors, claiming that the secularization decrees of the 1830s only applied to the missions of Alta California (Rojo 1972, 110). The call for secularization was largely ignored in northern Baja California, where the Dominicans—greatly reduced in number—managed to cling to their posts. At Mission Santa Catalina, the year 1834 offers herd estimates of one thousand cattle and six hundred sheep, by far the largest of the admittedly meager data available for the mission (Meigs 1935, 167; and see Lassépas 1859).

The year 1834 also marks our most detailed look at the Native population of Mission Santa Catalina in the form of a document titled "Padrón de la Mis. de Santa Catalina Virgen y Mártir" (Anonymous 1834). This *padrón*, or census, is the only one of its kind to survive from Mission Santa Catalina, though missionaries such as Caballero probably created one annually for each of the missions in the northern region. Today, the document appears to be missing a page, given that it lists a total of 211 individuals whereas earlier researchers had noted 239 (Meigs 1935; and see Panich 2010a, 240–41). Despite this discrepancy, the census shows that a significant number of Indigenous people continued to reside at Mission Santa Catalina into the 1830s. In fact, it was one of the most populous and stable missions of the time.* A separate account indicates that 250 people lived at the mission in 1834 (Lassépas 1859), a figure in keeping with the total of 239 from the padrón. Slight fluctuations would be expected depending on the season in which the total was acquired, as some Native people likely retired to lower elevations during the winter months when the padrón was recorded. Only Missions San Miguel and Santo Tomás were noted as having comparable Indigenous populations in the mid-1830s—both were said to be home to 254 individuals—but these numbers are of "doubtful accuracy." The only other firm population figure from this time is for Mission San Vicente, which counted 176 Native individuals in 1835 (Meigs 1935, 168).

Given the demographic challenges faced by Native communities across the Franciscan and Dominican mission systems, the 1834 census offers some insight into how residents at Mission Santa Catalina managed to maintain a relatively stable population (Panich 2010a, 244–46). One clue to the health of the mission is that—as with the earlier population figures—there are more adult women listed on the census than men, an important indicator of demographic viability (Cook 1976, 408–409; Jackson 1994, 110). By 1834, however, the mission's Native population was, on the whole, older than it had been in the early years. Relatedly, the census suggests that family size was relatively small. More than two-thirds of married couples, including Agueda and Isidoro, had two or fewer children. These two factors may have negatively impacted the ability of the mission's Indigenous population to reproduce itself over time (Jackson 1981, 310–11).

The padrón of 1834 also provides an important look into the ethnolinguistic composition of Santa Catalina's Native population. Each adult in the record was listed with a Spanish given name as well as a surname that in many cases was a Hispanicized version of his or her Indigenous shimul name. Based on my analysis of the twenty-six surnames listed on the document, twelve represent the names of prominent shimuls—many of which are present in Santa Catarina today—and another six are likely little-known shimuls, Native place names, or other Indigenous words (Panich 2009, 74–91; Panich 2010a, 246–51). Looking at the twelve most common surnames, listed in Table 3, we can

---

* Two other accounts, for example, suggest that Santa Catalina was home to some six hundred people in 1824 (Troncoso 1849, 20) and five hundred in 1828 (Pattie 1930, 268), but both figures are likely exaggerated (Panich 2010a, 242–44).

see that the mission's Native population subsumed a relatively high degree of ethnolinguistic diversity. Many of the most prevalent shimuls likely spoke Paipai—among them were the Jamsulch, Kwal-xwat, Xwa't, and Miyekwa. Though Kiliwa shimuls are conspicuously absent from the census, Jat'am is a predominantly Kumeyaay-speaking shimul (it is also present among the Cucapá and possibly the Paipai) and the surnames Guajalx and Cajualt may indicate Ko'alh, which is thought to be a dialect related to Kumeyaay (Field 2012; Mixco 2006). Taken together, the census suggests a large, predominantly Paipai-speaking population with a handful of individuals belonging to shimuls more closely related to other ethnolinguistic groups—in short, a scaled-up version of what we would expect a precontact community in this region to look like given traditionally exogamous marriage patterns.

Geographically, the most prevalent shimuls appear to have originated in locales within a roughly twenty-five-mile radius around the mission itself (Panich 2010a). This pattern aligns with the general parameters of Mission Santa Catalina's "tributary" area defined by Meigs (1935). Missionary recruitment at Santa Catalina seemingly did not undergo the same kind of constant outward expansion as at Mission Santa Clara and others in the San Francisco Bay region. At the same time, however, it is unlikely that the various shimuls listed on the census from Mission Santa Catalina were simply the remnants

Table 3. Surnames from Mission Santa Catalina padrón of 1834 with a summary of available ethnographic information

Census Information		Ethnographic Information	
Primary Spellings	No. of Individuals Listed	Common Ethnographic Spelling(s)	Primary Language(s) Spoken
Jatam	27	Jat'am, Hat'am	Kumeyaay, Cucapá
Jamsulchi	17	Jamsulch, Xamsulch	Paipai
Guajalx, Cajualt	16	Ko'alh, Ko'ał, Kwatl	Kumeyaay, Paipai
Colojuat	15	Kwal-xwat, Kulwat,	Paipai
Juat	9	Xwa't, Xwa:t'	Paipai
Millocoquac	7	Miyekwa	Paipai
Cuecupai	6	Kuweipai	Paipai
Guesac	6	Kwesak Qashaqsh	Paipai
Guecur, Cucur	6	Kekur	Paipai, Kumeyaay
Metsepa	5	Metesepa	Cucapá
Jamau	4	Xama'o	Paipai
Quenon	3	Qui noh	Kumeyaay

Source: Information on primary ethnographic sources can be found in Panich (2009, 75–82; 2010a, 248; and see Harrington 1985, reel 170).

of previously populous groups. Instead, the near constant conflict between colonial authorities and Native people from the Sierra Juárez suggests that it remained a refuge throughout the period. One estimate indicates that as many as two thousand unbaptized Indigenous people still lived in the Santa Catalina area in 1835 (Rodríguez Tomp 2002, 250). As discussed in the following chapters, early anthropologists and other observers found a wide variety of Native settlements in the region around the mission—including some tied to the shimuls listed on the census, such as Jamau, La Huerta, and San Isidoro— providing further evidence that the Spanish policy of reducción was never fully implemented in the Sierra Juárez. As noted for Alta California, I suspect that the Native inhabitants of Mission Santa Catalina maintained strong connections to certain communities outside of the colonial orbit, groups whom they relied upon for important social and physical resources.

This supposition is demonstrated by archaeological research at the site of Mission Santa Catalina, focusing on apparent Native habitation areas that were likely occupied into the 1830s (Panich 2009, 137–77; Panich 2010b). As at other missions throughout the Californias, faunal remains recovered from Mission Santa Catalina overwhelmingly represent introduced species, such as cattle, sheep, goats, and horses. However, small quantities of wild species were also present. These included regional food staples like quail, jackrabbit, cottontail rabbit, and desert rodents but also rarer species such as owl and mountain lion (Guía Ramírez 2010). At Mission San Vicente, which was also established in Paipai territory, archaeologists noted a similar pattern. There, the native species included small mammals such as cottontail and jackrabbit, as well as larger mammals like mountain lion, pronghorn, and mule deer. Given San Vicente's location near the coast, its faunal assemblage also included marine resources such as sea lion (Guía Ramírez 2008).

Connections with the coast were also evident at Mission Santa Catalina. Rock fish and marine shell—including red and black abalone—demonstrate ties to the Pacific Coast (Guía Ramírez 2010). Perhaps even more far flung exchange relationships are evidenced by *Olivella* shell beads, which are known to have been traded throughout the region in historic times (Gamble and Zepeda 2002). As noted in the previous chapter, obsidian artifacts from the mission can all be traced to geological source areas east of the Sierra Juárez, following the same pattern documented for precontact Paipai sites. The obsidian projectile points from the mission, together with one made from colonial-era bottle glass, similarly mirror those used in precolonial times (Gay et al. 2017; Panich 2011b; Panich et al. 2017).

The most abundant class of artifact from the mission site was locally made pottery. These humble fragments, most of which were undecorated, are almost indistinguishable from ancient varieties. To be sure, there is evidence of in-novation in vessel forms, but Native people manufactured these using the same paddle-and-anvil technique as their ancestors. Some sherds also indicate connections to outside regions; for example, painted buffwares and other dis-tinctive motifs speak to the exchange of materials and ideas with people living along the Colorado River. Nevertheless, analysis of the chemical composition of the ceramics from the mission site reveals that Indigenous potters created the vast majority of vessels with locally available clay (Panich and Wilken-Robertson 2013). Though individual potters likely came to the mission from throughout the region, this evidence points toward a coalescence of regional traditions at Santa Catalina (Panich 2010a; 2010b).

Santa Catalina's centrality in regional events is also demonstrated by its role in the rebellions that continued to undermine colonial control of Baja California well into the nineteenth century. In 1834, the year of the mission padrón, Native people of the Sierra Juárez and the Lower Colorado River area—probably representing various Paipai, Kumeyaay, and Cucapá groups—joined together in regional uprising. As described by Rojo, the Native war-riors charged down the arroyo from Santa Catalina to Mission San Vicente, "armed with bows and arrows as they usually were then" (1972, 57–60). This attack was followed by a year of unrest that engulfed the Sierra Juárez and the neighboring Sierra San Pedro Mártir. The regional politics of the uprising are of particular interest. Rojo states that Native people warned some civilian set-tlers to clear out in advance of the attack on Mission San Vicente while others, particularly the Kumeyaay leader Jatñil, defended the mission settlements against the Indigenous inhabitants of Santa Catalina and the rebel alliance. By the later years of the mission period, then, Native people in the Sierra Juárez appear to have settled into two distinct postures toward the colonial system: those who supported the missions and those who did not, a dichotomy still recalled by elders in Santa Catarina (Panich 2009, 126–27).

The members of this latter group eventually won out over the course of the next decade as the Dominicans ceded the interior missions to Native interests. Mission San Pedro Mártir had closed decades earlier, and Mission Santo Domingo was shuttered in 1839 (Magaña-Mancillas 1999). Mission Guadalupe was destroyed the following year during yet another uprising.* This rebellion was led by none other than Jatñil, who had helped Caballero establish the mission and defended it against Indigenous rebels just six years prior (Rojo 1972, 46; 2000, 83). His rationale for abandoning his truce with

---

* There is some indication that the attack may have occurred in October 1839 (Zarate 1993, 96).

the Dominicans centered on the interrelated issues of baptism and labor. According to an Indigenous woman who saved Father Caballero's life during the attack, Jatñil told her, "The one I'm looking for is the Father, because he's forcing baptism on the people of my tribe in order to enslave them in the mission just like you are without enjoying your liberty and living like horses" (Rojo 1972, 43).

Mission Santa Catalina was also destroyed in 1840, but the details of the attack are more difficult to piece together. Few official documents describe the event, though early Franciscan historican Zephyrin Engelhardt indicates that sixteen Native residents of the mission were killed in the uprising (1929, 666). Native people living near Santa Catarina who were interviewed by Meigs in the 1920s gave conflicting accounts (1935, 122–23). One Paipai man suggested that a neighboring Kiliwa group burned the mission when the people of Santa Catalina were away gathering piñon. In this version, the Kumeyaay leader Nicuárr and his warriors pursued the attackers into the Sierra San Pedro Mártir and slaughtered them in retribution. Others stated that the mission was destroyed during a general uprising that brought together Paipai, Kiliwa, Kumeyaay, and Cucapá people. Abelardo Ceseña, one of my consultants in Santa Catarina, related to me that groups hostile to the Dominicans infiltrated the mission's congregation and later joined with the general rebellion (Panich 2009, 218). This perspective aligns with that of another Paipai elder, Benito Peralta, who specified that Native people set fire to the mission as they fled during the attack (Garduño 1994, 113).

Other accounts offer still different perspectives, as indicated by the information given to Mauricio Mixco (1983) by Native consultants from the region. They too stated that Kiliwa individuals were responsible for the attack, though they saw the motivation stemming not from the colonial presence per se but rather from an ongoing feud between Paipai and Kiliwa clans over witchcraft killings. In the narrative recounted by Rufino Ochurte, Kiliwa warriors "arrived in [Santa Catalina] Mission territory (Paipai Country). They shot at each other killing many; they did many people in." After a brief pause in the battle, they snuck around the back of the mission and set fire to it after spotting some Paipai fighters who had taken refuge inside (Mixco 1983, 226). Whoever was responsible, the conflagration likely started in the thatched roof of the mission structures. Archaeological testing at the mission site confirmed the presence of a layer of burned debris directly above the packed earth floor (Panich 2009, 170) (Figure 14). A century later, the Kiliwa term for the mission ruins remained *Wa'iú-ichiú*, or "empty burned house" (Meigs 1935, 123).

FIGURE 14. Excavators from the local Paipai community rest during archaeological investigations at the site of Mission Santa Catalina. The interior of the room is at the level of the historic-period floor. Evidence of the burn layer associated with the destruction of the mission in 1840 is visible in the profile.

With the destruction of Missions Guadalupe and Santa Catalina in 1840—and the closing of San Pedro Mártir some time before—the Indigenous people of northern Baja California had solidified the mountainous interior as an Indigenous refuge. Though there are historical hints that Dominicans occasionally visited the abandoned missions throughout the 1840s and may have even attempted to revive Mission Santa Catalina in 1845, their project was essentially doomed (Lassépas 1859, 104; Magaña-Mancillas 1999, 202). As Native people at the coastal missions drifted away to join their compatriots in the sierra, the Dominicans slowly faced reality. Santo Tomás was the last to close its doors in 1849, after having been thoroughly looted by people heading north to the Alta California goldfields (Meigs 1935, 156).

By the 1840s, Santa Catarina had become a hub of Native activity in the region. It played a central role in many rebellions but was also home to a large—and relatively prosperous—population of Indigenous people. They included many Paipai speakers as well as others from neighboring Kumeyaay and Cucapá groups and perhaps still others who came to the Sierra Juárez to avoid the growing colonial centers closer to the coast. Like the Ohlone of the San Francisco Bay region and the Franciscans, the Paipai and their neighbors maintained an ambivalent relationship with the Dominicans. They clearly resented many aspects of missionization but also saw the mission as a way to maintain power in a rapidly shifting social milieu. As succinctly summarized by Mixco (1983, 7), "secularization ratified a *de facto* truce between Hispanic domination and Native freedom in Baja California."

Summary

The later years of the mission system presented many challenges for Indigenous communities. Although there is good evidence that the enculturation programs of both the Franciscans and Dominicans eased during this time, labor demands remained high. The health of mission populations varied greatly throughout the region—with some even experiencing demographic recovery by the end of the period—but by and large, the conditions of mission life had battered Native Californian communities (Kealhofer 1996). In the San Francisco Bay region, fewer than 8 percent of the tribally born people baptized at Bay Area missions were still associated with those institutions in 1834 (Milliken et al. 2009). To be sure, some of the missing people could have fled to refuge sites in the hinterlands, joined the region's secular settlements in the pueblos of San José or Yerba Buena (San Francisco), or may have been already working at regional ranchos, but the marked decline in population nevertheless underscores the severe impacts of the mission system for Native people. Other missions, such as Santa Catalina, seem to have been spared the worst. The paucity of records from northern Baja California frustrates any attempt to contextualize the seemingly healthy Indigenous population there, but the Native residents of Mission Santa Catalina likely benefited from the minimal missionary presence and their physical distance from colonial population centers.

Within these differing contexts, Native people did what they could to ensure basic survival but also to maintain some sense of community (Hull 2015). In the San Francisco Bay missions, people of Ohlone descent largely stuck together, intermarrying primarily with others speaking the same language while using the mission hierarchy and their status as Cristianos Viejos to maintain distinct identities. These dynamic groups of Ohlone speakers were at the core of the amalgamated populations noted by contemporary observers, typically associated with particular missions and known as *Doloreños*, *Clareños*, and *Chocheños*.* Those Indigenous people from the North Bay and

---

* Mission San Francisco de Asís eventually became known as Mission Dolores. Chocheño is apparently a colloquial form of San Joseño.

Central Valley who intermarried with Ohlone residents of the Bay Area missions likely saw themselves as joining these existing groups—communities that over time became the core of the Ohlone world. At Mission Santa Catalina, Native people drew on existing patterns of exogamous marriages to create a relatively large population that was predominantly Paipai but also included people of Kumeyaay and Cucapá descent. Nevertheless, the family clans represented by the shimul system remained important vectors of social identity, and competition between particular clans may have led to the eventual destruction of the mission at the hands of Native people.

As the mission system crumbled around them, Native Californians emerged bearing the scars of over seventy years of colonialism. Yet, they also carried with them a complex set of cultural practices that offered some flexibility in the uncertain days of the mid-nineteenth century. Armed with existing cultural knowledge of wild plant, animal, and mineral resources, those leaving the missions had also acquired newfound proficiency with agriculture, ranching, and industrial arts. Native people deployed these contrasting but perhaps complementary sets of experiences in localized ways, as will be discussed in the following chapter. For the Ohlone of the San Francisco Bay Area, the end of the missions offered only a brief respite from the struggles of colonialism, forcing them to use their accumulated knowledge to navigate an increasingly narrow path. In the Sierra Juárez, the Paipai faced fewer territorial impositions, but in both cases, Native Californians quickly put their experiences of the previous generations to work in service of forging their way in a new period of settler colonialism.

5

Staking Native Claims within Settler States

IN 1864, AN OHLONE MAN named Inigo was laid to rest along the shoreline of the San Francisco Bay. He had spent much of his life in the Franciscan mission of Santa Clara, but upon its closing in the mid-1840s, Inigo petitioned the Mexican government to grant him his ancestral village and the surrounding lands—what came to be known as Rancho Posolmi (Figure 15). There, he lived out his years with members of his immediate family and perhaps other Native individuals who had similarly endured the mission system. From his home near the bay, Inigo must have recognized a fundamental shift as the new city of Santa Clara rose up around the crumbling adobes of the former mission. Each year, more and more settlers appeared, dramatically altering the landscape of Inigo's homeland. We will never know exactly what Inigo thought of the changes he saw in his lifetime, but it is perhaps telling that when his time came, he chose to be buried not in the Catholic cemetery at Santa Clara but at the site of his ancestral village.

As others have noted (Shoup and Milliken 1999), Inigo's life serves as a poignant example of how one individual adapted to the shifting realities of Euro-American colonialism: the Spanish mission system, secularization under Mexican administration, and finally the onset of American settlement. Inigo was baptized at Mission Santa Clara in 1789, at age eight, during a time when tribal societies still dominated the San Francisco Bay Area. As the Spanish consolidated their control over the province during the ensuing decades, Inigo appears to have accepted life at the mission, as difficult as it must have been. Amid the high mortality of the mission community, eight of Inigo's eleven children died before they reached adulthood. Yet, Inigo persevered, eventually

FIGURE 15. Inigo, ca. 1860. Inigo spent his adult life at Mission Santa Clara and received the lands around his ancestral village as a land grant in the 1840s. Courtesy of Archives & Special Collections, Santa Clara University.

attaining the title of alcalde of the mission's large Indigenous population. And when the newly formed Mexican Republic began shutting down the missions in the 1830s, Inigo embraced another transition by becoming one of the few Native Californians to secure title to the ex-mission lands that the colonial regime had ostensibly held in trust for California Indians. In so doing, Inigo left the relative security of mission life to start over once again.

In this way, Inigo's life illuminates the broader contours of how Native people actively negotiated Euro-American colonialism, of which the missions were simply one part. From the early contacts through the end of the mission period, Inigo and his family drew on their own experience and cultural knowledge to make important decisions about how best to contend with their newfound circumstances. During the last twenty years of his life, Inigo and other former mission residents were confronted with a series of changes as far-reaching as those that their parents and grandparents had faced when they encountered the first Franciscan padres decades before. These new changes were wrought by American expansion, which embraced a fundamentally different vision of colonialism—settler colonialism—that had no room for Indigenous people. As the Gold Rush and successive waves of American settlement forever changed the region, Inigo and others like him sought out refuge in and around their ancestral territories. Facing both violence and dispossession, these resilient people staked a claim to the future.

Settler Colonialism in the Californias, 1840s–1900

As the mission system was secularized in the 1830s, most Native Californians officially lost their claim to their ancestral homelands even as they were legally emancipated from the mission system. In what amounted to a spectacular land grab, wealthy colonists secured between twelve million and thirteen million acres of prime real estate along the coasts and inland valleys of Alta California alone. Some eight hundred grants, awarded in parcels of up to forty-eight thousand acres each, were given out between 1834 and American annexation in 1846 (Clay 1999, 123–24; Hornbeck 1978, 376–78). A similar process unfolded in northern Baja California, but fewer details survive (Meigs 1935, 157–59). Across the region, these massive land grants supported the rise of private stock-raising enterprises, called ranchos. In many instances, the ranchos effectively replaced the missions—carrying on the same kinds of economic pursuits, on the same lands, and with the same labor pool. For many, the gendered and racialized labor roles of the mission era were simply transferred into the ranchos, where Native men worked as vaqueros and field hands while Indigenous women and children labored as domestic servants. Though living conditions and labor demands had changed little from the missions, the ranchos largely ignored the intertwined goals of religious and cultural conversion that had driven the Franciscan and Dominican projects (Silliman 2004). By the 1840s, the missions were all but abandoned and the ranchos were seemingly firmly entrenched in the economy of California.

Two events of the late 1840s fundamentally altered the nature of colonialism on the Pacific Coast of North America. First, in 1846, the onset of the Mexican-American War led to the American annexation of Alta California, a process codified with the signing of the Treaty of Guadalupe Hidalgo in February 1848. Just a week before the signing, gold was found at Sutter's Mill, setting off the California Gold Rush. Soon, the population of non-Native settlers in Alta California surpassed Native Californians for the first time in history. Whereas the missions were designed to integrate Indigenous people into the lowest rungs of the colonial order, the outsiders who arrived during and after the Gold Rush had a profoundly different idea about the place of Native Americans in society. Under the ideology of Manifest Destiny, white settlers sought to eliminate Indigenous people either by forced relocation to reservations or simply by violence. Soon after California gained statehood in 1850, eighteen treaties were haphazardly drawn up and signed, intending to remove Native people to reservations in the region's interior. These treaties were never ratified by the United States Senate (Heizer 1978b). Instead, state and federal policies encouraged settlers and local militias to exterminate Native Californian communities, leading to the deaths of thousands of Indigenous men, women, and children (Lindsay 2012; Madley 2016).

The genocide of the early American period was primarily waged against Native Californians living outside of the missionized coastal strip, but those who had directly experienced the missions were not spared the brunt of settler colonialism. In the remnants of Mexican California, including the Baja California peninsula, newly arrived settlers initially viewed Native people emancipated from the missions as an underclass of docile laborers who could maintain the slowly changing agrarian economy (Hurtado 1988; Phillips 2010). The growing urban centers also required laborers, and state and local governments passed a series of laws that prohibited "idleness" among California Indian populations. This push to reharness Native labor culminated in 1850 in the "Act for the Government and Protection of Indians" in California. This Orwellian piece of legislation provided for the legal indenture of Native children and, in combination with other state and local laws, perpetuated a state of unfree labor for Indigenous people (Madley 2016, 158–59).

At the same time that Native groups throughout the region faced further and further encroachment on their liberties and livelihood, the land was being pulled from beneath their feet. Though the process of granting private land claims initially began under Spanish authority, it accelerated as the century progressed. In the 1850s, the United States government, in the form of the General Land Office, extended the township and range system into California as surveyors set out to measure and divide those areas not previously claimed in the rancho period. The surveys were explicitly intended to facilitate the transfer of real estate—and thus the settlement of the countryside—and accordingly seldom included existing Native Californian communities (Panich et al. 2018e; Robinson 1948). In northwest Mexico, widespread land surveying came relatively late, in the 1880s, but similarly divided vacant land—the so-called *terrenos baldíos*—without recognizing the rights of Indigenous groups to their ancestral homelands. In Baja California, the task of surveying was given over to a series of private "colonization companies" which received one-third of the land surveyed as long as they attracted settlers to the region (Castillo-Muñoz 2017, 24–25; Goldbaum 1971, 12–16; Stephens 2018, 54–55). Even the creation of the international boundary line between the United States and Mexico served to fragment Native communities—particularly Kumeyaay and Cucapá groups—who had lived in the region from time immemorial (e.g., Castillo-Muñoz 2017, 19–20).

Given the changes to the nature of colonialism, the mid-nineteenth century is often the endpoint for the histories of Native Californian groups, particularly those who had labored in the missions. As the Anglo residents of Alta California mined the state's colonial history for the purposes of real estate speculation and tourism, California Indians were romanticized as relics of an earlier, simpler time (Kryder-Reid 2016; Lorimer 2016; Rawls 1984). Like Inigo, whom a local newspaper referred to as "devout, a good Indian" (*Evening News* 1916), the prevailing narrative suggests that Native Californians stoically bore their fate as traditional life inevitably gave way under the crushing weight of American settlement. Such images shaped much early scholarship on Native California, which assumed the extinction—or at least assimilation—of most formerly missionized groups during this time (e.g., Kroeber 1925). Yet, just as Native Californians outlasted the missions designed to unmake their societies, so too did they persevere in the tumultuous years of the late nineteenth century.

Native Negotiations

With secularization, Native Californians were emancipated from Franciscan and Dominican mission systems and many explicitly referenced this freedom as they shook off the yoke of colonial labor requirements and enculturation programs (Haas 1995, 38–44). Yet, with the increasing encroachment of settler colonialism, the Indigenous people of the formerly missionized zone had to make a choice. They could petition for independent land grants in their ancestral territories, work on the ranchos that had expropriated former mission lands, seek opportunity in the growing urban areas along the coast, or take refuge at the margins of colonial-held territory by joining or creating autonomous Indigenous communities (Lightfoot 2006; Panich 2019; Silliman 2004). Each of these options had its own challenges. Land grants, for example, were almost impossible to secure, let alone maintain in the face of malicious legal challenges, and autonomous communities were similarly under constant threat of dispossession. In the early years, ranchos likely offered the easiest transitions but like the missions before them, they were institutions that

survived only on the backs of Native laborers. And despite the relative independence of urban living, it came with the inherent cost of isolation from
ancestral homelands and community. Indigenous people leaving the missions,
then, carefully considered their options for a pathway forward, if they were
lucky enough to have a choice at all.

In some cases, however, Native Californians found that the most viable
option was to go underground. Many no doubt took stock of the horrific violence that white settlers unleashed against Indigenous people, particularly in
Alta California, and decided to turn their Native identities inward. Fearing
violence against their own families, they deployed the knowledge they had
acquired in the missions—the Spanish language, agricultural skills, and familiarity with the Catholic faith—to blend into the region's large mestizo
population. Though people of Hispanic ancestry faced their own persecution
in American California, they did not suffer the same kinds of genocidal violence aimed at Indigenous people. A common refrain during this dark time
was that it was "better to be a hated Mexican than a dead Indian" (Mendoza
2014, 122). The ignorance of white settlers facilitated this kind of passing
as they likely mistook many Native Californians for individuals of Mexican
descent (Field et al. 2013; Rizzo 2016, 317). Though the suppression of
outward Native identity was an intentional survival strategy throughout the
region, it has important methodological implications in the form of underre-
porting of California Indians in census documents and the seeming confirma-
tion of the myth of Indian extinction in the eyes of contemporary observers
(cf. Mancini 2015).

Social-Political Organization

After secularization, many Native people returned to their ancestral homelands where they maintained a variety of communities. Close to the centers of Spanish and Mexican California, some individuals, like Inigo, made
a legal claim to former mission lands. Though few claims were ultimately
successful (Hornbeck 1978, 388), the ability to secure legal title to ancestral
territories was an important first step in ensuring the persistence of specific
communities. North of San Francisco Bay, for example, an Indigenous man
named Camillo Ynitia gained title to the nearly nine-thousand-acre Rancho
Olompali, which was home to a large Native Californian community from
precontact times through the 1850s. Ynitia and most of those living there
after secularization relied on the Olompali land base for both sustenance and
autonomy, at least for a couple of decades (Carlson and Parkman 1986). A

short distance away, five Coast Miwok men emancipated from Mission San Rafael petitioned for title to Rancho Nicasio only to see their claim quashed by Mexican-era elites in 1843. Nevertheless, the Coast Miwok community there—known as Echa-tamal—persisted until the 1880s (Dietz 1976; Panich et al. 2018e). And farther west, along the shores of Tomales Bay, Coast Miwok people established a trading post with an American merchant nicknamed Tom Vaquero. There, intermarriage with an influential newcomer allowed local Coast Miwok people to retain control of the important village of Seglogue, which like Olompali and Echa-tamal, had likely been occupied continuously for countless generations (Schneider and Panich 2019).

For others, however, the onset of the American period and its attendant violence narrowed the options for self-determination. After the failure of the United States Senate to ratify the eighteen treaties of 1851, government officials organized a handful of "military reservations" in the Central Valley and in northern California. Decades later, in 1891, the government created another nine small reservations for groups in southern California after much public outcry. Although the reservations were not ideal, they offered some Native Californians a land base that sheltered them from the ongoing genocide and anchored economic and ceremonial pursuits (Bauer 2016a, 287–89; Heizer 1978a). Others struck out on their own, as in the example of Pomo communities in northern California who pooled their resources to purchase lands from which they could more effectively maintain social and political institutions (Schneider 2010). Regardless of how they obtained it, then, land was often the key to the persistence of Native Californian communities in the second half of the nineteenth century.

Subsistence Economies

With the onset of the Gold Rush and the ensuing population boom of non-Native settlers, many Native Californian communities lost control of their most productive habitats. To make matters worse, extractive economies choked streams and modified the landscape in dramatic ways, challenging Indigenous land-use patterns and traditional ecological practices. In certain locales, however, Native communities were able to blend old ways with new. At Tom Vaquero's trading post, in mid-nineteenth-century Marin County, archaeological research demonstrates a continued focus on aquaculture in the form of clam harvesting. The evidence also points to some continued use of burning as a landscape management practice at the same time that the site's residents consumed pork and other introduced foods (Schneider et al. 2018).

In northern Baja California, where the settler presence was minimal through the end of the nineteenth century, hunting and gathering remained important pursuits in the post-mission landscape (Meigs 1935, 158).

In other cases, Native Californians newly emancipated from the missions turned to the agricultural and domestic skills acquired in the missions as a way to buffer the changes of the mid-nineteenth century. Some used the continuities of labor between the missions and the post-secularization world to their advantage. Many individuals—particularly men, who could serve as vaqueros—worked at the private ranchos that sprang up across the region from the 1830s onward (Phillips 1993, 2010; Silliman 2004). Others, such as those who maintained communities in the growing urban areas of the former Spanish pueblos, worked as domestic servants (Farris 2018; Rizzo 2016, 336–56; Schaefer 2012). These gendered labor regimes of the post-secularization era served to fragment Native communities, and some Native Californian women turned to intermarriage with white settlers as a way to support their communities economically. This practice became increasingly risky amid the violence of the Gold Rush but it may have nevertheless helped to cement crucial alliances that allowed Native people to remain in their homelands (Hurtado 1988; Pérez 2018; Sousa 2015).

Technology and Material Culture

With the increasing number of settlers moving into California, Native people had access to an ever-expanding range of manufactured and imported goods. Conceptually, scholars have been slow to grapple with this archaeological record seemingly rendered mute by industrialization (Lightfoot 2006; Silliman 2010; Watkins 2017). In examining sites like the varied post-mission Coast Miwok settlements described above, the archaeology is clear. Native people used mass-produced items such as metal implements, white earthenwares, and glass bottles alongside objects that would have fit seamlessly within local precontact material traditions, such as obsidian implements and shell beads, well into the second half of the nineteenth century (Dietz 1976; Schneider 2018; Schneider and Panich 2017). While the latter are more typically understood as "Native" artifacts within longstanding archaeological assumptions about Indigenous material culture, the former are no less legitimately connected to the history of Native people. As Silliman (2010) demonstrates through his example of Rancho Petaluma, north of San Francisco Bay, one way to approach these issues is from the context of labor. Native Californians living in the nineteenth century often used the full extent of introduced material culture, ranging from the built environment to tableware, in the course of their work in increasingly shared spaces.

Ceremonial Life

Like material culture, ceremonial life in the second half of the nineteenth century included a mix of new and old. Although important questions remain about the full extent of religious conversion in the missions, some Native Californians continued to practice Catholicism after secularization. In 1879, for example, author Robert Louis Stevenson (1910, 106–107) visited Mission San Carlos, where he found a group of California Indians, probably local Rumsen or Esselen people, singing in Latin. Beyond the reach of the missions, Native religions and related ceremonial beliefs endured. In the Central Valley and adjacent foothills, accounts from the 1870s detail the continuation of annual mourning ceremonies—what observer Stephen Powers (1877) described as a "dance for the dead" that lasted several days and involved the use of an array of objects such as baskets, beads, and other ornaments. Archaeological deposits from north of San Francisco Bay similarly point toward the importance of Indigenous mourning practices, as indicated by the continued destruction through burning of personal effects into the rancho period and beyond (Alvarez and Parkman 2014; King 1966). Still other communities blended existing Indigenous religions to fit the new colonial circumstances, including the dislocating effects of wage labor. Such is the case of the Ghost Dance, which proliferated throughout California and neighboring states in the early 1870s and again in 1890, promising the return of the dead and the disappearance of white settlers. Though the ceremony was based on the Paiute round dance, the central Californian manifestation of the 1870 Ghost Dance was closely associated with a revival of the earlier Kuksu religion (Gayton 1930; Gifford 1926; Smoak 2006; Warren 2015).

Conflict

As they had in the mission period, Native Californians resisted the theft of their land, the violation of their communities, and the appropriation of their labor. Those living beyond the reach of the missions, such as the Yuki in northern California, responded in much the same way as their neighbors who witnessed founding of the initial Spanish settlements in the 1760s and 1770s. After Americans began stealing land and kidnapping women and children in the mid-1850s, the Yuki responded by killing unattended livestock. As the conflict escalated, the Yuki began taking aim at settlers themselves (Madley 2008). Far from the Hollywood stereotype, Yuki and other Native people in nineteenth-century California typically only attacked whites in retaliation for previous abuses. Though it was often a last resort, physical resistance to American expansion came at a catastrophically high price. California Indians who dared to kill white settlers or even livestock unwittingly participated in a cycle of violence that was quickly escalated by settlers intent on eliminating Indigenous groups. As detailed by recent scholarship on the nineteenth-century genocide in California (Lindsay 2012; Madley 2016), such "depredations" on the part of Native people were often used as the rationale for violent reprisals and the increasingly systematic war of extermination in the 1850s and 1860s. The outcome was both appalling and one-sided. "For every white man killed, a hundred Indians paid the penalty with their lives" (Heizer and Almquist 1971, 27).

O

The first several decades after the closing of the missions were a time of great upheaval for most Native Californian groups. Those who had tangled with the Franciscans and Dominicans found that they could keep their communities together by transitioning into the rancho system where the skills they learned in the missions were in high demand, at least in the early years. The arrival of the Americans dramatically changed the social and political landscape of the region, with a brutal campaign of erasure waged against interior tribes. Those along the coast who had participated in the missions and ranchos were spared from the most damaging violence but were nonetheless affected by the broader contours of settler colonialism. Many withdrew to the remote corners of their ancestral homelands, hoping to escape notice and to rebuild the foundations of their communities.

Staking Native Claims in the San Francisco Bay Area

After the secularization of the Franciscan missions in the 1830s, Ohlone families faced a number of challenges. Many of the Central Valley people who had previously resided at Missions Santa Clara and San José returned home as did members of the North Bay communities who had been at Mission San Francisco. Others, predominantly people of Ohlone descent or their relatives by marriage, stayed near the former missions and associated ranchos. The intent of the secularization decree and associated *reglamentos* notwithstanding, no Ohlone individuals from either Mission San Francisco or Mission San José received ex-mission lands from the Mexican government. Ohlone people from Mission Santa Clara, including Inigo, did receive four of the twelve grants that disposed of that mission's sixty-six thousand acres of land. (Milliken et al. 2009, 161; Shoup and Milliken 1999, 110–17). All four Native land grants—Ranchos La Purísima Concepción, Los Coches, Posolmi, and Ulistac—were given to men who were born in, or whose families hailed from, the precise areas for which they petitioned (Table 4). Other Ohlone people from Mission Santa Clara established rancherías on private ranchos, and a community of "free Indians" resided near the secular pueblo (Cambra et al. 2011, 35). Some may have also stayed near the former mission as indicated by a Tamien Ohlone vocabulary collected by a Jesuit instructor at the newly formed Santa Clara College in 1860 (Golla 2011, 165). Taken as a whole, Indigenous settlement patterns in the immediate post-secularization era demonstrate a strong connection to ancestral communities despite the impacts of missionization.

Near the ex-mission of San José, Native people remained without official land grants. A group of Cristianos Viejos, led by a man named Buenaventura who was born in the same region in the 1790s, received a short-lived communal license to farm along Mission Creek in the 1840s (Milliken et al. 2009, 161). This type of arrangement was noted on a map from 1855 that depicts "an agreed line between Estudillo and Indians" that separated rancho lands near San Leandro managed by the Estudillo family and some 3,904 acres that included fields cultivated by Native Californians during the 1840s (Gray 1855). It is unclear when these people lost their fields, but by 1856, Native families associated with Sylvester, one of the independent farmers of the area, were working for the Estudillos and their neighbor Guillermo

Table 4. Grants of mission lands to Native people in the San Francisco Bay area

Name of Land Grant	Date	Acres	Grantee(s)	Ethnolinguistic Affiliation	Baptismal Mission
La Purísima Concepción	1840	4,439	José Gorgonio and José Ramon	Bay Area Ohlone	Santa Clara
Posolmi	1844	3,042	Lope Inigo	Bay Area Ohlone	Santa Clara
Los Coches	1844	2,219	Roberto	Bay Area Ohlone	Santa Clara
Ulistac	1845	2,277	Macelo, Pio, and Cristobal	Bay Area Ohlone	Santa Clara

Source: Shoup and Milliken 1999, 113.

Castro (Schlichtmann 1988, 27). Little published archaeology exists for these ranchos or others closer to the former Mission San José, where Native people also found employment. Testing at the Suñol family rancho found that Native laborers there continued to employ obsidian tools and likely established their residential area on or near a precontact settlement (Luby 1995). A similar pattern, including the recovery of flaked glass tools, was noted during archaeological mitigation at an adobe associated with the Alviso family in Milpitas (Evans 2010). The new American government, however, quashed most existing land claims by the 1860s, and Mexican-era elites—and the Native people they relied on—lost most of their land holdings (Field et al. 1992, 424–25). Even without formal title to their homelands, Ohlone people and their kin coalesced along the southeastern shores of the bay during the mid-nineteenth century, creating new communities that brought together survivors of the various Bay Area missions (Cambra et al. 2011, 36).

Oral narratives collected by John Peabody Harrington in the 1920s offer some detail regarding life in the East Bay in the second half of the nineteenth century. The San Leandro-San Lorenzo area, for example, was home to many Native people. Among them was Angela Colos, who lived at the Estudillo family rancho as a young woman and whose parents married at Mission Santa Clara. She recalled seeing a Native man named Martín who gave sermons from a temescal near San Leandro (Harrington 1984, reel 36, 515). Another well-known Ohlone man, Pedro Alcantara* (also known as "Pedro Confessor"), continued to preach the Christian religion. He "traveled around much" in the early years, making stops near San Lorenzo among other locations, but eventually settled at the Pleasanton ranchería described at the end of this section (Harrington 1984, reel 37, 310, 828; reel 71, 434, 515). Farther south, near Newark and Alviso, Native people continued to use the marshlands much as they always had. Some newcomers recognized Ohlone people's traditional rights to the bayshore. As one Mr. Manyan told them, "It's your land." Yet, this was likely an exception to the rule and Ohlones in that area remained wary. Harrington's consultants recalled the practice of resisting the imposition of colonial bureaucracy by giving false names—"one said beans, and another rope, and another turnips"—to tax collectors. One man in

---

* This man was variably remembered as a Chocheño (by Angela Colos) or Clareño (by José Guzman). The ancestry of the Chocheño Pedro Alcantara (SJS Baptism 1292) is unstated but was almost certainly Bay Area Ohlone given the ethnolinguistic composition of the mission at the time of his baptism in 1804. The Clareño Pedro Alcantara (SCL Baptism 4892) was of the Luecha Ohlone group. It is also possible that the man recalled by Angela Colos and José Guzman was the well-known Pedro Alcantara of Mission San Francisco (SFD Baptism 553), who lived at least into the 1850s (Milliken et al. 2009, 195–96). Given the relative ages of the three men, the Chocheño Pedro Alcantara is most likely the man in question.

particular, José Catarino, wondered, "Why do they want to know my name?"
He proceeded to employ the fanciful surnames of Cresta-de-Gallo, Pisa-Flor,
Zancas-de-Caballo, and possibly others when interacting with the priest at
the ex-mission of San José (Harrington 1984, reel 71, 505–506, 512–513).

While the southern reaches of San Francisco Bay offered some refuge from
the changes sweeping the region, Ohlone people no doubt felt the squeeze of
the Gold Rush in rapidly expanding urban areas such as San Francisco, which
saw its non-Native population skyrocket in the late 1840s. Some families
remained associated with Mission San Francisco, as documented by baptisms
performed there in the 1840s and 1850s. Of the eight California Indian families whose children appear in the sacramental records, at least half can be
traced to Ohlone individuals (Milliken et al. 2009, 183–84). Others moved
farther south on the peninsula where they worked as laborers, often for Mexican elites who had managed to hold onto land after the American annexation.
According to the 1852 California state census, for example, most of the Native men, women, and children living in the San Francisco–San Mateo region
were associated with only a handful of colonial families. These groups are frus-
tratingly hard to identify as most are simply listed in aggregate, as in the case
of "21 Indians," including 17 men and 4 women, associated with ranchero
José Chico Sanchez (California 1852, roll 4, 483). Among those named with
sufficient detail to be identified in mission records were Juan Diego, a former
Native resident of Mission San Francisco, his wife Rosalia, and "13 Indians"
under the age of 21, presumably their children (California 1852, roll 4, 464;
Milliken et al. 2009, 191).

The documentary record for Native Californians living in the San Francisco Bay Area thins even more during the 1860s and 1870s. Despite the
relatively large numbers of Native people living on the San Francisco peninsula in the 1852 California census, few of those listed for San Francisco in
the 1870 federal census were born in California. San Mateo County counted
only eight Native individuals in that year, a figure that is contradicted by
the recollections of Nels Nelson's informants who recalled some of the shell
mounds "south of San Mateo as having been occupied by the Indians as late
as 1870" (Nelson 1909, 347). For Santa Clara County, the 1860 United States
Census lists approximately 160 people classified as "Indian"—counting individuals originating outside of California—but the county had only three
California-born Indians listed in the 1870 federal census (Kehl and Yamane
1995; Milliken et al. 2009).[*] Although Alameda County, in the East Bay,

---

[*] The figures vary slightly between Kehl and Yamane (1995) and Milliken et al. (2009). Kehl
and Yamane examined the original census documents whereas Milliken et al. drew their data from

retained roughly equivalent numbers of Indians from 1860 to 1870, my comparison of census rolls for those decades found almost no continuity in individuals listed as "Indian" (U.S. Census 1860a, 1860b, 1870a, 1870b). In other words, the total figures indicate a relatively stable Native population, but the individuals listed are almost completely different from one decade to the next. This pattern, combined with the seeming disappearance of Native people from Bay Area counties like San Mateo and Santa Clara, is reflective of an Indigenous population occupying the far margins of society.

Federal census records' limited utility for tracking Native Californians during this time has several interconnected causes. The first is migration as many Native people are listed as laborers or farm hands—jobs that were likely only temporarily held. It is also probable that census takers simply missed or ignored some Indigenous people. Of those who are on census rolls, many are listed without surnames, which makes them difficult to track with confidence. And even having surnames may not be sufficient to identify Native women who changed their names with marriage (Kehl and Yamane 1995). It is also likely that Native Californians passed as Mexicans, given the extreme violence and discrimination faced by Indigenous people during this time. For example, from the 1830s into the 1860s, settlers routinely abducted Native children and sold them into servitude. Though most of the children originated outside the missionized zone, many found themselves working in the greater San Francisco Bay Area (Heizer and Almquist 1971, 40–41). Their presence no doubt made an impression on Ohlone people. Angela Colos, who had been associated with Mission San José, recalled seeing "[a] wagon filled with Indian children coming down from Martinez . . . They were bringing them *como animal* [like animals] to be brought up by Spanish Californians . . . They wanted some water to drink. They were naked" (Harrington 1984, reel 37, 488). It was not until 1873, when Native Californians finally secured the right to testify against whites, that the unfree labor conditions finally started to abate (Madley 2014, 660–61).

With these caveats in mind, I analyzed the 1860 and 1870 United States Census records for Santa Clara and Alameda Counties in an attempt to understand how Native people navigated these turbulent times (U.S. Census 1860a, 1860b, 1870a, 1870b). As noted above, very few individuals conclusively appear in both decades. The clearest case is Mary Moore. In 1860, she was listed as nine-year-old "Minnie Moore," living in Oakland (Alameda County) with the Moore family who had come to California from Pennsylvania. Her

summary statistics. My examination of the primary evidence corresponds to the information given by Kehl and Yamane.

ethnicity is listed as Indian and she is noted as having been born in California. That she was a single California Indian child in a household of white settlers suggests that she may have been abducted from her biological family. She appears in the 1870 census as eighteen-year-old servant "Mary A. Moore" living with members of the same Moore family, though the Moores by this time had split into two households. She was still recorded as Indian, but her birthplace was now listed as Mexico. By 1880, Mary had completed her transformation, as she is listed as white, with Mexico as her birthplace (U.S. Census 1880). Though she remained a domestic servant for members of the Moore family, the census records demonstrate a gradual but ultimately successful move up the racial hierarchy of the time.

Other possible matches between the 1860 and 1870 census rolls suggest that passing as non-Native was a relatively common strategy. Guadalupe Berryessa, for example, was listed as a teenaged Indian servant in Alviso Township (Santa Clara County) in 1860 but he appears as a white farmer in the same township a decade later. Previous genealogical work suggests Guadalupe Berryessa had Indigenous ancestry from the Monterey area but was most often identified as *razón*, or white (Kehl and Yamane 1995, 25–27).* Within Alameda County, I found two other possible instances of passing. One was an eight-year-old Indian girl known only as Rosa, who lived with the Torres family in San Leandro in 1860 and who may be the same person as a seventeen-year-old servant named Rosa Keston, who was living in Oakland a decade later. In 1870, Rosa is listed as being white, but her birthplace reads "Cal Native Indian." Lastly, an Indian man named Marin Jesus, recorded in 1860, may be M. Jesus, living in the same township in 1870 but who was listed as white with a Mexican origin. Aside from Guadalupe Berryessa, the exact tribal origins of these individuals are unknown, but their experiences likely mirror those of Bay Area Ohlone people during this time.

I found no other conclusive evidence of individuals who appeared on both the 1860 and 1870 census rolls for Alameda or Santa Clara County, though the lack of surnames for many Native individuals precludes a definitive statement on the subject. For example, two Indian men listed as living in Santa Clara County in 1860 may appear in Alameda County in 1870. Both Pedro Antonio Real and Domingo Ruis are recorded as twenty-something Indian

---

* A similar case involves Guadalupe Bernal, who was also listed as an Indian servant in San Jose in 1860. A Guadalupe Bernal listed as a white San Jose farmer in the 1870 census is probably the same Guadalupe Macsimo Bernal baptized as *gente de razón* at Mission Santa Clara in 1839 (SCL Baptism 9944), grandson of a leather-jacket soldier and member of the prominent Bernal family of Santa Clara Valley. Another possible match is Yadalupe Bernal, who was listed in 1870 as a white fruit farmer in Alameda County.

men living in San Jose (Santa Clara County) in 1860 and are missing from the 1870 Santa Clara County rolls, which contain very few people of Native descent. However, two forty-year-old Indian men living near Pleasanton (Alameda County) in 1870 are named Pedro and "Doming." Even though the lack of surnames from the 1870 enumeration makes a secure link impossible—particularly since Hispanic given names were a lasting legacy of the mission system for many Native Californians—the ages generally align and there are no Native Pedros or Domingos from the 1860 Alameda County rolls who might have been enumerated a decade later.

Given that Pedro and Domingo would have been born in the late mission period, it may be possible to trace them back to the Franciscan establishments using the Early California Population Project database (Huntington Library 2006). Of the handful of men named Domingo baptized at Missions Santa Clara or San José and who lack death records—and who therefore would have been alive to see secularization—there is only one whose age matches the Domingo of 1860 and 1870. José Domingo was baptized at Santa Clara as a newborn on October 25, 1829 (SCL Baptism 8310). He was the son of Bibiano and Hilaria, both of whom were the mission-born children of Ohlone parents (SCL Baptisms 1301 and 5657, respectively). Hilaria herself seems to have maintained a relatively high status in the mission community (Peelo et al. 2018b).* Pedro is harder to match as several men named Pedro baptized at Missions Santa Clara and San José were living at the time of secularization. However, limiting the search to Pedro Antonio—the name that appears on the 1860 Santa Clara County rolls—offers two possibilities, both from Mission Santa Clara. The first was born in 1829 to Ohlone parents (SCL Baptism 8298)† while the other was born a decade later to parents who hailed from the Central Valley (SCL Baptism 9991).‡ Though it does not resolve the question of his origin, the 1880 federal census lists an Indian man named "Padro Antonio" living near Pleasanton, which may help to secure the connection to Mission Santa Clara (U.S. Census 1880).

---

* Bibiano's father was not known to the missionary who recorded his baptism, but his mother was from the Ohlone ranchería of San Juan Bautista (just south of the mission) and was baptized as a teenager in 1780 (SCL Baptism 918). Hilaria's parents, Queip and Coecaqe (baptized as Quincio and Cecillia, SCL Baptisms 4995 and 5439), were both from the important Ohlone community of Tayssen and were among the last Ohlone to be baptized at Mission Santa Clara.

† The father was also named Pedro Antonio and was baptized at the ranchería of San Joseph as a one-year-old on the first day of Santa Clara baptisms in June 1777 (SCL Baptism 10). The mother was named Guassem and was from the district of San Carlos, which encompassed rancherías south of what is today San Jose. She was baptized as Quiteria in 1803 (SCL Baptism 4431).

‡ The parents, José and María Francisca, are both listed as *Tulareño* neophytes, but their baptism numbers were not recorded.

Whatever their background, Pedro and Domingo were, by 1870, part of
an important Native hub of the late-nineteenth-century San Francisco Bay
Area. Indeed, the hills south of modern-day Pleasanton had attracted many
former mission residents as they were pushed off bayshore lands during the
1850s and 1860s. The largest Pleasanton-area settlement was called Alisal
and was closely associated with the Bernal family ranch. Along with Native
settlements near Niles (El Molino) and Sunol, these communities were home
to many Ohlone individuals as well as others with whom they had forged
connections in the missions, including people of Yokuts, Bay Miwok, Plains
Miwok, and Coast Miwok descent. As Indigenous communities across the
region fragmented in the American period, Native people living near Pleasanton used marriage and godparenting as ways to ensure group cohesion
(Field et al. 1992; Leventhal et al. 1994; and see Cambra et al. 2011 for further genealogical details). Still, Ohlone people continued to seek each other
out as indicated by the statement of one former Alisal resident in the 1920s:
"The Clareños were much intermarried with the Chocheños. The dialects
were similar" (Harrington 1984, reel 36, 197). Some, like Francisco Luecha
and José Luecha from Mission Santa Clara, even converted their ancestral
community name to their surname, perhaps to retain an important affiliation in the multiethnic milieu of the late nineteenth century (Harrington
1984, reel 36, 593–94). Ohlone people living in the region also kept their
Indigenous language alive; a Costanoan vocabulary recorded at Niles in 1884
is nearly identical to similar documents from San Lorenzo and Mission San
José (Beeler 1961).

Over the course of the late nineteenth century, Alisal was home to a vibrant Native community, where certain Indigenous practices were revitalized
at the same time that people adapted to the new realities of the American
period. A prime example is the meshing of the central Californian Kuksu
religion, which had been important at Mission San José, with the messianic
Ghost Dance of the 1870s (Collier and Thalman 1991, 235; Smoak 2006,
116). At least three teachers—one of whom, Tciplitcu, was likely Ohlone—
fanned out from the Pleasanton area to proselytize among the interior Miwok
groups to the east (Gifford 1926, 400–402). The Alisal community itself was
oriented around a centrally located sweat lodge, or temescal, in which the
Kuksu dances were held. The fiestas would draw Native people from as far
away as Sonoma and San Rafael. After the Hearst family purchased the land
on which the community was living, wealthy Americans from San Francisco
would come by train to watch the Kuksu dances (Harrington 1984, reel 36,
42; reel 71, 508, 521–22). The final known Kuksu dance at Alisal was held in
1897. Three years later, the sweat lodge was torn down after the death of José

Antonio, the last recognized captain of the Alisal ranchería, in keeping with Indigenous traditions (Field et al. 1992, 426; Galvan 1968, 12). His wife, Jacoba, seems to have taken on some of his leadership duties, as was common in Native California. Yet, by this time, the increasing urbanization of the San Francisco Bay Area was steadily encroaching on the hilly refuge afforded by Alisal and neighboring communities.

From secularization to the dawn of the twentieth century, Bay Area Ohlone people faced a new set of challenges spurred by the advance of American settler colonialism. Though the promises of secularization were almost immediately broken by Mexican-period elites, Native people were able to fall back on the skills learned in the missions to maintain economic continuity in California's agrarian economy. In the late 1840s, the dual revolutions of American annexation and the Gold Rush quickly transformed the region, and Ohlone families and their relations sought refuge in the hills of the southeastern Bay Area as the demographic and political changes radiated outward from the north. There, they found common cause at Alisal and other interrelated rancherías. Indigenous religion thrived at the same time that agricultural work remained an important source of livelihood despite the rapid urbanization of San Francisco, Oakland, and San Jose. The lives of individual Ohlone are difficult to see against the backdrop of the region's demographic and economic growth during this time, but Native people maintained significant social identities based on precontact and mission ancestry even as they intermarried with each other to perpetuate their contemporary community.

Staking Native Claims in the Sierra Juárez

The Dominican missions of northern Baja California met various ends—destruction, sacking, or just gradual abandonment—over the course of the 1830s and 1840s. These institutions never reached the size or influence of their counterparts in Alta California, but like the Franciscan establishments north of the newly surveyed border, most were effectively shuttered by 1850. Some people drifted away to seek opportunities in urban areas as evidenced by the presence of Native people from Baja California working as servants in Old Town, San Diego, in the 1830s. The small California Indian community there even included a man named Pelegrino Camacho from Mission Santa Catalina (Farris 2018). Other Native people chose to remain near the former mission complexes. One group was said to reside along the coast north of El Rosario in 1849, and others remained in the area near Mission Santo Tomás from

FIGURE 16. "Relics of the Santo Tomas Mission and their Guardian, Lower California." Magic lantern slide, publisher unknown. Probably late nineteenth century. From
the collection of the author.

the 1840s into the 1870s (Gabb 1867; Hohenthal 2001, 12; Parker 1876)
(Figure 16). However, most of Baja California's remaining Native populations
returned to ancestral villages, either by choice or by intimidation as they were
pushed off fertile agricultural lands (Meigs 1935).

The one mission where this pattern did not hold was Mission Santa Catalina. Though the mission itself was destroyed by Native rebels, the place
it occupied—*Jaca-tobojol*, in the Native language—remained an important
crossroads of Indigenous life. Like Alisal in the San Francisco Bay Area, Santa
Catarina (as it came to be known) attracted a wide range of Native people
by offering the promise of community and a refuge from settler colonialism.
Though referred to today as the Paipai, this group—like so many throughout
the Californias—was known historically by the name of the mission with
which they had been associated. As early as 1852, local Mexican officials were
using the phrase "el tribu de Santa Catarina" to describe the people residing
on the former mission lands (Castro 1852). Nearly two decades later, a newspaper account referred to the group as the "Catarineños" (Shipek 1965, 27).

The Catarineños did not face the same demographic pressures as their
compatriots in the San Francisco Bay Area. One enumeration put the population of the entire frontera at 2,872 in 1857. Of that total, at least 2,500

were Indians,* a figure that generally squares with other period estimates (Lassépas 1859, 47; Shipek 1965, 52). The mountainous interior of northern Baja California provided the setting for a range of refuge communities from the international border near Tecate to the northern reaches of the Sierra San Pedro Mártir. In the Paipai homelands, some families returned to their ancestral villages near San Isidoro and Jamau, but many remained near the ruins of Mission Santa Catalina (Garduño 1994, 61). By 1870, roughly 80 individuals were living at Santa Catarina whereas eight Native families were established near the former mission fields in the San Miguel valley.† The same accounts from 1870 also describe neighboring groups, including the Kiliwa, some of whom continued to live in the high elevations near the former mission of San Pedro Mártir and could occasionally be found working in the salt mines of San Quintín. Another group, numbering some 100 individuals, was living near Valle de la Trinidad in their "wild state" (Shipek 1965, 27, 29, 42). Given their location, these too were probably people of Kiliwa descent.

Despite the new international border between the United States and Mexico, Native people continued patterns of mobility that took them, or culturally important goods, between southern California and Baja California. Individuals involved in regional exchange networks conveyed materials such as abalone, shell beads, and other items from the Pacific Coast of Baja California northeast to Yuma territory along the Colorado River well into the 1860s (Taylor 1864, 34). In other instances, individuals themselves moved north into Alta California, as noted by the Kumeyaay leader Jatñil, who stated that many members of his tribe went north during the Gold Rush of 1849 (Rojo 1972, 46). Others remained in Kumeyaay lands near the growing city of San Diego. One man from Mission Santa Catalina, José Manuel Polton Hatam, who lived in San Diego with his wife Juana, even became the captain of the city's urban Indian community in the 1860s and 1870s (Carrico 2008, 124–27). It is notable that he retained his clan name, Jat'am, which had featured so prominently in the mission's 1834 census; in fact, the document lists a José Manuel Jatam who was married to a woman named Juana, perhaps indicating that the two made the trek northward together. Yet, the flow of people was more often southward as Native families being pushed off their land in the United States sought refuge with kin south of the border. Delfina Cuero (1968), a well-known Kumeyaay woman, recalled that her grandparents and other coastal Kumeyaay moved to

---

* This total likely omitted the populous Cucapá of the Colorado River Delta. A report from 1870 gave the Cucapá alone a population of 3,420 individuals (Castillo-Muñoz 2017, 13; Henderson 1964, 189).

† These figures come from two separate accounts so it is possible they refer to the same people.

Baja California as white settlers forced them out of the coastal valleys near San Diego sometime in the late nineteenth century.

Still, Indigenous people in northern Baja California were not immune from dispossession. Settlers across the region bought and sold property with little regard for the sovereignty of the land's original inhabitants or the intent of the secularization decree. In the early years, many former mission tracts, often consisting of lands occupied by Indigenous people, were deeded over to colonial soldiers in repayment for debts owed to them. This process began in the Spanish period but accelerated from the 1830s onward (Castillo-Muñoz 2017, 20–22; Lassépas 1859, 225; León Velazco 2010; Meigs 1935, 155–59). Documents from the 1850s make clear that local officials saw the Indigenous residents of the former mission lands as a deterrent to incoming settlers. For example, a military administrator of northern Baja California lamented, "We can populate these missions with families that could make good use of these lands, but savage Indians are currently occupying the land. No families want to go near them, because they are afraid of the Indians" (Castillo-Muñoz 2017, 21). In the case of Santa Catalina, the area was awarded to an outsider, Ricardo Palacias, in 1855, though the new owner seems not to have ever maintained a permanent presence there (Lassépas 1859, 104).

As in Alta California, Native communities were often either displaced or forced to work as laborers for the putative owners of the land. By the 1860s, foreign interests, in the form of the colonization companies, began to survey and partition the terrenos baldíos of northern Baja California. Though ultimately unsuccessful, these promotional schemes peaked in the 1880s alongside a land boom in neighboring southern California. Native people recognized the threat posed by these companies and, in 1887, banded together to petition the government to stop the theft of their land (Garduño 2003, 16–17). Their complaint was unsuccessful, and the Paipai and their neighbors were typically described as a docile and available labor force in documents produced to sell the region to foreign investors and settlers (Bendímez Patterson 1989, 66; Castillo-Muñoz 2017, 20–30; Goldbaum 1971; Nordhoff 1888). For example, one account from 1870 noted that the "domesticated Indians" of Santa Catarina would be "useful as laborers on the ranchos" (Shipek 1965, 27). Yet, even as their labor was in demand, the mobility of Native people threatened settler interests. Traditional hunting and gathering activities were now considered illicit acts of trespass and theft as demonstrated by the case of a group of Native people who were detained by Jacob Hanson, a Norwegian immigrant, in the 1880s while on their way to the annual piñon harvest in the Sierra Juárez (Garduño 2003, 14).

Despite the overall paucity of information about the daily lives of Native people during the second half of the nineteenth century, regional leaders are surprisingly visible in the historical record. One reason for this pattern likely stems from the unique nature of secularization of northern Baja California's missions, which can be seen as a concession to the fact that many groups remained autonomous despite nearly seventy years of Dominican proselytization. Some regional leaders, Jatñil and Nicuárr among them, rose to power in the late mission period, creating alliances between various lineages and across ethnolinguistic boundaries—relationships that may have persisted into the late nineteenth century in some cases. Another reason for the visibility of Native leaders after secularization is that Mexican officials encouraged communities made up of several shimuls to recognize a single political leader. Whereas mission-period documents refer to local leaders as *capitán*, noting a leadership role at the head of a particular ranchería or shimul, later leaders were called *general*. These generales were intended to mediate between the Mexican government and larger Indian "nations" and, therefore, did not necessarily reflect internally defined sociopolitical roles that continued to be based on shimul affiliation (Alvárez de Williams 2004; Garduño 1994, 193–95; Magaña Mancillas 2005, 114–15; Owen 1962, 157).

The exact sequence of political succession in Santa Catarina is unclear, but documents from the period identify several Native leaders. A letter from 1852, for example, indicates that one Capitán Bellota of the Tribu de Santa Catarina had died and his replacement—a Native man named Bartolo Salgado, "for whom, according to reports, the aforementioned people have some respect"—was appointed by a Mexican official. The letter goes on to state that "in this virtue, the authorities of this frontier will consider him and aid in his good management so that he keeps the tribe in order and occupied" (Castro 1852). By 1866, the community seems to have been under the leadership of El General Clemente who had been appointed by Mexican President Benito Juárez on the recommendation of the authorities of the frontera. Manuel Rojo remarked that Clemente was "an uncommon natural talent" with "very good judgement" (Rojo 2000, 115). Just five years later, however, another leader was chosen for the Native community of Santa Catarina. This man, named Chueco, was apparently nominated by a committee of Indigenous authorities from nearby communities like La Huerta (Rojo 2000, 61). Though appointed by outsiders, the presence of these leaders in the documentary record speaks to the relative power that Indigenous groups in northern Baja California maintained in the wake of secularization.

Other clues to the nature of Native communities during the second half of the nineteenth century come from early ethnographic notes and word lists collected by the Smithsonian Institution and others. For example, William Gabb (1867) collected linguistic information from several groups in the region, noting that Kiliwa people could be found living near San Quintín and that the "H'taam" continued to live near Mission Santo Tomás. Another word list from Santo Tomás, collected in 1876, bears a later note saying that it is "almost identical with the Hta-am of Wm M. Gabb," suggesting that the same family or families lived there a decade later (Parker 1876). The most useful linguistic document for understanding the interior world of the Sierra Juárez is a word list collected in December 1884, entitled "Vocabulary of the Language Spoken at Santa Catarina." While this document no doubt points toward the enduring importance of Santa Catarina as a regional hub, the linguistic information was actually collected in San Diego from a Native woman who had married a Paipai man and lived for some years in Santa Catarina. She stated that, of the various rancherías or tribes living at Santa Catarina, "Hata-am," "Kwal-a-whut," and "A-whut" were the most prominent (Henshaw 1884). These names clearly represent particular shimuls—Jat'am, Kwal-xwat, and Xwa't—listed in the mission padrón of 1834 (see Table 3), indicating a large degree of residential stability over the course of fifty years.

For the first three decades after the collapse of the missions, the Native inhabitants of the Sierra Juárez likely encountered only a handful of settlers. These newcomers divided the land according to new rules and often ran cattle across Paipai territories (Bendímez Patterson 1989) but they themselves were outnumbered demographically. Even as late as 1887, Ensenada—one of the region's largest urban centers—counted only fourteen hundred residents (Henderson 1964, 197). As in Alta California, this equation quickly shifted with the discovery of gold. Though there had been scattered reports of mineral wealth in the Sierra Juárez dating back decades, the first major strikes near Santa Catarina occurred in the early 1870s. Other minor deposits were worked on both slopes of the Paipais' highland territory throughout the period, with the biggest local gold rush occurring near El Álamo in 1888 and 1889. Few accounts of these nineteenth-century gold-mining activities directly describe the participation of Native people, but they were present as both miners and laborers (Carrico 2008, 81; Chaput et al. 1992; Lingenfelter 1967). One recollection of life in Sierra Juárez gold-mining towns states, "Most of the Indians around El Álamo just lived out in the open, they didn't have houses. They wore just about the same clothing they do now, only then they had no shoes" (Owen 1963, 384). This account, which also mentions Native women engaging in sex work, suggests that Paipai individuals at El Álamo and other boom towns did not integrate into the mainstream of settler society.

Overall, the experiences of Native people in the Baja California gold strikes mirrored the broader strategies of avoidance and selective engagement employed by the Paipai and their neighbors after the collapse of the missions. Individuals present in the documentary record are largely those people—appointed

generales and early anthropological consultants—who made the choice to interact with colonial authorities or other settlers. The bulk of the region's Indian
population, however, are discussed only in aggregate, if at all. This posture is
reflective of an inward turn, away from the failed colonial policies and their attendant conflicts witnessed in the mission period. As described by Paipai elder
Benito Peralta, who heard the stories from his forebears, "So what the Native
people did was to leave the best lands, those good for agriculture, and they took
hold of the uplands. But I say that they did this for a certain reason, for in those
times they did not practice agriculture nor raise livestock. Then, following the
wild fruits, they took hold of the uplands, where the agaves and other wild
plants were better, they took hold of that" (Bendímez Patterson 1989, 54).

The rugged Sierra Juárez offered the context for Paipai families and other
Native people to keep to themselves while remaining in their ancestral homelands, or at least in those of their compatriots (Garduño 1994, 51–54). There,
community structure coalesced around particular settlements, such as Santa
Catarina, where a critical mass of families offered support and sustenance
even as the shimul system continued to shape social identity. At the close of
the century, one local observer reported some twenty Indigenous rancherías
in northern Baja California (Alvárez de Williams 2004, 108). Though no
systematic archaeological evidence exists to illuminate daily life during this
time, findings from Kumeyaay communities immediately to the north in Alta
California show that closely related Native people used similar mountainous enclaves to keep their communities and cultural traditions alive despite
being "pushed into the rocks" by a growing settler population (Hildebrand
and Hagstrum 1995; Shipek 1988). Demographic pressures were less immediate in Paipai territory, and Native families were able to continue to visit a
wide variety of places along the coasts as they sought to reclaim autonomy
in the wake of missionization. Nevertheless, amid the political and demographic changes of the nineteenth century, the Paipai continued a pattern
of coalescence—initiated by the establishment of Mission Santa Catalina in
1797—that more and more firmly rooted them to their mountain homelands.

Summary

By the end of the nineteenth century, Native Californians clung to often tenuous claims at the margins of a new, but already deeply entrenched, settler
society. How they came to occupy such a space reflects a lengthy process of
both dispossession and a concerted strategy to retain autonomy in the face of
further change. The initial years after the secularization of the Franciscan and

Dominican mission systems offered Native people certain continuities within the familiar, yet similarly exploitative, rancho economy that developed all across the formerly missionized regions. Given the ubiquity of ranchos, which typically eschewed the religious and cultural proselytization of the missions, many Indigenous families found ways to remain in their ancestral homelands—and some, like Inigo, even managed to work within the colonial system to gain legal title to their home villages. From the vantage point of the early 1840s, both the Ohlone and Paipai likely saw opportunities to reestablish the very communities and lifeways that the missionaries had sought to destroy.

The Treaty of Guadalupe Hidalgo in 1848 fundamentally changed future options for both groups. After the annexation of Alta California by the United States, many Native people faced a vicious campaign of physical violence and legal machinations from incoming Anglo settlers. Though spared the most horrific abuses, the Ohlone of the San Francisco Bay Area nonetheless suffered the loss of many of their ancestral homelands to settlers pouring into the region during and after the Gold Rush. By the 1870s, Ohlone people and allied Native Californians established a series of refuge communities in the hills beyond the former mission of San José. In northern Baja California, in contrast, the Paipai and their neighbors capitalized on the small settler population of the interior to maintain residence in a broad constellation of places in and around the Sierra Juárez—consisting of ancestral shimul territories and newer multiethnic communities—that had given them sustenance during the Dominican mission period. In both regions, Native people relied on these communities, whether newly established or built on centuries-old foundations, to provide support, nourishment, and the perpetuation of traditions within the context of rapidly changing circumstances.

Though they often lacked legal title to their lands, the residents of places like Alisal and Santa Catarina also used aspects of their geographical marginalization to their advantage. Certainly, minimizing contact with settlers was a way to avoid exploitation—or worse. But by keeping to themselves and by occupying lands less attractive to newcomers, residents of these communities managed to avoid interference in their daily lives. Like Indigenous groups throughout the Borderlands, Ohlone and Paipai families had firsthand experience with the highly controlled social environments of the missions and clearly found them wanting. Their low visibility in the documentary record of the second half of the nineteenth century is part and parcel of the same pattern, but some instances of intentional noncooperation can be detected in the archives. Examples include the refusal of Ohlone individuals to give their names to priests or tax collectors or the decades-long practice of Paipai people using their shimul affiliations as surnames.

All across the former California colonies, Native people quietly adapted to the new settler states that were being constructed around them. By the close of the nineteenth century—two generations removed from the closing of the missions—the Ohlone and Paipai were still living in their ancestral territories. They preserved their communities by maintaining intimate ties, solidified through ceremony and kinship, to other Native groups. Their daily lives were shaped by the wisdom of their ancestors but simultaneously in-corporated strategic decisions about how to face the shifting constraints of colonialism and dispossession. Having weathered a seemingly never-ending stream of structural and direct violence since the first permanent colonies were founded in the 1760s and 1770s, Native Californians were in many cases finally able to plan for a stable future. In the years that followed, how-ever, these communities came under increased scrutiny from outsiders who sought to define what it meant to be Indian. As detailed in the next chapter, government agents and anthropologists crisscrossed the region, often making far-reaching decisions based on essentialist assumptions about what Native Californian societies should look like.

6

Divergent Pathways in the Twentieth Century

JOSÉ GUZMAN WAS AWAY WHEN he heard that the anthropologist was back. José had been working at Niles on a crew running a steam-powered threshing machine. It was hard work, especially for someone his age, but at least he was able to see some of the other Native men who still lived in the area around Alisal. Being the fourth of July, the foreman let everyone off early. Instead of celebrating with the other workers, José caught a ride to the southern reaches of Pleasanton—an area where the highway and railroad tracks followed the creek down to Sunol. Once home, he opened a window to let the air circulate and waited on the back porch until things cooled off. That's when the anthropologist arrived. Harrington, as he called himself, had recently traveled from San Francisco—a trip that involved a ferry, a streetcar, and ultimately a train, topped off with a chicken dinner at the Colombo Restaurant. If José had eaten that evening, he did not say. Despite the late hour, Harrington was eager to follow up on the issue of the giant footprints, those legendary depressions in the local bedrock that José and his father had visited years ago. There was one at Niles, near the old path to Mission San José. Another was right by the Pleasanton Ranchería—just past the houses of Rustico and José Antonio—and a third was on Brushy Peak, toward the San Joaquin River. Though he remained somewhat suspicious of Harrington, he explained the footprints to his enthusiastic guest. The year was 1925, and José knew that the knowledge his father had given him would be lost, that something meaningful would be gone forever, if he did not tell Harrington what he knew. He spoke with the anthropologist late into the night.[*]

A quarter of a century earlier, in 1900, José Guzman, his friends, and relatives were relatively secure in their place in the new political and social order that had transformed California since the Americans had arrived. These survivors had created a network of communities in the hills beyond Mission San José, maintaining a strong attachment to the homelands of their ancestors, who had joined the mission nearly one hundred years prior, around 1800. Their refuge—centered on Pleasanton, Niles, and Sunol—included the descendants of the Cristianos Viejos, those Ohlone people whose ancestral territories were close to Mission San José as well as others from Missions Santa Clara and San Francisco. While they had largely kept their distance in the mission system, intermarriage with Central Valley groups became more common over the course of the nineteenth century as Alisal attracted Indian people who faced dispossession throughout the region. Yet, in the span of two short decades, things had fallen apart. The deaths of key community members in the early 1900s were followed by further settler expansion into the area, and in the mid-1910s, a fire consumed the homes of many remaining residents of the Alisal community. Though Harrington and other anthropologists visited Guzman and several additional elders living in the area during the opening decades of the twentieth century, they viewed them as isolated remnants rather than a cohesive population. This mischaracterization has haunted the Ohlone ever since.

Nearly 550 airline miles to the southeast, the Paipai of Santa Catarina encountered Harrington the year after his evening visit to José Guzman's home near Pleasanton. There, several different individuals spoke with the anthropologist, detailing ethnonyms, place names, and political structure. From his notes, it is clear Harrington considered them to be a living community. Berkeley anthropologists were also keenly interested in the Paipai. After Edward Gifford and Robert Lowie, two Cal professors, encountered a Paipai doctor in southern California in the winter of 1921–1922, Alfred Kroeber encouraged geographer Peveril Meigs III to visit the extant Native groups of northern Baja California—including the Paipai settlements of Santa Catarina and San Isidoro—during his fieldwork in 1928 and 1929. Although the Indigenous people who spoke to Harrington and Meigs certainly noted places that were no longer occupied, the conversations often centered on the current disposition of important regional centers, such as La Huerta, Arroyo

---

[*] This vignette is closely based on Harrington's field notes for July 4, 1925 (Harrington 1984, reel 71, 444–45).

León, and Santa Catarina. These communities were, in the late 1920s, similar to what Alisal had been a generation earlier: places where Native people from relatively diverse backgrounds came together to find common ground amid an ever-encroaching settler presence. The rugged mountain homelands of the Paipai and their neighbors offered two major advantages compared to other Native Californian groups in the missionized zone who, up to the late nineteenth century, had largely followed similar paths in weathering sustained colonialism. One was the space necessary to forestall complete territorial dispossession; the other was to provide a sufficiently isolated backdrop against which to fit the mold of California Indians expected by early anthropologists.

Negotiating Sustained Colonialism, 1900–1950s

By the onset of the twentieth century, the full contours of settler colonialism were already in place across most of California and Baja California. Through violence or the threat of violence, settlers had pushed Native populations to the far margins of society. The newly vacated lands they left behind were quickly divided up and sold into private hands, leading to the expropriation of vast tracts of Indigenous territory. Although the United States government did establish some reservations, most Native Californian groups had to find ways to stay connected to their lands and to each other through informal means. In practice, groups often sought refuge by moving to remote reaches of their ancestral territory where the local environment or economic conditions had prevented large-scale colonial settlement. Within these enclaves, many communities adopted a strategy of minimal visibility. Yet, as a new century dawned and the nation states of the United States and Mexico had seemingly extended themselves into the last remaining corners of the North American continent, some in the dominant society began to seek out Native Californians who had successfully weathered the previous 130 years of colonialism.

The discipline of anthropology has a long and often troubled relationship with Indigenous peoples. In the United States, anthropology developed its distinctive "four fields" approach largely through the study of the Indigenous groups of the Americas. Much of the work was seen as salvage anthropology— that is, research conducted specifically to document Native cultures before they melted away in the face of modernity. As discussed above, the early anthropological study of Native California was buoyed in part by a romanticized notion of a dying race. Following the lead of Alfred Kroeber, many scholars turned their attention to Native people who could remember a time before the arrival of Europeans in what came to be known as the memory culture methodology (Lightfoot and Parrish 2009, 78). That the supposedly inevitable extinction of Native Americans did not come to pass is one of the central tenets of this book, but the fieldwork conducted under the early memory culture methodology still offers a unique insight into California Indian life during the late nineteenth and early twentieth centuries. This corpus of anthropological work, moreover, has in many cases had profound impacts on the way that governmental agencies and society at large have come to view Native Californian groups.

Social-Political Organization

In the early twentieth century, land became a major concern for Native Californian communities seeking to preserve their social and political institutions. The demographic catastrophe of the nineteenth century—caused by the synergistic effects of disease, violence, and cultural suppression—had passed and populations were stabilizing. Yet, many communities found themselves without legal title to the land they had always called home. In 1905–1906, United States Special Indian Agent Charles E. Kelsey visited dozens of Native communities across California in order to develop a census of landless Indigenous groups. In his report to the Commissioner of Indian Affairs, he wrote, "These Indian settlements are for the most part located upon waste or worthless land as near as possible to the ancestral home. These remnants of each stock or tribe or band occupy today almost exactly the same territory their ancestors did a century ago" (Heizer 1979, 137).

At the same time that groups across the region were fighting the uphill battle to obtain land, government policies whipsawed Native Californian communities in the United States. One controversial policy was the Indian Reorganization Act of 1934, which sought to impose Western-style governments on tribes across the nation. California groups did not universally accept the reorganization, and those that did often implemented tribal councils in ways that promoted local understandings of leadership and consensus (Bauer 2016a, 290–91). In Mexico, Indigenous groups gained some land rights as part of a nationwide movement of *indigenismo*, but the resulting government policies remained oriented toward the eventual integration of Native communities into the larger political and economic structures of the nation (Dawson 2004; de la Peña 2005). Aside from the Cucapá, who obtained an *ejido*, or communal landholding, in the 1930s, the Indigenous groups of northern Baja California still struggled for legal title to their lands. To comply with national agrarian reforms, they established formal tribal governments, similar to the reorganization in Alta California. In this system, the generales were replaced by *comisariados* in dealing with outsiders—particularly government officials—although separate traditional leaders often helped to manage internal affairs (Magaña Mancillas 2005, 115–16).

Subsistence Economies

Though most Native Californians in the missionized zone had by now been pushed to the margins of the settler society, they still carried with them knowledge of the landscape. Delfina Cuero (1968, 27–34), for example, described how her family continued to collect shellfish, hunt rabbits, and gather wild plants near San Diego even as the city expanded rapidly in the early twentieth century. This ecological knowledge was passed down from her mother and grandmother, who herself had spent time in the mission system as a young girl. Nevertheless, government regulation of hunting and fishing impacted Native people in other parts of California, who suddenly found that they were breaking the law by continuing their ancestral subsistence practices (Bauer 2009, 177–78). Some worked within those restrictions to maintain connections to important natural resources, including Coast Miwok and Southern Pomo people who continued to make a living from the sea by operating important fishing enterprises out of Bodega and Tomales Bays well into the twentieth century (Schneider 2007; 2019). Agriculture remained an important source of work, and in a distant echo of the mission period, Native Californians throughout the region continued to work as vaqueros, whose knowledge of the landscape and horse handling abilities kept them in high demand (Hogeland and Hogeland 2007, 36–41; Panich 2017).

Technology and Material Culture

By the dawn of the twentieth century, most observers assumed that Indigenous material culture traditions were a thing of the past. A notable exception was Ishi, a Yahi/Yana man who spent the final years of his life, from 1911 to 1916, working with anthropologists at the University of California. Though his treatment raises important ethical issues, Ishi is renowned for his flint-knapping skill. Among other objects, he produced finely crafted projectile points out of obsidian and glass that still inspire awe in observers (Shackley 2000). Of course, other Native Californians also continued various technological traditions as documented in the ethnographic literature of the time (e.g., Kroeber 1925). In southern California and neighboring Baja California, individuals from several groups maintained Indigenous pottery traditions, both as part of a growing part of their economic livelihood and simply for their own uses (Griset 1990; Meigs 1972; Porcayo Michelini 2018b; Rogers 1936). Basketry also remained an important skill in many Native communities, with outsiders increasingly interested in purchasing items for display in their homes or in museums. In fact, the early twentieth century was something of a golden age of California Indian basketry, with well-known weavers such as Mabel McKay gaining widespread attention for their craft (Bibby 2012; Shanks and Shanks 2006). In these ways, Native Californians used the knowledge handed down over generations to persevere despite the continuing pressures of colonialism and attendant economic hardships.

Ceremonial Life

The rapid growth of anthropological fieldwork in California during the early twentieth century documented the widespread continuation, or at least recollection, of Indigenous ceremonial practices throughout the region (Kroeber 1925). Some held closely to the key religions that existed prior to the arrival of the Europeans. Others, such as the curing ceremonies documented among interior Miwok groups in the 1920s, had their roots in precontact times but also incorporated aspects of the Ghost Dance of the late nineteenth century (Gifford 1926; and see Smoak 2006). And all across California and Baja California, mourning ceremonies connected communities to their ancestors. Schneider, for example, describes an early twentieth-century coastal event at Tomales Bay that brought together people from numerous tribes for the purposes of feasting, celebrating, and mourning (2018, 88). Even government agents spoke of the enduring connection between Native Californians and their ancestors through the perpetuation of the annual mourning ceremony (Heizer 1979, 137).

Still, Native ceremonial practices were subject to the same pressures of assimilation and subjugation that affected other areas of life. In some cases, elders made the difficult decision not to continue them, even though the younger generation often remained receptive. Delfina Cuero, born around the turn of the last century, tells about the Kumeyaay women's puberty ceremony in which she did not participate. "I would have gone through with it if they had asked me. I believe in it, but they didn't ask me" (Cuero 1968, 39). And to be sure, some Native people practiced Christianity. Among the Payómkawichum, however, Christianity was considered a distinct belief system that had to be kept separate from existing Indigenous religion. The two were not compatible, according to local leader Rejinaldo Pachito, but neither was it impossible to practice both simultaneously (White 1963, 136–37).

Conflict

Discrimination against California Indians continued unabated into the twentieth century, and many communities kept memories of the previous centuries' atrocities alive through oral narratives (Bauer 2016b). Yet, direct violence was far below the levels of unrestrained brutality of the early American period, and some of the most intense conflicts between Native people and newcomers moved to the courts. The California Indians Jurisdictional Act of 1928, for example, let the State of California sue the federal government on behalf of tribes over the eighteen unratified treaties of 1852. After the resolution of that case, in the early 1940s, several California tribes not subject to the original treaties brought their own suit against the federal government under the Indian Claims Commission Act of 1946 to seek compensation for the lands illegally taken from them. With the help of anthropologists Alfred Kroeber and Robert Heizer, the tribes argued that individual Native Californian groups had always maintained defined territories to which they were permanently attached and which they had never willingly ceded. They won their case in 1959. Heizer recalled that the whole ordeal seemed "a little silly." There was never any doubt on either side, he said, "that the Indians had, indeed, owned California, and that it had been taken from them without compensation by the United States Government" (Heizer 1978a, iii).

O

For Native Californians, the first half of the twentieth century was a time of divergent pathways. Some groups caught the attention of anthropologists, who recorded their daily lives in minute detail, hoping to catch a glimpse of what California had been like before the arrival of Europeans. Government agents similarly relied on essentialist assumptions about Indigenous cultures to provide land and other forms of assistance to California Indians who were still suffering from the wounds of the previous century. Yet, those Native Californians who did not meet the expectations of anthropologists or the government continued to fall victim to the policies of erasure, though this time the injuries came from the pen rather than the sword. And through it all, Native people found ways to continue, drawing on their experience to forge a path forward.

Decades of Dispossession in the San Francisco Bay Area

By 1900, most of the San Francisco Bay Area Ohlone were either living in the extended Native community near Pleasanton or isolated within the large settler cities that had sprung up in the second half of the nineteenth century. Among the latter were the Evencio and Alcantara families, both of whom had Ohlone ancestors associated with Mission San Francisco. The Evencio family had lived in nearby San Mateo since secularization, but Pedro Evencio—born at Mission San Francisco in the mid-1820s—died in 1896. His son, Joseph Evencio, followed a decade later. The Alcantara family had been associated with Missions San Francisco and Santa Clara in the second half of the nineteenth century. Marie Buffet, daughter of Bernardino Alcantara, lived in the city of San Francisco into the 1920s, apparently passing as a white woman (Milliken et al. 2009, 190–96). Like Inigo of Mission Santa Clara, these individuals caught the public's attention as romanticized icons of a bygone era, and their deaths were widely publicized in the local press. Unbeknownst to most of the dominant society's casual observers, a relatively large group of Native people continued to live on the edge of the greater San Francisco Bay Area.

This community was centered at Alisal but also included a constellation of related Indigenous settlements nestled in the hills beyond the former mission of San José. This area had initially served as a refuge from the influx of Anglo-American settlers who flooded the Bay Area in the wake of the Gold Rush. Yet, the area around Alisal soon became the site of a concerted Indigenous revitalization movement that was perhaps most publicly expressed in the melding of the Kuksu religion and the Ghost Dance in the 1870s onward. The death of the traditional leader of Alisal, José Antonio, in 1900 was followed in short succession by that of Custiniano, the leader of the Native community at Sunol, who died in 1904 (*San Francisco Call* 1904, 4). Despite these setbacks, the residents of Alisal entered the new century as a distinct community. A document produced by the Northern California Indian Association in 1904, intended to call attention to the plight of landless Indians in California, estimated a population of seventy individuals, with another eight at Niles. An additional twenty-five Ohlone people were enumerated in the nearby towns of Danville and Byron in Contra Costa County (Heizer 1979, 99–100). A local history from the same year suggested that both Alisal and Niles each counted "half a hundred persons," pointing toward a total population of the area of at least one hundred individuals (Country Club 1904, 35).

During this time, the Bay Area Ohlone fell under the jurisdiction of the Bureau of Indian Affairs (BIA), which was responding to public outcry over the poor treatment of Native Californians. To assess the situation, Special Indian Agent Kelsey tallied the residents of California Indian settlements up and down the state during 1905 and 1906. His methodology seems to have been based in part on the 1900 federal census as he used that document for his claim that Santa Clara and San Francisco Counties had no Indian residents. The only Bay Area settlements Kelsey personally visited were those near Pleasanton and Niles, where he enumerated some eighteen families totaling forty-two individuals (Kelsey 1971, 1–4). These figures are no doubt low, but his census does include Angela Colos and "Joe Gooseman" (José Guzman), who later became well-known anthropological consultants. More important, perhaps, is the fact that the Kelsey census establishes the Pleasanton-Niles population as an entity recognized by the government as an extant California Indian community, one that came to be known as the Verona Band of Alameda County. Although Kelsey's report provided the basis for the purchase of lands for many Native Californian groups, the Verona Band and other Ohlone groups were completely ignored.

Tragedy struck the Alisal community in the mid-1910s, when a fire caused by work along the nearby Western Pacific Railroad consumed several homes. By this time, the community was already dispersing as the pressures of living in the Bay Area continued to mount. The 1910 federal census recorded the presence of Alisal, referred to in that document as "Indian Town," but recorded only seventeen individuals of Native descent living there at the time (U.S. Census Bureau 1910). Most of the former residents were able to remain in the southeastern Bay Area and to maintain ties to the Niles-Sunol-Pleasanton region in particular. A government report from 1923 offered a tally of thirty individuals associated with the Verona Band. Just four years later, however, the BIA's Sacramento superintendent, Lafayette Dorrington, unilaterally decided that there was no need for the BIA to purchase land for their ranchería (Cambra et al. 2011, 48–53; Milliken et al. 2009, 208). Dorrington's indifference was not limited to the Bay Area Ohlones, but his decision to write off the Verona Band effectively severed the federal government's involvement in the affairs of San Francisco Bay Area Indigenous groups without any official act of Congress. Though they themselves did not recognize it as such, the combination of bureaucratic ineptitude and governmental indifference of the 1920s marked the end of Ohlone peoples' status as official Indians (Field et al. 1992, 418).

At about the same time that Dorrington abandoned the Ohlone, Western science did the same. Established in the early twentieth century, the Department of Anthropology at the University of California (later, the University of California, Berkeley) set about recording California Indian lifeways under the leadership of Alfred Kroeber. Following the precedent of earlier, journalistic chroniclers of Native California (e.g., Powers 1877), the memory culture approach employed by the Berkeley anthropologists excluded most of the groups whose ancestors had been associated with the Spanish, and later Mexican, missions along the coastal strip. Despite visiting Alisal himself in 1909 (not to mention sharing a patron with the Verona Band, Phoebe Apperson Hearst), Kroeber largely ignored the Native people living just a short distance from Berkeley. In his monumental *Handbook of the Indians of California*, Kroeber declared with scholarly authority, "The Costanoan group is extinct so far as all practical purposes are concerned" (1925, 464).

Thus, the Ohlone were dealt a double blow in the mid-1920s: an extinction sentence from anthropology and a de facto termination of acknowledged status by the BIA. Ohlone people, however, were not fazed by the outsiders' proclamations. As detailed in federal documents, members of the Verona Band routinely enrolled with the BIA when allowed to do so. In the late 1920s and early 1930s, for example, officials working as part of the California Indians Jurisdictional Act of 1928 sought to enumerate all Native Californians who had ancestors subject to the eighteen unratified treaties of 1851–1852. The heads of the Ohlone families of the East Bay—who were still living near Pleasanton, Sunol, and Niles—enrolled as either "Ohlones" or the "Mission San José Tribe." As time passed, tribal members ensured that children born after 1928 continued to be enrolled with the BIA. By 1951, the California Indian Roll included some forty individuals as part of the Mission San José tribe (Cambra et al. 2011; Kroeber and Heizer 1970; Milliken et al. 2009, 206–19). Clearly, Ohlone families were determined to define their own identities.

Some individuals similarly worked with anthropologists to preserve important linguistic and cultural traditions. Despite Kroeber's declaration of Ohlone extinction, the list of anthropologists who visited Alisal in the early twentieth century reads like a Who's Who of early California anthropology: in addition to Kroeber himself, C. Hart Merriam visited there in 1909 and 1910, and Edward Gifford passed through in 1914 (see Field et al. 1992, 426; Leventhal et al. 1994, 310). This research, however, primarily centered on linguistic reconstruction and, at least in its published form, is of little use for documenting life at Alisal during the time in which the fieldwork was conducted. Kroeber only minimally refers to his linguistic work there (e.g., Kroeber 1910), presaging his later extinction proclamation. Merriam (1967), for his part, seems to have ignored the core Ohlone population of the community in favor of the descendants of Central Valley groups, whose ancestors had intermarried with Ohlone families during the late mission period and its aftermath. Still, Merriam met and interviewed many of the important figures from the early-twentieth-century community, like José Guzman, Angela Colos, and "Joe Benoko" (José Binoco).

The fieldwork of greatest importance, however, was conducted by the most reclusive of the early California anthropologists, John Peabody Harrington. Working for the Bureau of American Ethnology, Harrington first visited the Pleasanton area in August 1921 but returned multiple times over the course of the 1920s and early 1930s. There, he conducted linguistic and ethnographic interviews with Angela Colos and José Guzman, along with additional consultation with knowledgeable elders Susana Nichols and José Binoco, among others (Figure 17). Although Harrington's fieldwork in Pleasanton was not as extensive as his research with people living directly to the south—he conducted far-reaching interviews with Mutsun and Rumsen speakers—his consultants' testimonies nonetheless flesh out our understanding of Bay Area Ohlone life in the first half of the twentieth century. For example, Harrington's field notes offer rich information regarding Indigenous ceremonies, such as descriptions of Kuksu dances and traditional sweat lodges, or *tupentak* in the Chocheño language. Other accounts described the construction of tule thatch houses and the details of basketry making, which often incorporated red woodpecker scalps. Still other conversations describe the preparation of native foods—such as sturgeon caught near Alviso, which could be dried for storage—as well as a wealth of ethnobotanical knowledge, including detailed information regarding soaproot and acorns (Harrington 1984, reel 36). That members of the Ohlone community still commanded this wide range of knowledge into the 1920s and 1930s is a testament to their resilience in the face of dispossession.

Harrington also recorded important details about local ethnonyms. His consultants often referred to people based on their affiliation with particular missions, such as the Clareños or Chocheños. Ohlone consultants also recalled the Native terms for particular groups. As one explained, "The [Indian] name of the Chocheños is Lisiánis," a term Harrington most often wrote as Lisyánes. Though his notes suggest some uncertainty, the name seems to have been used to refer to the original inhabitants of the area around Mission San José, whom his consultants referred to as Cristianos Viejos (Harrington 1984, reel 36, 384–404). Angela Colos, for example, stated that the "Lisyánes were the San José—this name covered up as far as [San] Lorenzo . . . The Doloreños were not Lisyanes, nor were the Clareños" (Harrington 1984, reel 36, 535). Harrington's notes contain the ancestral affiliations of most of the key individuals living near Pleasanton at the time and even some who had been deceased for many years. Despite the far-reaching transformations of the previous century

FIGURE 17. Angela Colos, a Chocheño speaker and resident of the Alisal ranchería. Photographed by John P. Harrington in 1921. Courtesy of the National Anthropological Archives, Smithsonian Institution [91–30287].

and a half, these discussions reveal that Ohlone people living in the 1920s and 1930s still traced their relationships back to ancestral territories even as their sociopolitical life coalesced around their hilly enclaves in the southeastern reaches of the San Francisco Bay Area. There, individuals from many backgrounds joined the core of Ohlone Cristianos Viejos from local Bay Area missions, primarily through intermarriage. This group came to be called Muwekma, or *la gente*, as Harrington's consultants put it. Their descendants, members of today's Muwekma Ohlone Tribe, continue to use the term inclusively (Field et al. 1992, 414).

Nevertheless, the realities of early twentieth-century life posed challenges for the intergenerational transmission of knowledge. Facing the constant threat of discrimination, some East Bay Ohlone people continued to pass as non-Native. Although many families enrolled with the BIA during the same time that Harrington was conducting fieldwork, some of his consultants recalled the practice of passing. One individual, according to other consultants, wanted "to be white." Harrington, for his part, could not entice the man to speak in his Native language (Harrington 1984, reel 36, 540; reel 37, 299). In another instance, a woman who left Alisal for San Leandro and San Lorenzo was said to speak in *la pura idioma*. But upon her return, she was living with a Mexican man and speaking only Spanish (Harrington 1984, reel 36, 570). Even one of Harrington's most knowledgeable consultants, Angela Colos, faced the challenge of language loss: her parents would not speak to her in their Native languages. Her linguistic knowledge came from her grandparents and apparently from her stepfather, whose parents were Chocheño-speaking Cristianos Viejos from Mission San José (Harrington 1984, reel 37, 536; Milliken 2009, 199). The need to keep a low profile, or even passing as Mexican, was recalled by numerous individuals who came of age in the early to mid-twentieth century. For instance, one East Bay Ohlone man recalled losing childhood friends once his Native Californian heritage became known (Hedges 2019, 94–113; Milliken et al. 2009, 212–14).

The realities of making a living also exerted a centrifugal force on the Ohlone community. Harrington's field notes chart the moves that families and individuals made throughout their lifetimes, often as the result of opportunities to work for white settlers. Many individuals, particularly men, continued to labor in the agricultural sector, which kept them moving throughout the year. Based on his visits in 1909, Merriam stated that José Binoco "works from ranch to ranch, usually from Pleasanton to Livermore" (1967, 369). Of those Alisal residents whose occupations were listed in the 1910 federal census, all were laborers relying on "odd jobs" (U.S. Census Bureau 1910). In other cases, random events cost the Ohlone important cultural knowledge. In 1921, Ramona Marine Sanchez, who was a member of a prominent Ohlone family at Alisal, died unexpectedly, severing an important generational connection (Field et al. 1992, 427–28). The failure of Harrington and other anthropologists to document the underlying community structure—though he repeatedly referred to the "Pleasanton Ranchería"—was later used as evidence by the United States government in its decision to deny the Muwekma Ohlone Tribe's petition to reinstate their federally recognized status (Office of Federal Acknowledgment 2002).

A lingering question centers on the fate of Ohlone people not directly associated with Alisal. For example, the Northern California Indian Association census from 1904 lists sixty-five "Costanoans" on the San Francisco peninsula—thirty at San Mateo and thirty-five at Redwood City (Heizer 1979, 106). Despite those seemingly significant figures, Kelsey did not visit either community during his fieldwork of 1905–1906, instead reiterating the estimate of fifteen Indians in all of San Mateo County published in the 1900 United States census. Many years later, Native people who enrolled with the BIA under the California Indians Jurisdictional Act of 1928 listed their affiliation as Mission Santa Clara, and some living on the San Francisco peninsula enrolled simply as "Mission" Indians. Another group of twelve individuals listed their affiliation as "Redwood City" (Kroeber and Heizer 1970; Milliken et al. 2009, 206). Little else is known about these individuals, but they may have been associated with the Evencio or Alcantara families or may represent other individuals who had been affiliated with Missions Santa Clara or San Francisco. What is clear is that these people continued to assert their Ohlone identity in the face of bureaucratic and scholarly indifference, revealing both the enduring affiliations maintained by Native communities and also the challenges of documenting those connections to satisfy the byzantine and essentialist federal acknowledgment process today.

Throughout the first half of the twentieth century, Native people living in the southern and eastern Bay Area maintained important linguistic and cultural traditions and continued to recognize themselves as a distinct community even after the government and anthropologists had decided otherwise. Among today's Muwekma community, this time is known as the "Families Period," during which large extended families served to connect the community in place of a formal land base. As in earlier times, marriage and godparenting were key social mechanisms by which people maintained their connections (Cambra et al. 2011; Field et al. 1992; Milliken et al. 2009; Ramirez 2007). Most families were able to stay in the broader region around the former settlement at Alisal by residing in cities such as San Jose, Milpitas, and Fremont, and certain elders were recognized stalwarts of tribal identity. One such individual was Trinidad Marine, the sister of Ramona Marine Sanchez, and a relative of José Antonio and Jacoba, the last traditional leaders of the Alisal community (Field et al. 1992, 427–28). Many women worked in the home and continued to use the natural resources of the Bay Area for medicine and food. Though discrimination remained a constant presence, men often took jobs in the burgeoning Bay Area economy and, when duty called, in the armed forces. In fact, several Muwekma men served in World War I and World War II (Cambra et al. 2011; Milliken et al. 2009). Through it all, holidays and life events like births and marriages brought multiple generations together, cementing bonds that had been stretched thin by over a century and a half of colonialism.

By the 1950s, the descendants of the thousands of Bay Area Ohlones who were baptized at Missions San Francisco, Santa Clara, and San José were difficult for most outsiders to identify against amid the region's massive postwar suburban expansion. As they gradually lost their land base at Alisal during the preceding decades, Ohlone people made do by selectively participating in the settler society and maintaining their tribal connections through extended family events. Some were involved in the suit brought under the Indian Claims Commission during the late 1940s and 1950s, including a Bay Area California Indian Council that seems to have counted descendants of the Verona Band among its members (Milliken et al. 2009, 220). Still, in the eyes of most observers and the United States federal government, the Ohlone by this time had ceased to exist as a unified group. Although families continued to ensure strong connections, their erasure, for all intents and purposes, was complete.

Defending a Homeland in the Sierra Juárez

The Native residents of the Bay Area and northern Baja California both entered the twentieth century inhabiting hilly enclaves. The Paipai, however, were able to maintain control of their lands more successfully as the decades passed. By 1900, Native people had established several enduring population centers in northern Baja California's mountainous interior. These areas offered refuge for families and individuals escaping growing urban centers on both sides of the international border. As one Native consultant asserted, the "people of La Huerta take in all the San Diego and Campo Indians" (Harrington 1985, reel 170, 228). But it was not just La Huerta that was open to Indigenous refugees. Delfina Cuero and her family followed her grandparents south into the Sierra Juárez in the early years of the new century. She recalled, "In those days the Indians didn't know anything about a line [the border]. This was just a place in the whole area that had belonged to the Indians where nobody told us to move on" (Cuero 1968, 54). Local people knew well that the Sierra Juárez was Native ground. The challenge was to keep it that way.

One major impediment was the slow but steady march of settler demography, which had inverted the ratios of the previous century. Though fewer than ten thousand settlers lived in the entire state of Baja California in 1910, estimates suggest there were only about six hundred Indians in the Sierra

Juárez in 1919 (Henderson 1964, 195; Nelson 1921, 8). Such population figures are complicated by patterns of seasonal mobility, wage labor, and non-cooperation on the part of Indigenous people, but nonetheless speak to the struggle to keep land in Native hands. Over the course of the early twentieth century, the gradual coalescence of the Indigenous communities continued, with places like Santa Catarina, La Huerta, and a handful of others taking on ever greater roles in the region's Indigenous landscape. These places were visited by a series of anthropologists beginning in the early 1900s and with increasing frequency from the 1920s onward. In contrast to the Ohlone of the urban San Francisco Bay Area, nearly all early anthropological observers remarked on the persistence of specific communities and the various cultural traditions practiced among their residents. The Paipai and their neighbors likely never saw the results of these early ethnographic forays, but this kind of research almost certainly bolstered their claims to the land in the realm of public opinion.

Still, anthropological observers of Native Baja California found it difficult to parse the distinctions between extant social groups, traditional shimuls, languages spoken, and externally applied ethnonyms—particularly given the complex processes of sociopolitical coalescence playing out in the region. This was especially true for the multiethnic community of Santa Catarina, where Paipai was the most common language but families and individuals still viewed membership in a specific shimul as the primary vector of social identification. The nineteenth-century communal identity as Catarineños was likely reserved for dealings with outsiders whereas the term Paipai was applied more broadly to encompass people speaking a similar language and residing at a number of named settlements. Within either category, however, each individual belonged to one of several distinct shimuls which in many ways continued to structure most social interaction in the Native world of the Sierra Juárez. A clear example of the failure of outsiders to grasp this layered identity is present in traveler Arthur North's (1908, 1910) discussion of the so-called "Yumas" who lived around the ruins of Mission Santa Catalina and the "Pai-pais" who resided in the canyons between there and Mission San Vicente.

Harrington conducted linguistic fieldwork in Baja California in the 1920s, recording the names of many important places and social groups, though he too struggled to comprehend the crosscutting layers of sociopolitical organization and ethnolinguistic affiliation that knit together the Native people of the Sierra Juárez. His field notes are notoriously difficult to parse but they nonetheless highlight the continued importance of the shimul system for the Paipai and their neighbors (Harrington 1985, reel 170). Multiple consultants stressed the difference between language groups and surnames, or *apellidos*, which were often individuals' ancestral shimul names (e.g., Harrington 1985, reel 170, 395, 402). The process of using shimul names as surnames was already evident a century earlier as demonstrated on the mission padrón of 1834. In fact, many of the shimuls noted by Harrington and other early ethnographers were the same ones given by Native people living at Mission Santa Catalina during the Dominican period (see Table 3). By the early twentieth century, some surnames were Hispanicized versions of traditional clan names (Jat'am became Tambo, for example), but many individuals still used the original shimul names and almost all consultants could at least remember the Indigenous forms (and see Garduño 2003).

The early ethnographic work also offers a picture of the changing geographic distribution of the Paipai and their neighbors in the early to mid-twentieth century (Meigs 1939; Hohenthal 2001; Kelly 1942; Owen 1962). Most researchers used the general framework of Kroeber's memory culture methodology, which provides some insight into continuities with earlier times. This is particularly useful in terms of understanding the geography of different shimuls. The Jamsulch, for example, could be found in the region between San Vicente and San Isidoro, and many Ko'alh and Jat'am lived at La Huerta (Harrington 1985, reel 170; Meigs 1972, 1977). Yet, Santa Catarina remained the most populous Paipai settlement, with some thirty-six families associated with it in 1929 (Meigs 1935, 158). Prominent Santa Catarina families bore the Miyewkwa and Ko'alh apellidos, while Kwal-xwat families lived at nearby San Miguel. Some shimuls, such as the Kekur who lived previously near Santo Tomás, seem to have been displaced by the time anthropologists arrived.

Perhaps due to the deeply ingrained assumptions of memory culture interviews, few early anthropologists were able to fully tease apart the palimpsest of Indigenous memory and historical contingency manifested in their informants' answers regarding group territories. One of the most astute observers of the transformations in the region's Native geography was Ralph Michelsen, who wrote, "If a Paipai Indian were to draw a map of Paipai territory, he would probably draw a map of the area which contained people with whom he could converse. However, if he were asked to draw a map of *his* territory, he would probably draw a map of the places where he could go safely. It would conform neither to a map of the area where people speak his language nor to a map drawn by another Paipai of different parentage" (1991, 159). Keeping in mind this complexity, most Native consultants still viewed Santa Catarina as a distinctly Paipai place. This view proved to be enduring despite the fact that the life histories of individuals living there indicate that the broader community, inclusive of nearby San Miguel, was home to people who spoke not just Paipai, but also Cucapá, Kiliwa, Ko'alh, and Kumeyaay (Goldbaum 1984; Harrington 1985, reel 170; Henderson 1952). One of Harrington's consultants put it bluntly: "San Miguel people are a great mixture of tribes" (Harrington 1985, reel 170, 225).

Despite the coalescence of people at Santa Catarina and other regional settlements, the tensions captured by Michelsen simmered just beneath the surface for some individuals. Such animosity may have found a vehicle in the Mexican Revolution of 1911. In that year, filibusters led by Ricardo Flores Magón captured many of the region's most important cities. As they moved southwest toward Ensenada, they passed through Paipai and Kiliwa territories. Some Native individuals joined the rebels, but others were sympathetic to the federal cause. As interpreted by anthropologist Roger Owen (1963), the broader sociopolitical conflict was of little import to those who joined the Magonistas as their actual intent was to use their newfound revolutionary allies to execute a powerful hechicero living at Santa Catarina—a plan that was apparently successful—and to strengthen the relative position of their allied shimuls. Other sources, however, suggest that Native people who rode with the Magonistas were simply fighting against their marginal position in Mexican society (Castillo-Munoz 2017, 54–57). A Kiliwa narrative confirms this perspective, "Hunger! The people were hungry! It was said that the government did nothing to improve matters. It would have to be removed . . . In that distant time these Indians had no authority" (Mixco 1983, 234–35). Whatever their motive, participation in the revolution came at a terrible cost as federal forces massacred nine Paipai and Kiliwa men at the Paipai ranchería of Jamau after the Magonistas' retreat. These troubling events are only rivaled by the burning of Mission Santa Catalina in local oral narratives, although the two have become somewhat conflated with the passing of individuals who lived through either time (Mixco 1983; Owen 1963; Panich 2009, 131).

Oral narratives and early ethnographic work also reveal the contours of daily life for the Paipai and other Native groups (Bendímez Patterson 1989, 2008; Cuero 1968; Hohental 2001; Hicks 1963; Joël 1976; Magaña Mancillas 2005; Meigs 1939). Although most families grew crops—corn, beans, melons, wheat, and other vegetables—hunting and gathering remained important pursuits. Acorns and piñon were especially important in local cuisine (Figure 18). Harvest time brought people from many different communities together. Residents of Santa Catarina who I spoke with in 2008 recalled traveling to the higher elevations of the Sierra Juárez, near Campo Nacional, to collect piñon in the mid-twentieth century. The harvest lasted from the middle of August to the end of September, during which time several burros would be loaded with nuts. They kept enough of the harvest for their own use over the winter and sold the surplus to local ranchers. Often, they met people from La Huerta and El Mayor (a Cucapá settlement) as well as other Paipai in the piñon groves. These occasions were almost universally remembered fondly. Tears came to the eyes of one woman as she spoke of climbing the tall pines to knock down the cones.

As with piñon and acorn harvests, trips to the coast were an important opportunity to visit friends and family. Several Paipai and Ko'alh women I spoke with in 2008 remembered traveling the old trail that followed the arroyo between Santa Catarina and San Vicente as children in the 1940s and 1950s. The families would travel on horseback and on burro, often passing the night with relatives or friends along the way. Some families would spend part of the winter at the coast collecting abalone, although others apparently stayed in San Vicente where people grew various crops. Such coastal trips were an important part of the seasonal round for most twentieth-century communities of the Sierra Juárez (Cuero 1968). As recalled by Paipai elder Benito Peralta, hunting—often with bow and arrow—remained an enjoyable

FIGURE 18. Petrocinia, preparing acorns outside her home in Santa Catarina. Photographed by John P. Harrington in 1926. Courtesy of the National Anthropological Archives, Smithsonian Institution [91–32058].

and economically important pursuit (Bendímez Patterson 1989, 48–53). Deer and rabbit were the principal sources of meat for most Indian families in those days. Indeed, Owen noted a distinct ambivalence toward subsistence agriculture in Santa Catarina, perhaps due to the hunting and gathering history of the local people and the abundance of local wild foods: whether or not one plants crops, "no one starves in the mountains" (Owen 1962, 39). The ability of Native people to continue hunting and gathering practices was facilitated by the minimal extent of ecological change associated with agriculture and invasive species. Though localized disturbances were present, historical ecological research at the end of the twentieth century concluded, "Today's vegetation, especially the brushland, forest, and desert scrub ecosystems, have remained largely pristine since the initial Spanish explorations" (Minnich and Vizcaíno 1998, 101; and see Wilken Robertson 2018 for an excellent survey of the twenty-first century ethnobotany of Native Baja California).

Residents of Santa Catarina maintained other important traditions that had their roots in precontact times. One of the most notable was pottery, which is well represented in the photographs and field notes of many early visitors like Harrington and his friend Edward H. Davis. Meigs, who conducted his fieldwork in the 1920s, observed that traders would visit the Native communities of the Sierra Juárez to procure ceramic vessels for the Ensenada tourist market (1939, 37). Paipai potters also sold their wares to neighboring ranchers at the same time that they continued to make pottery for their own domestic uses, such as storage and cooking (Hinton and Owen 1957; Panich and Wilken-Robertson 2013; Wade 2004). An account from the 1950s noted that the pottery then being produced and used in Santa Catarina and other Paipai settlements was indistinguishable from the ceramics found in local precontact archaeological sites (Henderson 1952, 9). Ethnographic collections of Paipai ceramics from around the same time include objects, such as ollas and smoking pipes, that have antecedents going back centuries as well as other items that incorporated elements of Euro-American vessels (Griset and Ferg 2010; Porcayo Michelini 2018b). Taken together, these windows on Paipai ceramic production reveal a dynamic but unbroken tradition.

Native people also maintained many religious and ceremonial practices. Of the most important were annual mourning ceremonies, called *keruk*, though other fiestas and dances were common throughout the region (Hohenthal 2001; Meigs 1939; Michelsen and Owen 1967; Cuero 1968, 36–37). David Goldbaum, a prominent settler, described a mourning ceremony he witnessed at Santa Catarina early in the twentieth century in which the deceased, his house, and all it contained were burned and his horses distributed among the living (1984, 22–23). Aside from some residents of La Huerta, almost all of the region's Native people—including the Paipai—denied any practice of Catholicism or Christianity more broadly, despite the sporadic activity of Protestant missionaries (Hinton and Owen 1957). Hechiceros remained a source of awe well into the twentieth century, as noted by Juan Mishkwish, a Kumeyaay man from northern Baja California. "He said an hechicero can make people sick by poison, and that they have today not as much power as they had in the old days, but people are afraid of them still" (Meigs 1974, 21). The events of 1911, in which members of different shimuls conspired to execute an hechicero near Santa Catarina, attest to the power such individuals held over their communities (Owen 1963). As late as 1949, anthropologist William Hohenthal met Paipai individuals who assiduously avoided one hechicero in particular (2001, 314). Most, however, used their powers for curing, as noted by a Paipai doctor named Jackrabbit interviewed in the winter of 1921–1922. He described how, by consuming jimsonweed, he had gained the ability to cure snake bites and arrow wounds (Gifford and Lowie 1928). According to Paipai visited by Meigs in 1929, the Paipai hechiceros were the best curers in the region (Meigs 1977, 17).

During the opening decades of the twentieth century, many Paipai joined the broader Mexican economy. Given their intimate knowledge of the sierra, Native men were in high demand as vaqueros and sheepherders for livestock-raising enterprises of various sizes (Garduño 2003; Meigs 1939; Owen 1962). Paipai elders I spoke with in Santa Catarina recalled that their fathers and other male relatives missed many of the happy trips to harvest acorns and piñon while they were away working for Mexican ranchers. Others noted that knowledge of livestock was one of the principal benefits of missionization, a notion that aligns with early ethnographies which stressed the importance of the horse for residents of the Sierra Juárez as a means of both economic and physical mobility (Hohenthal 2001, 130; Panich 2017). Women too participated in the cash economy. Benito Peralta's mother, for example, supported their family by taking in laundry from settlers in nearby El Álamo (Bendímez Patterson 1989, 19). Other women worked as domestics in the region's growing cities and periodically joined other Native people from the Sierra Juárez who traveled to the Mexicali area during the winter months to harvest cotton (Owen 1962, 17–18). Paipai consultants I spoke with recalled that in the old days people would make the trip from Santa Catarina or San Miguel, taking three to four days on foot or sometimes less if horses or pack animals were available. In later times, a truck would come to San Miguel to pick up workers and to take them to the cotton fields.

The Paipai slowly began to engage in other aspects of Mexican society as well. A school was established at the settlement of San Miguel in 1925.

Benito Peralta recalled that, since they did not speak Spanish, he and other children at first understood nothing at all but that they soon began learning the new language (Bendímez Patterson 1989, 43–45). When Harrington visited the community a few years later, he photographed seventeen students standing with their teacher in front of the humble adobe structure. Later observers found the school closed, but by mid-century, most residents of Santa Catarina were at least bilingual—speaking Spanish and one or more Native languages—and many could read and write (Hinton and Owen 1957, 92). Far from signaling acculturation, Paipai participation in the Mexican cash economy and rural educational programs represented another way to make life in the Sierra Juárez work. As Michelsen and Owen note, "The Indians of Baja California have always welcomed innovations. They will examine, and seriously consider, anything which may aid them in the constant attempts to maintain, prolong, or better their lives . . . They welcome Protestant missionaries, anthropologists, travelers, hunters and anyone else who finds his way to Santa Catarina" (1967, 39).

As the twentieth century progressed and outsiders encroached upon many Indigenous rancherías, the Paipai consolidated their community around the former mission. By 1930, the non-Native population of Baja California grew to 48,327 and reached 79,908 a decade later. Indigenous people numbered roughly one thousand individuals during this time. Outside of the Cucapá ejido, granted in 1937–1938, San Miguel—probably together with residents of Santa Catarina—was the most populous Indian settlement, followed by the nearby communities of La Huerta, Valle de la Trinidad, and Arroyo León (Henderson 1964, 211–13). Even San Miguel—home to many Paipai and their kin in the century after the destruction of Mission Santa Catalina—was abandoned in favor of Santa Catarina during the 1950s due to changes in the local water table after a large earthquake (Alvárez de Williams 2004, 109).

Though most of the rapidly growing settler population remained along the coast, the question of land tenure is central to understanding the persistence of the Paipai and other Native groups in Baja California. By the mid-twentieth century, local Native people considered the principal communities of Santa Catarina, La Huerta, and others to be *reservas indígenas*. The legal nature of such landholdings seems to have been based on promises made decades earlier in the Benito Juárez era or later in the nineteenth century. Goldbaum, for example, claims to have seen in 1897 a document from a government agency granting the people of Santa Catarina the right to the lands on which they lived and cultivated crops (Goldbaum 1984, 22; and see Bendímez Patterson 1989, 64). The situation on the ground was tenuous at best, however, with local Mexican officials occasionally acceding to Native statements of sovereignty when they occupied marginal lands (Hinton and Owen 1957, 91; Hohenthal 2001, 313–14). As described by one observer, "Except for the Cocopas, who live on ejidos on the Colorado Delta, remaining Indian communities simply occupy lands, some of which are quite marginal, by the prescriptive right of possession" (Henderson 1964, 298). Whereas smaller Indigenous rancherías were slowly absorbed by Mexican landholdings, the reserva of Santa Catarina was "vigorously protected" by its residents through mid-century (Owen 1962, 16).

Summary

Though arising through independent local developments, the parallel historical trajectories charted by Ohlone and Paipai people from the 1770s onward began to diverge widely in the early twentieth century. A crucial factor was simply space. Both groups had relied on their ancestral homelands to sustain important refuge communities during and after the mission period. In the San Francisco Bay Area, the network of settlements around Alisal marked an enduring connection to Ohlone homelands while simultaneously offering individuals from neighboring groups a place to turn to when things got bad, which they did with increasing frequency. In northern Baja California, Santa Catarina played a similar role for the Paipai and their neighbors despite having been the site of a Dominican mission for over a generation. Yet, by the early 1900s, Alisal was unraveling. The informal arrangements with local landowners could no longer be maintained and white settlers encroached even farther into the East Bay hills. The Sierra Juárez, in contrast, attracted only scattered non-Native interests and at a slower pace than the rapidly urbanizing San Francisco Bay region. Thus, the Paipai were able to define their reserva—whether or not it represented a legal land claim—within a sparsely populated region where large tracts of land remained essentially open range.

Labor was another, directly related factor. Both areas remained largely agrarian into the second half of the nineteenth century, and both groups could therefore utilize the skills their ancestors acquired in the missions to navigate the colonial landscape. Even though the historical record is comparatively sparse, the surviving documents indicate that many residents of Alisal took on seasonal agricultural labor at farms throughout the East Bay. In the Sierra Juárez, similar work was common, occasionally taking people far from Santa Catarina to pursue jobs as vaqueros, as sheep herders, or to pick cotton and other crops. Native people also retained traditional ecological knowledge, allowing them to gather important food and medicinal resources as they moved across the landscape. The ability to use agrarian labor regimes to maintain a foothold in one's ancestral territory gradually diminished in the urbanizing Bay Area even as it remained a viable option in the Sierra Juárez.

Other factors of life are difficult to compare, in large measure due to the nature of the evidence. Without a doubt, the fundamental assumptions of the memory culture methodology employed by most anthropological observers color what we know about these two communities in the early twentieth century. Believing that the Ohlone were culturally extinct, most Berkeley anthropologists felt that the residents of Alisal and related settlements could not offer useful information about supposedly traditional lifeways and therefore made only cursory linguistic investigations. Other Ohlone enclaves, such as that near Redwood City, appear to have been totally ignored. Even Harrington, who more clearly understood the persistence of Ohlone people into the twentieth century, was primarily concerned with linguistic data such as the names of particular groups or places. In the Sierra Juárez, in contrast, most anthropologists found communities that met their expectations of what Indigenous societies should look like. Though in many cases anthropologists focused primarily on elements they felt were reflective of precontact times, such as kinship terms or ceremonial practices, the mere act of pursuing these kinds of ethnographies ensured that the archives contain a relatively rich level of detail regarding daily practices.

The existing evidence clearly demonstrates that people in both regions continued to view themselves as distinct Indigenous groups, belying the work of anthropologists and other officials who came to define what it meant to be Indian. In the San Francisco Bay Area, science and government both pronounced the Ohlone extinct in the 1920s, a judgment that Ohlone people refused to concede but that the dominant society all too easily accepted. In the Sierra Juárez, local Mexican officials saw the Paipai as a relatively cohesive and distinct social group, and Santa Catarina was recognized as a hub of Indigenous culture among many academics, tourists, and adventurers. These distinctions notwithstanding, most anthropologists followed the lead of Kroeber and others by failing to see beyond their essentialist blinders when it came to charting the future of Indigenous cultures. North, for example, proclaimed that the extinction of the Native groups of Baja California was, in the early years of the twentieth century, "near at hand" (1908, 241). Five decades later, survival of Indian communities in the Sierra Juárez was unanticipated by anthropologists, who saw their assimilation as "inevitable" (Hinton and Owen 1957, 101; and see Owen 1963, 390). These statements reflect the scholarly biases of the time—a period when acculturation theory was at the forefront of the social sciences—but their perpetuation in more recent scholarship and popular understandings of Native Californian societies has very real implications for the continued cultural and political autonomy of the region's Indigenous people.

Conclusion

Persistent Peoples

AS I WAS FINISHING THE manuscript for this book, I had the pleasure of sitting on an Indigenous Peoples Day panel discussion that also included two Ohlone leaders and the ethnohistorian of the Muwekma Ohlone Tribe. We were discussing the complex Native history of the southern San Francisco Bay region and in particular Santa Clara University (SCU), where I work. The room was filled with more than 150 SCU students, staff, and faculty, as well as interested community members. The conversation ranged from the archaeological heritage of Mission Santa Clara to the American-period erasure of Ohlone people from the Bay Area to ways the university could address the legacy of colonialism through scholarships and other measures. The final speaker was Monica V. Arellano, the vice chairwoman of the Muwekma Ohlone Tribal Council. In concluding the formal presentations, she did not need to rehash the facts and figures related to her ancestors' experiences under Spanish, Mexican, and American rule—the hard evidence of the injustices of colonialism. Instead, she offered an official welcome to the tribe's ancestral homeland and described several revitalization efforts that tribal members are leading. She ended with a brief statement on behalf of her community: "We're strong, we're resilient, and we're still here." In the span of a few short minutes, Vice Chairwoman Arellano had cut directly to the heart of the matter: Ohlone people have maintained their communities and they never left their homeland. They have persisted.

The Muwekma Ohlone Tribe and other Ohlone organizations have spent the past several decades fighting against the structures of settler colonialism that have sought to erase them from the Bay Area landscape. The Muwekma, in particular, have been active in the struggle to regain federal acknowledgment. Their journey mirrors the challenges faced by many California tribes following the United States federal government's termination policy of the mid-twentieth century. Termination, as envisioned by the government, would end the special status of Native American groups. The process, moreover, was intended to be one of detribalization: tribal governments would be dissolved and communal assets would be divided among individuals. In California, thirty-six rancherías were terminated under the policy, though dozens more— like the Ohlone community at Alisal—had been effectively terminated earlier in the twentieth century (Castillo 1978). It was not long, however, before termination began to have an opposite effect. The termination of tribal status ultimately fostered renewed Native refusal of forced assimilation, a resistance that coincided with the broader civil rights movements of the 1960s and 1970s. By the 1980s, Native communities up and down California were demanding reacknowledgement and jurisdiction over their ancestral territories (Bauer 2016a, 292). Though their quest for federal acknowledgment has stalled, the Bay Area Ohlone and related groups are at the forefront of the contemporary movement to reassert Native Californian control of cultural and natural resources (Field al. 1992, 413–14).

In northern Baja California, the Paipai and others must similarly negotiate the structures imposed by the settler government. Despite outward celebration of indigenismo during much of the twentieth century, Mexican policy remained firmly oriented toward integration and acculturation. Even now, in a new era of multiculturalism, Indigenous identity in Mexico—as in the United States—is legally defined by outsiders (Dawson 2004; de la Peña 2005). While Native groups in Baja California are pressured to perform indigeneity in order to assert their rights, official categories often conflict with the localized ways that Native people articulate their identities in relation to the state, long-term economic activities, and occupation of their ancestral homelands (Muehlmann 2013).

In the Sierra Juárez, the Paipai and their Kiliwa and Kumeyaay neighbors have maintained control of a handful of reserves, even as many of the rancherías that sustained people into the early twentieth century have been taken over by mestizo populations (Alvárez de Williams 2004). Yet, these places are almost universally remembered as Native homelands—places where relatives lived and died or where people would stop on trips outside of their home community. This landscape continues to nurture a sense of identity even as settler landholdings creep closer and closer to the remaining Indigenous enclaves (Garduño 2003, 21–22). Households in Santa Catarina often consist of alternating generations, as elders watch over their grandchildren so that adults in their twenties and thirties can leave to work in the agricultural sector or in cities like Ensenada and still have their children grow up in the community. Although many residents express frustration over the failure of government assistance programs—which, like the Dominican mission system two centuries prior, fail to account for local understandings of autonomy and social organization—members of the community view their lives as being intimately tied to the Native world of the Sierra Juárez. As Owen noted more than a half century ago, "The Paipai choose to remain Paipai" (1962, 41).

Patterns of Persistence

Clearly, the Ohlone and Paipai have persisted as social groups. But what does it mean to have persisted? Though the particulars differ across California, the overall pattern demonstrated in the preceding chapters is the same as the one identified by Vice Chairwoman Arrellano in her address to the SCU community. Native Californians are still here and they never left. This is the macrolevel message of this book. The interwoven patterns of persistence visible in the particular histories of the Ohlone and Paipai have important parallels in the complex mosaic of Indigenous peoples of California and across North America. Yet, if we focus our attention on any two Native Californian groups, the simple fact of survival is complicated by diverse strategies of survivance that played out in localized circumstances. Across the region, Native Californians worked within and against ever-shifting colonial structures to ensure the continuation of their communities, families, and traditions but they did so in ways that made sense within their own culturally defined worldviews and fit the particular historical moment. A tension exists, then, between the broad patterns common to all persistent peoples and the more intimate choices made by any single group as it managed the constraints and opportunities of dynamic relations with their Indigenous neighbors and non-Native colonists.

A benefit of the comparative approach is that the juxtaposition of particular case studies may highlight points of convergence between seemingly different trajectories. In some instances, it may be possible to detect how differences in colonial structures resulted in distinct patterns of social organization and external acknowledgment that continue to have relevance decades or centuries later (Lightfoot 2005). Yet, internal dynamics within Native societies also affected the long-term processes of sustained colonialism. In charting Indigenous-colonial interactions in the American Southwest/ Northwest Mexico across more than four centuries, anthropologist Edward

Spicer asserted that colonial entanglements cannot "be explained by any simple formula" and instead must be understood as stemming from the local circumstances that structured each encounter (1962, 17). However, the fact that many Indigenous societies he studied continued to maintain distinct identities despite the long history of missionization and incorporation into nation states led Spicer to look for commonalities that drove the continuation of self-determination (and see Spicer 1971). Among the most important, in his view, were "continued residence on their land and common experiences in the struggle for autonomy" (Spicer 1962, 578). These observations have largely stood the test of time.

Importance of Homelands

Much has been written about the enduring relationship between peoples and their homelands. In a particularly insightful comment, writer Hugh Brody addresses long-held beliefs about the relative nature of hunter-gatherer and farming societies. In the classic stereotype, farmers are literally rooted to a specific territory by their crops whereas hunters and gatherers roam freely from place to place. "However, the stereotype has it the wrong way around. It is agricultural societies that tend to be on the move; hunting peoples are far more firmly settled. This fact is evident when we look at these two ways of being in the world over a long time span—when we screen the movie of human history, as it were, rather than relying on a photograph" (Brody 2000, 7). This observation is borne out by the history of California over the past 250 years: several empires have come and gone whereas Native people have remained.

The pressures of colonialism have failed to uproot Native Californians—who today comprise some 109 federally recognized tribes in the United States, eight more communities in Baja California, plus the dozens of unacknowledged tribes like the Muwekma Ohlone—who all have managed, often against incredible opposition, to maintain a physical connection to their ancestral homelands. This feat was front and center in the suit presented to the Indian Claims Commission by California tribes in the mid-twentieth century. Although it stopped short of granting full financial compensation for the lands that were taken, the government conceded that Native people held fast to their territory, even in the mission period. In its decision, the Commission wrote, "We gather from the evidence that with few exceptions no tribelet voluntarily completely abandoned its tribal home" (Heizer 1978a, 129).

These findings have only been strengthened by recent scholarship. Most Native Californian groups who were associated with missions found ways, such as fugitivism or the manipulation of the paseo system, to maintain ties to their homelands and the important places and resources they held (Schneider 2015b; Panich and Schneider 2014). As the missions closed down in the 1830s and 1840s, groups who had witnessed the founding of missions in their core territories—including the Ohlone and the Paipai—remained closely associated with those places despite the scars of colonialism. The ability of Native people to stay in their homelands became more difficult within the growing settler nations of nineteenth-century United States and Mexico. Both the Ohlone and the Paipai carved out enclaves that allowed them to retain social and cultural autonomy within their ancestral lands. Alisal and Santa Catarina were certainly smaller than the total extent of their residents' ancestral territories, but viewed from the perspective of the people who inhabited the communities at the time—few of whom ever witnessed the precolonial landscape—such locales represented enduring regional connections. Contextualized within deep Indigenous histories, both settlements reflected aspects of earlier settlement patterns with primary residential areas surrounded by working landscapes and places of ceremonial importance.

As the twentieth century progressed, Ohlone people faced increasingly difficult choices about the physical form of their community. Without an official reservation or even a critical mass of privately held land, the only way to keep their community going was, ironically, to disperse. Most remained in the general area, with seasonal labor practices providing an avenue to continued engagement with the land through mid-century. In the 1960s, many families previously associated with Alisal came together to save the Ohlone Cemetery, originally a campo santo of Mission San José, from destruction during the construction of Interstate 680 (Medina 2015). More recently, Bay Area Ohlone have been actively working to revitalize the Chocheño language as well as other important cultural practices such as Indigenous cuisine. Ohlone people are also at the forefront of public movements to protect ancestral sites from development and to recenter Indigenous people in the interpretation of the region's colonial history (Elias 2018; Galvan 2013; Galvan and Medina 2018; Keenan 2018; Zappia 2018, 385–86) (Figure 19). Some have even formed a land trust to begin the process of reclaiming territory in the urban core of the Bay Area, one parcel at a time (NoiseCat 2018). As argued by anthropologist Michelle Lelièvre (2017), Native peoples' continued engagement with their homelands, even in the face of erasure, is itself an act of sovereignty.

In the Sierra Juárez, the Paipai similarly watched as important places fell into the hands of non-Native interests over the course of the nineteenth and twentieth centuries. As one Native resident put it, "The foreigners got in, they settled, they filled this land" (Mixco 1977, 223–24). Still, the core

FIGURE 19. Andrew Galvan at Mission San Francisco, where his great-great-great-great grandfather was baptized in 1794. Since 2004, Andrew has served as curator of the mission. Courtesy of Andrew Galvan.

community of Santa Catarina offered a refuge to those who had been displaced, gradually gaining more importance in the Native world of northern Baja California. The geography of Santa Catarina is centered on the area immediately surrounding the former mission site, but even today, some residents continue to reside in outlying hamlets that more closely align to their ancestral shimul territories. Across the reserva, many people rely on the landscape for their economic livelihood, ranging from cattle ranching to the collecting of clay that will ultimately be used for artisanal pottery to the harvesting of palmilla (*Yucca schidigera*) for the manufacture of cosmetics (Graham 2019; Wilken-Robertson 2018, 218–21) (Figure 20). Local place names remain in use and carry with them important cultural meanings, and elders recall the locations of older settlements and ancient ancestral sites. As Paipai elder

Benito Peralta told archaeologist Julia Bendimez Patterson in the 1980s, "I was born here, I was raised here, and I will die here" (1989, 19). This sentiment was echoed by a local official, Feliciano Cañedo, with whom I worked two decades later. He affirmed, "This is our land. We were born here and we will die here" (Panich 2009, 5).

FIGURE 20. Teresa Castro Albañez making pottery with the paddle-and-anvil technique. Santa Catarina, 2008.

Struggles for Autonomy

Another common experience among the Indigenous groups who have faced centuries of colonialism along the North American borderlands has been what Spicer (1962) calls "the oppositional process." That is, by defending their way of life against military domination and directed culture change, Native groups in many cases strengthened their resolve to remain distinct social and political entities. In some ways, this tension was present in the contradictions of the colonial systems themselves: the missions were designed to enculturate, but as Indios, Native people were an entire class of people separate from colonial society. Similarly, United States government policy on Native Americans has been marked by frequent swings between elimination, removal, and assimilation. Within these shifting structures, Native Californians have steadfastly insisted on their own autonomy in various ways. As others have shown, opposition to colonialism was not simply a response to domination but rather Indigenous groups drew on localized landscapes, knowledge, and memory to define their own communities (Den Ouden 2005; Liebmann and Murphy 2010; Schneider 2015b)

Native resistance to Spanish colonization took many forms. These varied chronologically over the course of the mission period and geographically across the expanse of Alta and Baja California (Castillo 1989). In the San Francisco Bay region, Ohlone people found ways to push back against the mission system despite the comparatively heavy colonial presence and the wide geographic imprint of mission recruitment. Whereas many Ohlones physically fought the Spanish in the late eighteenth century, their tactics changed as large numbers of Native groups from California's interior became associated with the San Francisco Bay Area missions, starting in the 1800s. The arrival of more distant Native Californians altered the calculus for Ohlone people, who resented the colonial presence in their homelands but must have also recognized that they were rapidly becoming outnumbered in the missions themselves. Thus, the later mission revolts in central California were almost all led by individuals from the Central Valley or the North Bay. Ohlone people, for their part, seem to have leaned on the missions for political stability while simultaneously undermining the Franciscans' enculturation program by maintaining cultural traditions in the relative privacy of the mission rancherías.

In the Sierra Juárez, local Native groups put up near constant armed resistance against the missions and their enculturation projects, paradoxically opening up spaces for Indigenous autonomy (Magaña Mancillas 2001). Native people who came together to fight the Spanish created enduring alliances between representatives of all four of the region's major ethno-linguistic groups—Paipai, Kiliwa, Kumeyaay, and Cucapá. Though membership in particular shimuls seems to have structured some individuals' participation in these conflicts, regional practices that connected different groups—exogamous marriages, communal mourning ceremonies, and seasonal economic pursuits—likely facilitated the creation of military alliances at different moments in the history of colonization. In this way, the shimul system remained a primary vector of social identity at the same time that broader distinctions between Native Californians and colonists reinforced macroscale fields of identification and affiliation.

In both regions, Native people also practiced more understated forms of noncooperation. The archaeological record is replete with evidence for the refusal of Native Californians to cede cultural traditions such as the use of stone tools, the exchange of beads, and the mourning of the dead. From within the regimented worlds of the mission system, Native people quickly learned that names were political. Nineteenth-century Ohlone refused to reveal their true names to priests and American tax collectors, and the Paipai insisted upon having their shimul affiliations recorded along with the names given to them at baptism as in the 1834 census from Mission Santa Catalina. Post-mission censuses from the Bay Area similarly reflect the preference of Native people to evade bureaucratic entanglement—simply take stock of the seemingly random appearance and disappearance of large numbers of California Indians from early American period census records.

The refusal to succumb to missionary and settler colonial programs extended to the resolve of Native Californian groups to stay connected to the landscape even without legal property rights in the eyes of colonial powers. Through oral narratives, historical documents, and archaeological materials, it is clear that Native people continued to engage with culturally meaningful places despite the increasingly partitioned colonial landscape. Ranging from the mission-era manipulation of the paseo system to the hunting and gathering practices of the twentieth century that crosscut settler property lines, the Ohlone and Paipai were present in ways that defied colonial expectations. The determination of Native people to set their own social and physical boundaries stymied colonial agents from the first missionaries all the way through to twentieth-century anthropologists. In this way, the oppositional process facilitated macroscale differentiation at the same time that Native people exploited newcomers' ignorance about Indigenous social organization and subsistence economies as a form of resistance in and of itself (cf. Scott 2009; Welch 2017, 18).

Communities of Perseverance

The idea of an enclave subsumes both of the above factors: a land base from which a group can maintain its distinction from others, often through the process of opposition to colonialism or other forms of domination. But the persistence of Indigenous communities across generations is not simply the natural result of the passage of time; rather, communities are reproduced through human agency as people navigate historically contingent social structures and cultural attitudes to go about their daily lives. Communities, moreover, are active aggregations of individuals and families who can turn to each other for mutual support and a sense of belonging (Hull 2015; Hull and Douglass 2018; and see Canuto and Yaeger 2000). These insights help to contextualize the apparent differences between Indigenous communities in the twenty-first century and those living in California prior to the arrival of Europeans.

Recent reevaluations of late precontact California suggest that people lived in relatively small-scale polities but remained connected through regional economic, ceremonial, and kinship ties. During the early years of the colonial period, these core communities were undermined by high mortality rates at the same time that members of many formerly distinct groups came to live together in the mission rancherías. Mission residential communities differed in some ways from the ones Native people had left behind—they were, at a minimum, larger and more diverse—but nonetheless provided the resources needed for perseverance in a repressive colonial context (Lightfoot 2018). By living in close proximity with others from similar backgrounds, mission residents were able to find marriage partners, continue culturally meaningful ceremonial obligations, and obtain important raw materials from beyond the mission walls that they could use for the preparation of familiar cuisine and material culture. They could, in other words, create community. This pattern of making do, forged in the missions, was recreated in countless other contexts: at ranchos, in cities, on reservations, and in the refuge communities of Alisal and Santa Catarina.

One of the fundamental ways of reproducing one's community is, of course, to reproduce. Given the pronounced demographic and territorial losses of the time, postcontact communities grew out of, but did not precisely replicate, those that came before. Instead, Native people turned to existing exogamous marriage practices and regional economic and ceremonial connections to enlarge the field of possible marriage partners at the same time that the total population of potential spouses was becoming more circumscribed. These intimate strategies are evident in the documentary record for Spanish and

Mexican California, including the missions of the San Francisco Bay Area and Mission Santa Catalina in Baja California. The patterns of coalescence represented in the mission marriage and census records demonstrate that Native people of each generation looked to the future of their communities as they sought spouses and created families, while the evidence for the continuation of mourning ceremonies throughout colonial California similarly reveals the connections they maintained to those who had come before.

With the closing of the missions, Native Californians were no longer subject to the policy of reducción that had been implemented with varying degrees of success by the Franciscans and Dominicans. Some people, particularly those who had entered the mission system relatively late in time, opted to return to ancestral communities on the edge of the colonial world. But for others, the missions had been founded in the center of their original territories. Ohlone people, and those with whom they had forged familial connections at regional missions, maintained community via a constellation of interconnected settlements in the southeastern Bay Area. There, they welcomed members of other ethnolinguistic groups and combined local religious ceremonies with Pan-Indian revival movements in the late nineteenth century. Their land base was slowly eroded in the early twentieth century, but the people themselves never severed ties, reforming decades later as the Muwekma Ohlone Tribe and closely related entities. In northern Baja California, the residents of Santa Catarina similarly offered a refuge to their neighbors and the resulting community has retained its role as a central node in the Paipai world nearly two centuries after the destruction of the mission.

As archaeologist Kathleen Hull (2015) has argued, the high mortality rates suffered by Native Californians in the colonial era have become something of a red herring for discussions of cultural continuity within the realms of federal acknowledgment and popular opinion. Rather than simply enumerating the number of survivors to gauge the authenticity of contemporary Native groups, we must also consider long-term patterns of community sustainability in which Indigenous families and individuals made use of the often restricted social and material resources available to them to ensure a baseline quality of life. There is no denying that colonialism has negatively impacted Native Californians but it is also possible to see surprising continuities in social organization. The Ohlone community at its most tenuous point in the mid-twentieth century was fundamentally rooted in Indigenous understandings of social organization and community. Though they were reduced in total number and had lost sizeable amounts of territory, the Ohlone of that time remained organized into large extended families that were connected to each other by marriage and by ceremonial obligations, a pattern that extends centuries into the past. The experiences of the Paipai reflect a similar story, albeit one that is more fully represented in the ethnographic and historical records. In both cases, people relied on their homelands and were bolstered by opposition to colonialism, but it was ultimately the communities themselves that persevered.

An End to Terminal Narratives

Today, a full two decades into the twenty-first century, the Ohlone and Paipai continue to build on the accumulated knowledge of the past to contend with the challenges of sustained colonialism in localized, culturally specific ways. Yet, the fact that we are discussing extant Native Californian groups at all in the year 2020 would have surprised many of the outsiders who interacted with Ohlone and Paipai communities over the past 250 years. From the earliest missionaries to twentieth-century anthropologists, nearly all expected that Native Californian societies would eventually fade in the face of supposed progress. These deeply entrenched ideas carried Spanish missionaries around the world to the Americas, drove countless settlers across the continent, and lured generations of anthropologists out of their universities and into Native communities. Such are the deep and intertwined roots of terminal narratives.

By the third decade of twentieth century, however, many observers determined that the narrative had come to an end. In his oft-cited *Handbook of the Indians of California*, Kroeber put it plainly: "The tribes dedicated to mission life are gone" (1925, 888). This broad-brush proclamation was repeated in various local histories and ethnographic summaries across California and Baja California. The inevitability of Indian extinction in California was coming to pass as predicted by generations of historians who chronicled the supposed demise of Native Americans from the Atlantic Coast westward across the continent (Mancini 2015; O'Brien 2010). Historical scholarship is, in many ways, a collection of stories that those of us in Western society tell ourselves (Scott 2009, 8). For most of the past 250 years, newcomers to California have been telling a similar tale: one of primitive societies whose claim to the region was quickly, if tragically, undermined by their own biological and cultural susceptibility to the influence of "civilization" (Rawls 1984). The cumulative effect has been that outsiders have been declaring Native Californians to be extinct for nearly a century despite their continued presence throughout the region.

Part of the pervasiveness of the myth of Indian extinction is rooted in deeply essentialist understandings of Indigenous cultures and identities. Even

Kroeber later acknowledged that Native California *people* were alive and well. Rather, in his estimation, "It is their aboriginal culture which has essentially died" (Kroeber and Heizer 1970, 2). This too gets it wrong. What Kroeber and many others failed to understand is that continuity does not equal stasis (Ghisleni 2018). As the examples of the Ohlone and the Paipai demonstrate, each group present today has persisted in its own fashion. Through a careful sifting of the evidence, it is possible to see the clues they left along the way: archaeological deposits that speak to the importance of tradition, the documents where they inserted their own Indigenous sense of identity, and the landscapes inscribed with meaning by oral narratives. By following these varied trajectories, it is possible to trace both the Ohlone and the Paipai from their precontact origins through to the present day. Their stories overlap and diverge along the way but both tell the tale of continuity.

In closing, I propose a different end to the terminal narrative: one in which we—as members of settler society—examine our own tightly held mythologies of conquest and racial superiority. From the missions to the twentieth century, newcomers to California have perpetuated the erasure of Indigenous peoples through violence, removal, scholarship, and the byzantine requirements for federal recognition. For their part, Native people have consistently undermined these colonial programs and attitudes to maintain their own communities. Yet, the echoes of earlier policies are present in the fact that Native Californians—like other Indigenous groups worldwide—are still left with the burden of proof when forced to demonstrate their own identities in the realms of popular opinion and governmental acknowledgment. There, they face an impossible standard: to have survived required change yet change precludes survival (Miranda 2013). As the examples in this book demonstrate, however, change and persistence are part of the same process. No two groups have followed the same pathways to the present but this fact does not invalidate their persistence.

Vice Chairwoman Arellano put it clearly: Native Californians are still here and they are resilient. Given the history of the past 250 years, I have no doubt that people will be saying the same thing for decades and centuries to come.

References

Acebo, Nathan, and Desireé Reneé Martinez. 2018. "Towards an Analytic of Survivance in California Archaeology." *Procedings of the Society for California Archaeology* 32: 144–52.

Allen, Mark W. 2012. "A Land of Violence." In *Contemporary Issues in California Archaeology*, edited by Terry L. Jones and Jennifer E. Perry, 197–215. Walnut Creek, CA: Left Coast Press.

Allen, Mark W., Tsim D. Schneider, Christopher Morgan, Kathleen L. Hull, and Kenneth M. Ames. 2016. "Structured Tumult: A Review Forum for Robert L. Bettinger's Book, Orderly Anarchy: Sociopolitical Evolution in Aboriginal California." *California Archaeology* 8 (1): 111–25.

Allen, Rebecca. 1998. *Native Americans at Mission Santa Cruz, 1791–1834: Interpreting the Archaeological Record.* Perspectives in California Archaeology. Institute of Archaeology: University of California, Los Angeles.

Allen, Rebecca. 2010. "Alta California Missions and the Pre–1849 Transformation of Coastal Lands." *Historical Archaeology* 44 (3): 69–80.

Allen, Rebecca, R. Scott Baxter, Linda Hylkema, Clinton Blount, and Stella D'Oro. 2010. *Uncovering and Interpreting History and Archaeology at Mission Santa Clara.* Report to Santa Clara University, Santa Clara, CA.

Alvarez, Susan H., and E. Breck Parkman. 2014. "A Clamshell Disk Bead Manufacturing Kit from CA-SON-2294/H, Petaluma Adobe State Historic Park, Sonoma County, California." *Proceedings of the Society for California Archaeology* 28: 197–205.

Alvárez de Williams, Anita. 2004. *Primeros Pobladores de la Baja California: Introducción a la Antropología de la Península.* Mexicali: Centro INAH Baja California.

Ambro, Richard D. 2003. *They Danced in the Plaza: The Historical Archaeology of Notre Dame Plaza, Mission San Francisco de Asís (Dolores), 347 Dolores Street, San Francisco, California.* Report to Mercy/Charities Housing California, San Francisco.

Anderson, M. Kat. 2005. *Tending the Wild: Native American Knowledge and the Management of California's Natural Resources.* Berkeley: University of California Press.

Anonymous. 1834. *Padrón de la Mis. de Santa Catalina Virgen y Mártir.* Manuscript on file, Saint Albert's Priory, Oakland, CA.

Archibald, Robert. 1978. *The Economic Aspects of the California Missions.* Washington, DC: Academy of American Franciscan History.

Arkush, Brooke S. 1993. "Yokuts Trade Networks and Native Culture Change in Central and Eastern California." *Ethnohistory* 40 (4): 619–40.

Arkush, Brooke S. 2011. "Native Responses to European Intrusion: Cultural Persistence and Agency Among Mission Neophytes in Spanish Colonial California." *Historical Archaeology* 45 (4): 62–90.

Arrillaga, José Joaquín. 1797a. *Letter to El Marqués de Branciforte, September 30.* C-A 14:10. Bancroft Library, University of California, Berkeley.

Arrillaga, José Joaquín. 1797b. *Letter to El Virrey de México, October 9.* C-A 14:11. Bancroft Library, University of California, Berkeley.

Arrillaga, José Joaquín. 1804a. *Letter to José de Iturrigaray, May 8.* C-A 25:292. Bancroft Library, University of California, Berkeley.

Arrillaga, José Joaquín. 1804b. *Letter to José de Iturrigaray, July 1.* C-A 25:300. Bancroft Library, University of California, Berkeley.

Arrillaga, José Joaquín. 1804c. *Letter to José de Iturrigaray, October 24.* C-A 25:302–303. Bancroft Library, University of California, Berkeley.

Arrillaga, José Joaquín. 1804d. *Letter to José Manuel Ruiz, November 17.* C-A 25:244. Bancroft Library, University of California, Berkeley.

Arrillaga, José Joaquín. 1969. *José Joaquín Arrillaga: Diary of His Surveys of the Frontier, 1796.* Baja California Travels Series 17, edited by John W. Robinson and translated by Froy Tiscareno. Los Angeles: Dawson's Book Shop.

Aschmann, Homer. 1959. *The Central Desert of Baja California: Demography and Ecology.* Ibero-Americana 42. Berkeley: University of California Press.

Aschmann, Homer. 1974. "A Late Recounting of the Vizcaíno Expedition and Plans for the Settlement of California." *Journal of California Anthropology* 1 (2): 174–85.

Asisara, Lorenzo. 1989. "The Assassination of Padre Andrés Quintana by the Indians of Mission Santa Cruz in 1812: The Narrative of Lorenzo Asisara." Edited and translated by Edward D. Castillo. *California History* 68 (3): 116–25.

Atalay, Sonya. 2006. "No Sense for the Struggle: Creating a Context for Survivance at the NMAI." *American Indian Quarterly* 30: 597–618.

Aviles, Brian A., and Robert L. Hoover. 1997. "Two Californias, Three Religious Orders and Fifty Missions: A Comparison of the Missionary Systems of Baja and Alta California." *Pacific Coast Archaeological Society Quarterly* 33 (3): 1–28.

Barco, Miguel del. 1973. *Historia Natural y Crónica de la Antigua California.* Edited by Miguel León-Portilla. México DF: Universidad Nacional Autónoma de México.

Barr, Juliana. 2007. *Peace Came in the Form of a Woman: Indians and Spaniards in the Texas Borderlands.* Chapel Hill: University of North Carolina Press.

Barr, Juliana. 2017. "There's No Such Thing as 'Prehistory': What the Longue Durée of Caddo and Pueblo History Tells Us about Colonial America." *The William and Mary Quarterly* 74 (2): 203–40.

Basgall, Mark E. 1979. "To Trade, or Not to Trade: A Pomo Example." *Journal of California and Great Basin Anthropology* 1: 178–82.

Bauer, William J., Jr. 2009. *"We Are All Like Migrant Workers Here": Work, Community, and Memory on California's Round Valley Reservation, 1850–1941.* Chapel Hill: University of North Carolina Press.

Bauer, William J., Jr. 2016a. "California." In *The Oxford Handbook of American Indian History*, edited by Frederick E. Hoxie, 275–99. Oxford: Oxford University Press.

Bauer, William J., Jr. 2016b. *California through Native Eyes: Reclaiming History.* Seattle: University of Washington Press.

Bean, Lowell John. 1976. "Social Organization in Native California." In *Native Califor-nians: A Theoretical Retrospective,* edited by Lowell John Bean and Thomas C. Black-burn, 99–123. Menlo Park, CA: Ballena Press.

Bean, Lowell John, and Thomas C. Blackburn, eds. 1976. *Native Californians: A Theoretical Retrospective.* Menlo Park, CA: Ballena Press.

Bean, Lowell John, and Thomas F. King, eds. 1974. *'Antap: California Indian Political and Economic Organization.* Ramona, CA: Ballena Press.

Bean, Lowell John, and Harry Lawton. 1976. "Some Explanations for the Rise of Cultural Complexity in Native California with Comments on Proto-Agriculture." In *Native Californians: A Theoretical Retrospective*, edited by Lowell John Bean and Thomas C. Blackburn, 19–48. Menlo Park, CA: Ballena Press.

Bean, Lowell John, and William Marvin Mason. 1962. *Diaries and Accounts of the Romero Expeditions in Arizona and California, 1823–1826.* Palm Springs, CA: Palm Springs Desert Museum.

Bean, Lowell John, and Sylvia Brakke Vane. 1978. "Cults and Their Transformations." In *Handbook of North American Indians*, vol. 8, *California*, edited by Robert F. Heizer, 662–72. Washington, DC: Smithsonian Institution.

Beebe, Rose Marie, and Robert M. Senkewicz. 2015. *Junípero Serra: California, Indians, and the Transformation of a Missionary*. Norman: University of Oklahoma Press.

Beechey, Frederick W. 1831. *Narrative of a Voyage to the Pacific and Beering's Strait, Vol. 2.* London: H. Colburn and R. Bentley.

Beeler, M. S. 1961. "Northern Costanoan." *International Journal of American Linguistics* 27 (3): 191–97.

Bellifemine, Viviana. 1997. "Mortuary Variability in Prehistoric Central California: A Statistical Study of the Yukisma Site, CA-SCL-38." Master's thesis, San Jose State University.

Bendímez Patterson, Julia. 1989. *Historia Oral: Benito Peralta de Santa Catarina, Comunidad Pai-Pai.* Cuadernos de Ciencias Sociales, Serie 4. Mexicali: Universidad Autónoma de Baja California, Instituto de Investigaciones Sociales.

Bendímez Patterson, Julia. 2008. *Raíces Profundas, Corazones Ancestrales: Historia Oral de María Emes Boronda.* Mexicali: Centro INAH Baja California.

Bennyhoff, James A. 1977. *Ethnogeography of the Plains Miwok.* Center for Archaeological Research at Davis, no. 5, University of California, Davis.

Bennyhoff, James A. 1994. "Central California Augustine: Implications for Northern California Archaeology." In *Toward a New Taxonomic Framework for Central California Archaeology: Essays by James A. Bennyhoff and David A. Fredrickson*, edited by Richard E. Hughes, 65–74. Contributions of the Archaeological Research Facility 52, University of California, Berkeley.

Berger, John. A. 1948. *The Franciscan Missions of California.* Garden City, NY: Doubleday & Company.

Bernard, Julienne, and David. W. Robinson. 2018. "Contingent Communities in a Region of Refuge." In *Forging Communities in Colonial Alta California*, edited by Kathleen L. Hull and John G. Douglass, 113–32. Tucson: University of Arizona Press.

Bettinger, Robert L. 2015. *Orderly Anarchy: Sociopolitical Evolution in Aboriginal California*. Berkeley: University of California Press.

Bibby, Brian. 2012. *Essential Art: Native Basketry from the California Indian Heritage Center*. Berkeley, CA: Heyday.

Bickford, Virginia. 1982. "European Artifacts from a Chumash Cemetery, CAL-LAN-264." Master's thesis, California State University, Long Beach.

Blackburn, Thomas C., and M. Kat Anderson. 1993. *Before the Wilderness: Environmental Management by Native Californians*. Menlo Park, CA: Ballena Press.

Bourdieu, Pierre. 1977. *Outline of a Theory of Practice*. Cambridge: Cambridge University Press.

Bourdieu, Pierre. 1990. *The Logic of Practice*. Stanford, CA: Stanford University Press.

Braje, Todd J., Tom D. Dillehay, Jon M. Erlandson, Richard G. Klein, and Torben C. Rick. 2017. "Finding the First Americans." *Science* 358 (6363): 592–94.

Broadbent, Sylvia M. 1972. "The Rumsen of Monterey: An Ethnography from Historical Sources." In *Miscellaneous Papers in Archaeology*, 45–93. Contributions of the Archaeological Research Facility 14, University of California, Berkeley.

Broadbent, Sylvia M. 1974. "Conflict at Monterey: Indian Horse Raiding 1820–1850." *Journal of California Anthropology* 1: 86–101.

Brody, Hugh. 2000. *The Other Side of Eden: Hunters, Farmers, and the Shaping of the World*. New York: North Point Press.

Brown, Alan K. 1994. "The European Contact of 1772 and Some Later Documentation." In *The Ohlone Past and Present: Native Americans of the San Francisco Bay Region*, edited by Lowell John Bean, 1–42. Menlo Park, CA: Ballena Press.

Brown, Alan K. 2001. "Introduction." In *A Description of Distant Roads: Original Journals of the First Expedition into California, 1769–1770*, edited and translated by Alan K. Brown, 3–146. San Diego: San Diego State University Press.

Brown, Kaitlin M. 2018. "Crafting Identity: Acquisition, Production, Use, and Recycling of Soapstone during the Mission Period in Alta California." *American Antiquity* 83 (2): 244–62.

Buscaglia, Silvana. 2017. "Materiality and Indigenous Agency: Limits to the Colonial Order (Argentinian Patagonia, Eighteenth-Nineteenth Centuries)." *International Journal of Historical Archaeology* 21: 641–73.

Byrd, Brian F., Shannon Dearmond, and Laurel Engbring. 2018. "Re-Visualizing Indigenous Persistence during Colonization from the Perspective of Traditional Settlements in the San Francisco Bay-Delta Area." *Journal of California and Great Basin Anthropology* 38 (2): 163–90.

California State Library. 1852. *1852 California State Census*. Sacramento, CA.

Cambra, Rosemary, Alan Leventhal, Monica V. Arellano, Sheila Guzman Schmidt, and Gloria Arellano Gomez. 2011. "An Ethnohistory of Santa Clara Valley and Adjacent Regions; Historic Ties of the Muwekma Ohlone Tribe of the San Francisco Bay Area and Tribal Stewardship over the Mission Santa Clara Neophyte Cemetery: Clareño Muwékma Ya Túnneshte Nómmo [Where the Clareño Indians are Buried] Site." In *Final Report on the Burial and Archaeological Data Recovery Program Conducted on a Portion of the Mission Santa Clara Indian Neophyte Cemetery (1781–1818): Clareño Muwékma Ya Túnncšte Nómmo {Where the Clareño Indians Are Buried} Site (CA-SCL-30/H), Located in the City of Santa Clara, Santa Clara County, California*, written by Alan Leventhal et al. Report to Pacific Gas and Electric Company, Santa Clara, CA.

Cañizares, José de. 1952. "Putting a Lid on California: An Unpublished Diary of the Portolá Expedition (Continued)." *California Historical Society* 31 (3): 261–70.

Canuto, Marcello A., and Jason Yaeger, eds. 2000. *The Archaeology of Communities: A New World Perspective*. London: Routledge.

Carlson, Pamela McGuire, and E. Breck Parkman. 1986. "An Exceptional Adaptation: Camillo Ynitia, the Last Headman of the Olompalis." *California History* 65 (4): 238–310.

Carrico, Richard L. 1997. "Sociopolitical Aspects of the 1775 Revolt at Mission San Diego de Alcalá: An Ethnohistorical Approach." *Journal of San Diego History* 43 (3): 143–57.

Carrico, Richard L. 2008. *Strangers in a Stolen Land: Indians of San Diego County from Prehistory to the New Deal*. San Diego: Sunbelt Publications.

Carrico, Richard L. 2018. "Kumeyaay Inscriptive Art at Three Spanish Colonial Period Sites in San Diego: Cultural Continuity, Syncretic Behavior, or Resistive Art?" *Rock Art Papers* 19: 81–92.

Castillo, Edward D. 1978. "The Impact of Euro-American Exploration and Settlement." In *Handbook of North American Indians*, vol. 8, *California*, edited by Robert F. Heizer, 99–127. Washington, DC: Smithsonian Institution.

Castillo, Edward D. 1989. "The Native Response to the Colonization of Alta California." In *Columbian Consequences*, vol. 1, *Archaeological and Historical Perspectives on the Spanish Borderlands West*, edited by David H. Thomas, 377–94. Washington, DC: Smithsonian Institution Press.

Castillo-Muñoz, Verónica. 2017. *The Other California: Land, Identity, and Politics on the Mexican Borderlands*. Berkeley: University of California Press.

Castro, Gregg. 2014–2015. "Mission Accomplice (But NOT Accomplished)." *News from Native California* 28 (2): 59–62.

Castro, Manuel de Jesús. 1852. *Untitled Manuscript*. M-M 21:535. Bancroft Library, University of California, Berkeley.

Cavender Wilson, Angela. 1998. "Grandmother to Granddaughter: Generations of Oral History in a Dakota Family." In *Natives and Academics: Researching and Writing about American Indians*, edited by Devon A. Mihesuah, 27–36. Lincoln: University of Nebraska Press.

Chaput, Donald, William Mason, and David Zárate Loperena. 1992. *Modest Fortunes: Mining in Northern Baja California*. Los Angeles: Natural History Museum of Los Angeles.

Chavez, Yve B. 2017. "Indigenous Artists, Ingenuity, and Resistance at the California Missions After 1769." PhD diss., University of California, Los Angeles.

Chilcote, Olivia. 2015. "Pow Wows at the Mission: Identity and Federal Recognition for the San Luis Rey Band of Luiseño Mission Indians." *Boletín: Journal of the California Missions Studies Association* 31 (1): 79–87.

Cipolla, Craig N. 2013. "Native American Historical Archaeology and the Trope of Authenticity." *Historical Archaeology* 47 (3): 12–22.

Cipolla, Craig N. and Katherine Howlett Hayes, eds. 2015. *Rethinking Colonialism: Comparative Archaeological Approaches*. Gainesville: University Press of Florida.

Clay, Karen B. 1999. "Property Rights and Institutions: Congress and the California Land Act of 1851." *Journal of Economic History* 59 (1): 122–42.

Collier, Mary E. T., and Sylvia B. Thalman. 1991. *Interviews with Tom Smith and Maria Copa: Isabel Kelley's Ethnographic Notes on the Coast Miwok Indians of Marin and Southern Sonoma Counties, California*. Miwok Archaeological Preserve of Marin Occasional Paper no. 6, San Rafael, CA.

Cook, Sherburne F. 1960. "Expeditions to the Interior of California, Central Valley, 1820–1840." *University of California Anthropological Records* 20 (5): 151–213.

Cook, Sherburne F. 1976. *The Conflict between the California Indian and White Civilization*. Berkeley: University of California Press.

Coombs, Gary, and Fred Plog. 1977. "The Conversion of the Chumash Indians: An Ecological Interpretation." *Human Ecology* 5 (4): 309–28.

Cordero, Jonathan F. 2015. "Native Persistence: Marriage, Social Structure, Political Leadership, and Intertribal Relations at Mission Dolores, 1777–1800." *Journal of California and Great Basin Anthropology* 35 (1): 133–49.

Cordero, Jonathan F. 2017. "California Indians, Franciscans, and the Myth of Evangelical Success." *Boletín: Journal of the California Missions Foundation* 33 (1): 62–79.

Costello, Julia G., and David Hornbeck. 1989. "Alta California: An Overview." In *Columbian Consequences*, vol. 1, *Archaeological and Historical Perspectives on the Spanish Borderlands West*, edited by David H. Thomas, 303–31. Washington, DC: Smithsonian Institution Press.

Costo, Rupert, and Jeannette Henry Costo, eds. 1987. *The Missions of California: A Legacy of Genocide*. San Francisco: Indian Historian Press.

Country Club. 1904. *History of Washington Township, Alameda County, California*. Niles, CA: Woman's Club of Washington Township.

Crespí, Juan. 2001. *A Description of Distant Roads: Original Journals of the First Expedition into California, 1769–1770*. Edited and translated by Alan K. Brown. San Diego: San Diego State University Press.

Crosby, Harry W. 1994. *Antigua California: Mission and Colony on the Peninsular Frontier, 1697–1768*. Albuquerque: University of New Mexico Press.

Cuero, Delfina. 1968. *The Autobiography of Delfina Cuero, A Diegueño Indian*. Edited by Florence C. Shipek. Los Angeles: Dawson's Book Shop.

Curry, Benjamin A. 2018. "Cattle in the Garden: An Environmental and Archaeological History of Ranching at Rancho Refugio—Wilder Ranch." PhD diss., University of Arizona.

Cuthrell, Rob Q., Lee M. Panich, and Oliver R. Hegge. 2016. "Investigating Native Californian Tobacco Use at Mission Santa Clara, California, through Morphometric Analysis of Tobacco (*Nicotiana* spp.) Seeds." *Journal of Archaeological Science: Reports* 6: 451–662.

Dartt-Newton, Deana. 2011. "California's Sites of Conscience: An Analysis of the State's Historic Mission Museums." *Museum Anthropology* 34 (2): 97–108.

Dawson, Alexander S. *Indian and Nation in Revolutionary Mexico.* Tucson: University of Arizona Press.

Deetz, James. 1963. "Archaeological Investigations at La Purísima Mission." *Archaeological Survey Annual Report* 5: 161–241.

Den Ouden, Amy E. 2005. *Beyond Conquest: Native Peoples and the Struggle for History in New England.* Lincoln: University of Nebraska Press.

de la Peña, Guillermo. 2005. "Social and Cultural Policies Toward Indigenous Peoples: Perspectives from Latin America." *Annual Review of Anthropology* 43: 717–39.

Des Lauriers, Matthew R. 2011. "Of Clams and Clovis: Isla Cedros, Baja California, Mexico." In *Trekking the Shore: Changing Coastlines and the Antiquity of Coastal Settlement*, edited by Nuno F. Bicho, Jonathan A. Haws, and Loren G. Davis, 161–77. New York: Springer.

Des Lauriers, Matthew R. 2014. "The Spectre of Conflict on Isla Cedros, Baja California, Mexico," In *Violence and Warfare among Hunter-Gatherers*, edited by Mark W. Allen and Terry L. Jones, 204–19. Walnut Creek, CA: Left Coast Press.

Diekmann, Lucy, Lee M. Panich, and Chuck Striplen. 2007. "Native American Management and the Legacy of Working Landscapes in California." *Rangelands* 29 (3): 46–50.

Dietler, John, Heather Gibson, and Benjamin Vargas. 2018. "'A Mourning Dirge was Sung': Community and Remembrance at Mission San Gabriel." In *Forging Communities in Colonial Alta California*, edited by Kathleen L. Hull and John G. Douglass, 62–87. Tucson: University of Arizona Press.

Dietler, John, Heather Gibson, and James M. Potter, eds. 2015. *Abundant Harvests: The Archaeology of Industry and Agriculture at San Gabriel Mission.* SWCA Anthropological Research Paper no. 11, Pasadena, CA.

Dietz, Stephen A. 1976. "Echa-Tamal: A Study of Coast Miwok Acculturation." Master's thesis, San Francisco State University.

Dillon, Brian Dervin, and Matthew A. Boxt. 2013. "California Ceramic Traditions: An Introduction." *Pacific Coast Archaeological Society Quarterly* 47 (1 & 2): 1–10.

Douglass, John G., Kathleen L. Hull, and Seetha N. Reddy. 2018. "The Creation of Community in the Colonial Era Los Angeles Basin." In *Forging Communities in Colonial Alta California*, edited by Kathleen L. Hull and John G. Douglass, 35–61. Tucson: University of Arizona Press.

Duggan, Marie Christine. 2004. *The Chumash and the Presidio of Santa Barbara: Evolution of a Relationship, 1782–1823.* Santa Barbara, CA: Santa Barbara Trust for Historic Preservation.

Duggan, Marie Christine. 2016. "With and Without an Empire: Financing for California Missions Before and After 1810." *Pacific Historical Review* 85 (1): 23–71.

Duggan, Marie Christine. 2018. "Beyond Slavery: The Institutional Status of Mission Indians." In *Franciscans and American Indians in Pan-Borderlands Perspective: Adaptation, Negotiation, and Resistance*, edited by Jeffrey M. Burns and Timothy J. Johnson, 237–50. Oceanside, CA: Academy of American Franciscan History.

Dylla, Emily. 2017. "Hunters, Soldiers, and Holy Men: An Archaeological Study of Masculinities and Male Household Space at Mission San Antonio de Padua, Monterey County, California." PhD diss., University of Texas at Austin.

Eerkens, Jelmer W., Gregory S. Herbert, Jeffrey S. Rosenthal, and Howard J. Spero. 2005. "Provenance Analysis of *Olivella biplicata* Shell Beads from the California and Oregon Coast by Stable Isotope Fingerprinting." *Journal of Archaeological Science* 32: 1501–14.

Eerkens, Jelmer W., Eric J. Bartelink, Laura Brink, Richard T. Fitzgerald, Ramona Garibay, Gina A. Jorgenson, and Randy S. Wiberg. 2016. "Trophy Heads or Ancestor Veneration? A Stable Isotope Perspective on Disassociated and Modified Crania in Precontact Central California." *American Antiquity* 81 (1): 114–31.

Elias, Ishmael. 2018. "West Berkeley Shellmound," *News from Native California* 32 (1): 9–10.

Engel, Paul. 2019. "A Synthesis and Analysis of Radiocarbon Dates from Point Reyes National Seashore." Paper presented at the 53rd Annual Meeting of the Society for California Archaeology, Sacramento.

Engelhardt, Zephyrin, O.F.M. 1929. *The Missions and Missionaries of California*, vol. 1, *Lower California*. Santa Barbara, CA: Mission Santa Barbara.

Engstrand, Iris H.W. 1997. "Seekers of the 'Northern Mystery': European Exploration of California and the Pacific." *California History* 76 (2 & 3): 78–110.

Erlandson, Jon M., and Kevin Bartoy. 1995. "Cabrillo, the Chumash, and Old World Disease." *Journal of California and Great Basin Anthropology* 17 (2): 153–73.

Erlandson, Jon M., Torben C. Rick, Douglas J. Kennet, and Phillip L. Walker. 2001. "Dates, Demography, and Disease: Cultural Contacts and Possible Evidence for Old World Epidemics Among the Protohistoric Island Chumash." *Pacific Coast Archaeological Society Quarterly* 37 (3): 11–26.

Etheridge, Robbie. 2010. *From Chicaza to Chickasaw: The European Invasion and the Transformation of the Mississippian World, 1540–1715*. Chapel Hill: University of North Carolina Press.

Evans, Sally R. 2010. *Jose Maria Alviso Adobe Renovation Project—Phase III, CA-SCL-155/H (P-43-000167), City of Milpitas, Santa Clara County, CA*. Report from Archaeological Resource Service to City of Milpitas, CA.

Evening News [San Jose, California]. 1916. "When San Jose Was Young: A Series of Interesting Articles of an Historical Nature Prepared Especially for the News by a Well Known Author and Journalist: No. 51, Inygo of Inygo Ranch" 67 (134): 6. Dec. 4.

Evett, Rand R., Ernesto Franco-Vizcaino, and Scott L. Stephens. 2007. "Comparing Modern and Past Fire Regimes to Assess Changes in Prehistoric Lightning and Anthropogenic Ignitions in a Jeffrey Pine–Mixed Conifer Forest in the Sierra San Pedro Mártir, Mexico." *Canadian Journal of Forestry Research* 37: 318–30.

Farnsworth, Paul. 1989. "The Economics of Acculturation in the Spanish Missions of Alta California." *Research in Economic Anthropology* 11: 217–49.

Farris, Glenn J. 1988. "Recognizing Indian Folk History as Real History: A Fort Ross Example." *American Indian Quarterly* 13 (4): 471–80.

Farris, Glenn J. 1991. *Archaeological Testing in the Neophyte Housing Area at Mission San Juan Bautista, California*. Sacramento: Resource Protection Division, California Department of Parks and Recreation.

Farris, Glenn J. 2014. "Depriving God and the King of the Means of Charity: Early Nineteenth-Century Missionaries' Views of Cattle Ranchers near Mission La

Purísima, California." In *Indigenous Landscapes and Spanish Missions: New Perspectives from Archaeology and Ethnohistory*, edited by Lee M. Panich and Tsim D. Schneider, 154–71. Tucson: University of Arizona Press.

Farris, Glenn J. 2018. "The Diverse Community of the Pueblo of San Diego in the Mexican Period in California, 1821–1846." In *Forging Communities in Colonial Alta California*, edited by Kathleen L. Hull and John G. Douglass, 234–59. Tucson: University of Arizona Press.

Ferguson, R. Brian, and Neil L. Whitehead, eds. 1992. *War in the Tribal Zone: Expanding States and Indigenous Warfare*. Santa Fe, NM: School of American Research Press.

Ferris, Neal. 2009. *The Archaeology of Native-Lived Colonialism: Challenging History in the Great Lakes*. Tucson: University of Arizona Press.

Ferris, Neal, Rodney Harrison, and Michael V. Wilcox. 2014. *Rethinking Colonial Pasts through Archaeology*. Oxford: Oxford University Press.

Field, Les W. 1999. "Complicities and Collaborations: Anthropologists and the 'Unacknowledged Tribes' of California." *Current Anthropology* 40 (2): 193–209.

Field, Les W., Alan Leventhal, and Rosemary Cambra. 2013. "Mapping Erasure: The Power of Nominative Cartography in the Past and Present of the Muwekma Ohlones of the San Francisco Bay Area." In *Recognition, Sovereignty Struggles, and Indigenous Rights in the United States: A Sourcebook*, edited by Amy E. Den Ouden and Jean M. O'Brien, 287–309. Chapel Hill: University of North Carolina Press.

Field, Les, Alan Leventhal, Dolores Sanchez, and Rosemary Cambra. 1992. "A Contemporary Ohlone Tribal Revitalization Movement: A Perspective from the Muwekma Costanoan/Ohlone Indians of the San Francisco Bay Area." *California History* 71 (3): 412–31.

Field, Margaret. 2012. "Kumeyaay Language Variation, Group Identity, and the Land." *International Journal of American Linguistics* 78 (4): 557–73.

Fischer, John Ryan. 2015. *Cattle Colonialism: An Environmental History of the Conquest of California and Hawai'i*. Chapel Hill: University of North Carolina Press.

Flores Hernández, María, and Manuel Eduardo Pérez Rivas. 2018. "Spatial Analysis of Shell Midden Camps at La Jovita, Ensenada, Baja California." *Pacific Coast Archaeological Society Quarterly* 54 (3 & 4): 1–34.

Flores Santis, Gustavo Adolfo. 2014. "Native American Response and Resistance to Spanish Conquest in the San Francisco Bay Area, 1769–1846." Master's thesis, San Jose State University.

Fredrickson, David A. 1994. "Archaeological Taxonomy in Central California Reconsidered." In *Toward a New Taxonomic Framework for Central California Archaeology: Essays by James A. Bennyhoff and David A. Fredrickson*, edited by Richard E. Hughes, 90–103. Contributions of the Archaeological Research Facility 52, University of California, Berkeley.

Gabb, William M. 1867. *Cochimí and Kiliwa Comparative Vocabulary*. MS 1147. Washington, DC: Smithsonian Institution National Anthropological Archives.

Gallivan, Martin D. 2007. "Powhatan's Werowocomoco: Constructing Place, Polity, and Personhood in the Chesapeake, C.E. 1200–C.E. 1609." *American Anthropologist* 109 (1): 85–100.

Galvan Andrew A. 2013. "Old Mission Dolores, Under New Management: An Open Letter." *News from Native California* 26 (4): 11–13.

Galvan, Andrew, and Vincent Medina. 2018. "Indian Memorials at California Missions." In *Franciscans and American Indians in Pan-Borderlands Perspective: Adaptation, Negotiation, and Resistance*, edited by Jeffrey M. Burns and Timothy J. Johnson, 323–31. Oceanside, CA: American Academy of Franciscan History.

Galvan, Philip Michael. 1968. "The Ohlone Story." *The Indian Historian* 1 (2): 9–13.

Gamble, Lynn H. 2008. *The Chumash World at European Contact: Power, Trade, and Feasting among Complex Hunter-Gatherers*. Berkeley: University of California Press.

Gamble, Lynn H., and Chester King. 2011. "Beads and Ornaments from San Diego: Evidence for Exchange Networks in Southern California and the American Southwest." *Journal of California and Great Basin Anthropology* 31 (2): 155–78.

Gamble, Lynn H., and Irma Carmen Zepeda. 2002. "Social Differentiation and Exchange among the Kumeyaay Indians during the Historic Period in California." *Historical Archaeology* 36 (2): 71–91.

Garduño, Everardo. 1994. *En Donde se Mete el Sol: Historia y Situación Actual de los Indígenas Montañeses de Baja California*. México DF: Consejo Nacional para la Cultura y las Artes.

Garduño, Everardo. 2003. "The Yumans of Baja California, Mexico: From Invented to Imagined and Invisible Communities." *Journal of Latin American Anthropology* 8 (1): 4–37.

Garroutte, Eva Marie. 2003. *Real Indians: Identity and the Survival of Native America*. Berkeley: University of California Press.

Gay, Brandon M., Christopher Brito, and Ian Weir. 2017. "Portable XRF Analysis of Obsidian Projectile Points and Debitage from Paipai Territory, Northern Baja California." *Pacific Coast Archaeological Society Quarterly* 53 (2 & 3): 87–102.

Gayton, Anne H. 1930. "The Ghost Dance of 1870 in South-Central California." *University of California Publications in American Archaeology and Ethnology* 28 (3): 57–82.

Geiger, Maynard, and Clement W. Meighan, eds. 1976. *As the Padres Saw Them: California Indian Life and Customs as Reported by the Franciscan Missionaries 1813–1815*. Santa Barbara, CA: Santa Barbara Mission Archive Library.

Gerhard, Peter, and W. Michael Mathes. 1995. "Peregrinations of the Baja California Mission Registers." *The Americas* 52 (1): 71–80.

Ghisleni, Lara. 2018. "Contingent Persistence: Continuity, Change, and Identity in the Romanization Debate." *Current Anthropology* 59 (2): 138–54.

Gibson, Heather, John Dietler, and Alyssa Newcomb. 2018. "*Jacalitos de Tule*: Weaving Stories of Domestic Life at San Gabriel Mission." Paper presented at the 51st Annual Conference on Historical and Underwater Archaeology, New Orleans.

Giddens, Anthony. 1979. *Central Problems in Social Theory: Action, Structure and Contradiction in Social Analysis*. Cambridge: Cambridge University Press.

Gifford, Edward W. 1926. "Miwok Cults." *University of California Publications in American Archaeology and Ethnology* 18 (3): 391–408.

Gifford, Edward W. 1947. "California Shell Artifacts." *Anthropological Records* 9 (1): 1–132.

Gifford, Edward W. 1955. "Central Miwok Ceremonies." *Anthropological Records* 14 (4): 261–318.

Gifford, Edward W., and Robert H. Lowie. 1928. "Notes on the Akwa'ala Indians of Lower California." *University of California Publications in American Archaeology and Ethnology* 23: 339–52.

Goldbaum, David. 1971. *Towns of Baja California*. Translated by William O. Hendricks. Glendale, CA: La Siesta Press.

Goldbaum, David. 1984. "Noticia Respecto a las Comunidades de Indígenas que Pueblan el Distrito Norte de Baja California." *Calafia* 5 (3): 19–26.

Golla, Victor. 2011. *California Indian Languages*. Berkeley: University of California Press.

Graham, Margaret A., and Russell K. Skowronek. 2015. "Feeding the Congregation at Mission Santa Clara de Asís." *Boletín: Journal of the California Mission Studies Association* 31 (1): 184–202.

Graham, Michelle Donna. 2019. "Tangible Memories?: Pa'ipai Ceramic Traditions in Santa Catarina." PhD diss., Universidad Autónoma de Baja California.

Gray, Nicholas. 1855. *Map of a survey of lands situated between San Leandro and San Lorenzo Creeks, the Bay of San Francisco and the range of mountains to the east, exhibiting boundaries of the "Rancho San Leandro" and adjoining lands*. Land case 234 ND, 747. Land case map, F-524. Bancroft Library, University of California, Berkeley.

Greenwood, Roberta S. 1976. *The Changing Faces of Main Street: Ventura Mission Plaza Archaeological Project*. Report to the Redevelopment Agency of the City of San Buenaventura, CA.

Griset, Suzanne. 1990. "Historic Transformations of Tizon Brown Ware in Southern California." In *Hunter-Gatherer Pottery in the Far Southwest*, edited by Joanne M. Mack, 179–200. Carson City: Nevada State Museum.

Griset, Suzanne, and Alan Ferg. 2010. "Norton and Ethel Allen among the Paipai." *Journal of the Southwest* 52 (2 & 3): 395–416.

Guía Ramírez, Andrea. 2010. *Análisis de los Restos Arqueofaunístico Rescatados del Proyecto de Arqueología Histórica de la Misión de Santa Catalina Temporadas 2005, 2006 y 2007*. Manuscript on file, Santa Clara University, CA.

Guía Ramírez, Andrea. 2008. "Los Animales y el Desarrollo de las Misiones Bajacalifornianas (Resultado de un Estudio Arqueozoológico)." In *Memorias: Balances y Perspectivas de la Antropología e Historia de Baja California 2002–2004*, 241–46. Mexicali: Centro INAH Baja California.

Haas, Lisbeth. 1995. *Conquests and Historical Identities in California, 1769–1936*. Berkeley: University of California Press.

Haas, Lisbeth. 2011. *Pablo Tac, Indigenous Scholar: Writing on Luiseño Language and Colonial History, c. 1840*. Berkeley: University of California Press.

Haas, Lisbeth. 2014. *Saints and Citizens: Indigenous Histories of Colonial Missions and Mexican California*. Berkeley: University of California Press.

Hackel, Steven W. 1997. "The Staff of Leadership: Indian Authority in the Missions of Alta California." *The William and Mary Quarterly* 54 (2): 347–76.

Hackel, Steven W. 2003. "Sources of Rebellion: Indian Testimony and the Mission San Gabriel Uprising of 1785." *Ethnohistory* 50 (4): 643–69.

Hackel, Steven W. 2005. *Children of Coyote, Missionaries of Saint Francis: Indian-Spanish Relations in Colonial California, 1769–1850.* Chapel Hill: University of North Carolina Press.

Hackel Steven W. 2013. *Junípero Serra: California's Founding Father.* New York: Hill and Wang.

Hämäläinen, Pekka. 2008. *The Comanche Empire.* New Haven: Yale University Press.

Hantman, Jeffrey L. 2018. *Monacan Millennium: A Collaborative Archaeology and History of a Virginia Indian People.* Charlottesville: University of Virginia Press.

Harrington, John Peabody. 1984. "Costanoan Field Notes." *John P. Harrington Papers*, vol. 2, *Northern and Central California.* Washington, DC: National Anthropological Archives, Smithsonian Institution. Microfilm.

Harrington, John Peabody. 1985. "Diegueño and Paipai/Kiliwa Field Notes." *John P. Harrington Papers*, vol. 3, *Southern California and Basin.* Washington, DC: National Anthropological Archives, Smithsonian Institution. Microfilm.

Hartnell, William E. P. 2004. *The Diary and Copybook of William E. P. Hartnell: Visitador General of the Missions of Alta California in 1839 and 1840.* Edited and translated by Starr Pait Gurcke and Glenn J. Farris. Santa Clara: California Mission Studies Association.

Hayes, Katherine H., and Craig N. Cipolla. 2015. "Introduction: Re-Imagining Colonial Pasts, Influencing Colonial Futures." In *Rethinking Colonialism: Comparative Archaeological Approaches*, edited by Craig N. Cipolla and Katherine H. Hayes, 1–13. Gainesville: University Press of Florida.

Hedges, Alicia A. 2019. "Recognition Through Remembrance: A Consideration of Muwekma Ohlone Oral Histories with Kuksu-Associated Material Culture to Infer Precolonial Connections to Place." Master's thesis, San Jose State University.

Heizer, Robert F. 1941. "Archeological Evidence of Sebastian Rodríguez Cermeño's California Visit in 1595." *California Historical Society Quarterly* 20 (4): 315–28.

Heizer, Robert F. 1947. "Francis Drake and the California Indians, 1579." *University of California Publications in American Archaeology and Ethnology* 42 (3): 251–302.

Heizer, Robert F., ed. 1974. *The Destruction of California Indians.* Santa Barbara: Peregrine Smith.

Heizer, Robert F., ed. 1978a. *The California Indians vs. The United States of America (HR 4497): Evidence Offered in Support of Occupancy, Possession, and Use of Land in California by the Ancestors of Enrolled Indians of California.* Socorro, NM: Ballena Press.

Heizer, Robert F. 1978b. "Treaties." In *Handbook of North American Indians*, vol. 8, *California*, edited by Robert F. Heizer, 701–704. Washington, DC: Smithsonian Institution.

Heizer, Robert F., ed. 1979. *Federal Concern about Conditions of California Indians 1853–1913: Eight Documents.* Socorro, NM: Ballena Press.

Heizer, Robert F., and Alan J. Almquist, eds. 1971. *The Other Californians: Prejudice and Discrimination under Spain, Mexico, and the United States to 1920.* Berkeley: University of California Press.

Heizer, Robert F., and Albert B. Elsasser. 1980. *The Natural World of the California Indians.* Berkeley: University of California Press.

Henderson, David Allen. 1964. "Agriculture and Livestock Raising in the Evolution of the Economy and Culture of the State of Baja California, Mexico." PhD diss., University of California, Los Angeles.

Henderson, Randall. 1952. "Tribesmen of Santa Catarina." *The Desert Magazine* 15 (7): 5–11.

Hendry, George W. 1931. "The Adobe Brick as a Historical Source." *Agricultural History* 5 (3): 110–27.

Hendry, George W., and Margaret P. Kelly. 1925. "The Plant Content of Adobe Bricks: With a Note on Adobe Brick Making." *California Historical Society Quarterly* 4 (4): 361–73.

Henshaw, Henry Wetherbee. 1884. *Vocabulary of the Language Spoken at Santa Catarina, December 10, 1884.* MS 1128. Washington, DC: Smithsonian Institution National Anthropological Archives.

Herrera, Allison. 2019. "California History, Retold." *High Country News* 51 (7): 12–18.

Hicks, Frederic N. 1959. "Archaeological Sites in the Jamau-Jaquijel Region, Baja California: A Preliminary Report." *University of California, Los Angeles, Archaeological Survey Annual Report 1958–1959*: 60–68.

Hicks, Frederic N. 1963. "Ecological Aspects of Aboriginal Culture in the Western Yuman Area." PhD diss., University of California, Los Angeles.

Hildebrand, John A., and Melissa B. Hagstrum. 1995. "Observing Subsistence Change in Native Southern California: The Late Prehistoric Kumeyaay." *Research in Economic Anthropology* 16: 85–127.

Hildebrandt, William R., Kenneth R. Bethard, and David Boe. 1991. *Archaeological Investigations at CA-SCL-714/H: A Protohistoric Cemetery Area near Gilroy, California.* Report on file at the Northwest Information Center, Sonoma State University, CA.

Hinton, Thomas B., and Roger C. Owen. 1957. "Some Surviving Yuman Groups in Northern Baja California." *América Indígena* 17 (1): 87–102.

Hogeland, L. Frank, and Kim Hogeland. 2007. *First Families: A Photographic History of California Indians.* Berkeley: Heyday.

Hohenthal, William D. 2001. *Tipai Ethnographic Notes: A Baja California Indian Community at Mid-Century.* Edited by Thomas C. Blackburn. Novato, CA: Ballena Press.

Hoover, Robert L. 1989. "Spanish-Native Interaction and Acculturation in the Alta California Missions." In *Columbian Consequences*, vol. 1, *Archaeological and Historical Perspectives on the Spanish Borderlands West*, edited by David H. Thomas, 395–406. Washington, DC: Smithsonian Institution Press.

Hoover, Robert L., and Julia G. Costello. 1985. *Excavations at Mission San Antonio, 1976–1978.* Institute of Archaeology, University of California, Los Angeles.

Hornbeck, David. 1978. "Land Tenure and Rancho Expansion in Alta California, 1784–1846." *Journal of Historical Geography* 4 (4): 371–90.

Hudson, Travis, and Craig Bates. 2015. *Treasures from Native California: The Legacy of Russian Exploration.* Edited by Thomas Blackburn and John R. Johnson. Walnut Creek, CA: Left Coast Press.

Hughes, Richard E., and Randall Milliken. 2007. "Prehistoric Material Conveyance." In *California Prehistory: Colonization, Culture, and Complexity*, edited by Terry L. Jones and Kathryn A. Klar, 259–71. Lanham, MD: Altamira Press.

Hull, Kathleen L. 2009. *Pestilence and Persistence: Yosemite Indian Demography and Culture in Colonial California*. Berkeley: University of California Press.

Hull, Kathleen L. 2011. "Archaeological Expectations for Communal Mourning in the Greater Los Angeles Basin." *Journal of California and Great Basin Anthropology* 31 (1): 25–38.

Hull, Kathleen L. 2012. "Communal Mourning Revisited: A New Appraisal of Old Evidence." *California Archaeology* 4 (1): 3–38.

Hull, Kathleen L. 2015. "Quality of Life: Native Communities Within and Beyond the Bounds of Colonial Institutions in California." In *Beyond Germs: Native Depopulation in North America*, edited by Catherine M. Cameron, Paul Kelton, and Alan C. Swedlund, 222–48. Tucson: University of Arizona Press.

Hull, Kathleen L., and John G. Douglass. 2018. "Community Formation and Integration in Colonial Contexts." In *Forging Communities in Colonial Alta California*, edited by Kathleen L. Hull and John G. Douglass, 3–32. Tucson: University of Arizona Press.

Hull, Kathleen L., John G. Douglass, and Andrew L. York. 2013. "Recognizing Ritual Action and Intent in Communal Mourning Features on the Southern California Coast." *American Antiquity* 78 (1): 24–47.

Huntington Library. 2006. *Early California Population Project*, v. 1. Created by Steven W. Hackel, Anne M. Reid, et al. San Marino, CA: The Huntington Library, Art Collections, and Botanical Gardens.

Hurtado, Albert L. 1988. *Indian Survival on the California Frontier*. New Haven, CT: Yale University Press.

Hylkema, Mark G. 1995. *Archaeological Investigations at the Third Location of Mission Santa Clara de Asís: The Murguía Mission, 1781–1818 (CA-SCL-30/H)*. Oakland: California Department of Transportation, District 4, Environmental Planning.

Hylkema, Mark G. 2002. "Tidal Marsh, Oak Woodlands, and Cultural Florescence in the Southern San Francisco Bay Region." In *Catalysts to Complexity: Late Holocene Societies of the California Coast*, edited by Jon M. Erlandson and Terry L. Jones, 263–81. Perspectives in California Archaeology, vol. 6. Cotsen Institute of Archaeology, University of California, Los Angeles.

Hylkema, Mark G. 2007. *Santa Clara Valley Prehistory: Archaeological Investigations at CA-SCL-690, the Tamien Station Site, San Jose, California*. Center for Archaeological Research at Davis, no. 15, University of California, Davis.

Jackson, Robert H. 1981. "Epidemic Disease and Population Decline in the Baja California Missions, 1697–1834." *Southern California Quarterly* 63 (4): 308–46.

Jackson, Robert H. 1984. "Gentile Recruitment and Population Movements in the San Francisco Bay Area Missions." *Journal of California and Great Basin Anthropology* 6 (2): 225–39.

Jackson, Robert H. 1994. *Indian Population Decline: The Missions of Northwestern New Spain, 1687–1840*. Albuquerque: University of New Mexico Press.

Jackson, Robert H., and Edward Castillo. 1995. *Indians, Franciscans, and Spanish Colonization. The Impact of the Mission System on California Indians.* Albuquerque: University of New Mexico Press.

Jackson, Thomas L., and Jonathon E. Ericson. 1994. "Prehistoric Exchange Systems in California." In *Prehistoric Exchange Systems in North America*, edited by Timothy G. Baugh and Jonathon E. Ericson, 385–415. New York: Plenum Press.

Joël, Judith. 1976. "Some Paipai Accounts of Food Gathering." *Journal of California Anthropology* 3 (1): 59–71.

Johnson, John R. 2006. "The Various Chinigchinich Manuscripts of Father Gerónimo Boscana." In *San Diego, Alta California, and the Borderlands: Proceedings of the 23rd Annual Conference of the California Mission Studies Association*, edited by Rose Marie Beebe and Robert M. Senkewicz, 1–19. Santa Clara: California Mission Studies Association.

Jones, David S. 2015. "Death, Uncertainty, and Rhetoric." In *Beyond Germs: Native Depopulation in North America*, edited by Catherine M. Cameron, Paul Kelton, and Alan C. Swedlund, 16–49. Tucson: University of Arizona Press.

Jones, Terry L., and Al W. Schwitalla. 2008. "Archaeological Perspectives on the Effects of the Medieval Drought in Prehistoric California." *Quaternary International* 188: 41–58.

Jordan, Kurt A. 2008. *The Seneca Restoration, 1715–1754: An Iroquois Local Political Economy.* Gainesville: University Press of Florida.

Kasper, Kimberly, and Russell G. Handsman. 2015. "Survivance Stories, Co-Creation, and a Participatory Model at the Mashantucket Pequot Museum and Research Center." *Advances in Archaeological Practice* 3 (3): 198–207.

Kealhofer, Lisa. 1996. "Evidence for Demographic Collapse in California." In *Bioarchaeology of Native American Adaptation in the Spanish Borderlands*, edited by Brenda J. Baker and Lisa Kealhofer, 56–92. Gainesville: University Press of Florida.

Keenan, Harper Benjamin. 2018. "Visiting Chutchui: The Making of a Colonial Counterstory on an Elementary School Field Trip." *Theory & Research in Social Education.* DOI: 10.1080/00933104.2018.1542361.

Kehl, Jacquelin J., and Linda Yamane. 1995. *Ethnohistoric Genealogy Study: Tasman Corridor Light Rail Project, Santa Clara County, California.* Report to Woodward-Clyde Consultants, Oakland, CA.

Kelly, William H. 1942. "Cocopa Gentes." *American Anthropologist* 44: 675–91.

Kelsey, C. E. 1971. *Census of Non-Reservation California Indians, 1905–1906.* Berkeley: University of California Archaeological Research Facility.

King, Chester D. 1990. *Evolution of Chumash Society: A Comparative Study of Artifacts Used for Social System Maintenance in the Santa Barbara Channel Region before A.D. 1804.* New York: Garland Publishing, Inc.

King, Julia A. 2012. *Archaeology, Narrative, and the Politics of the Past: The View from Southern Maryland.* Knoxville: University of Tennessee Press.

King, Thomas F. 1966. "CA-SON-320: An Unusual Archaeological Site on Bodega Head, Sonoma County, California." Robert E. Schenk Archives of California Archaeology, no. 20. San Francisco.

Kotzebue, Otto von. 1821. *A Voyage of Discovery into the South Sea and Beering's Straits.* London: Longman, Hurst, Rees, Orme, and Brown.

Kroeber, Alfred L. 1910. "The Chumash and Costanoan Languages." *University of California Publications in American Archaeology and Ethnology* 9 (2): 237–71.

Kroeber, Alfred L. 1925. *Handbook of the Indians of California.* Bureau of American Ethnology Bulletin, no. 78. Washington, DC: Smithsonian Institution.

Kroeber, Alfred L. 1932. "The Patwin and Their Neighbors." *University of California Publications in American Archaeology and Ethnology* 49 (4): 253–423.

Kroeber, Alfred L. 1962. "Two Papers on the Aboriginal Ethnography of California: The Nature of Land Holding Groups in Aboriginal California." *University of California Archaeological Survey Reports* 56: 21–58.

Kroeber, Alfred L., and Robert F. Heizer. 1970. "Continuity of Indian Population in California from 1770/1848 to 1955." *Contributions of the University of California Archaeological Research Facility* 9: 1–22.

Kryder-Reid, Elizabeth. 2016. *California Mission Landscapes: Race, Memory, and the Politics of Heritage.* Minneapolis: University of Minnesota Press.

Lacson, P. Albert. 2015. "Making Friends and Converts: Cloth and Clothing in Early California History." *California History* 92 (1): 6–26.

Langsdorff, Georg Heinrich von. 1814. *Voyages and Travels in Various Parts of the World During the Years 1803, 1804, 1805, 1806 and 1807.* London: Henry Colburn.

Larson, Daniel O., John R. Johnson, and Joel C. Michaelsen. 1994. "Missionization Among the Coastal Chumash of Central California: A Study of Risk Minimization Strategies." *American Anthropologist* 96: 263–99.

Lassépas, Ulises U. 1859. *De la Colonización de la Baja California.* México DF: Imprenta de Vicente Garcia Torres.

Lasuén, Fermín Francisco de. 1965a. *Writings of Fermín Francisco de Lasuén, Volume 1.* Edited and translated by Finbar Kenneally. Washington, DC: Academy of American Franciscan History.

Lasuén, Fermín Francisco de. 1965b. *Writings of Fermín Francisco de Lasuén, Volume 2.* Edited and translated by Finbar Kenneally. Washington, DC: Academy of American Franciscan History.

Laylander, Don. 1987. "Sources and Strategies for the Prehistory of Baja California." Master's thesis, San Diego State University.

Laylander, Don. 1997. "The Linguistic Prehistory of Baja California." In *Contributions to the Linguistic Prehistory of Central and Baja California,* edited by Gary S. Breschini and Trudy Haversat, 1–94. Salinas, CA: Coyote Press.

Laylander, Don. 2015. "Three Hypotheses to Explain Pai Origins." *Pacific Coast Archaeological Society* 50 (3 & 4): 115–30.

Lelièvre, Michelle A. 2017. *Unsettling Mobility: Mediating Mi'kmaw Sovereignty in Postcontact Nova Scotia.* Tucson: University of Arizona Press.

León Velazco, Lucila del Carmen. 2001. "San Vicente en el Contexto de la Frontera." *Memorias: Balances y Perspectivas de la Antropología e Historia de Baja California* 2: 105–15.

León Velazco, Lucila del Carmen. 2007. "Resistencia Indígena en Baja California Misional." *Memorias: Balances y Perspectivas de la Antropología e Historia de Baja California* 8: 180–87.

León Velazco, Lucila del Carmen. 2010. "Indígenas y la Independencia de México." Paper presented at the XI Encuentro Binacional, Balances y Perspectivas, Ensenada.

Lepowsky, Maria. 2004. "Indian Revolts and the Cargo Cults: Ritual Violence and Re-vitalization in California and New Guinea." In *Reassessing Revitalization Movements: Perspectives from North America and the Pacific Islands*, edited by Michael Harkin, 1–60. Lincoln: University of Nebraska Press.

Leventhal, Alan. 1993. "A Reinterpretation of Some Bay Area Shellmound Sites: A View from the Mortuary Complex from CA-ALA-329, the Ryan Mound." Master's thesis, San Jose State University.

Leventhal, Alan, Les Field, Hank Alvarez, and Rosemary Cambra. 1994. "The Ohlone: Back from Extinction." In *The Ohlone Past and Present: Native Americans of the San Francisco Bay Region*, edited by Lowell J. Bean, 297–336. Ballena Press Anthropological Papers, no. 42. Menlo Park, CA: Ballena Press.

Leventhal, Alan, Diane DiGiuseppe, Melynda Atwood, David Grant, Rosemary Cambra, Charlene Nijmeh, Monica V. Arellano, Sheila Guzman-Schmidt, Gloria E. Gomez, and Norma Sanchez. 2011. *Final Report on the Burial and Archaeological Data Recovery Program Conducted on a Portion of the Mission Santa Clara Indian Neophyte Cemetery (1781–1818): Clareño Muwékma Ya Túnneste Nómmo {Where the Clareño Indians Are Buried} Site (CA-SCL-30/H), Located in the City of Santa Clara, Santa Clara County, California.* Report to Pacific Gas and Electric Company, Santa Clara, CA.

Levy, Richard. 1978. "Costanoan." In *Handbook of North American Indians*, vol. 8, *California*, edited by Robert F. Heizer, 485–95. Washington, DC: Smithsonian Institution.

Liebmann, Matthew, and Melissa S. Murphy, eds. 2010. *Enduring Conquests: Rethinking the Resistance to Spanish Colonialism in the Americas*. Santa Fe, NM: School for Advanced Research Press.

Lightfoot, Kent G. 1995. "Culture Contact Studies: Redefining the Relationship between Prehistoric and Historical Archaeology." *American Antiquity* 60 (2): 199–217.

Lightfoot, Kent G. 2005. *Indians, Missionaries, and Merchants: The Legacy of Colonial Encounters on the California Frontiers*. Berkeley: University of California Press.

Lightfoot, Kent G. 2006. "Missions, Furs, Gold and Manifest Destiny: Rethinking an Archaeology of Colonialism for Western North America." In *Historical Archaeology*, edited by Martin Hall and Stephen W. Silliman, 272–92. Oxford: Blackwell Publishing.

Lightfoot, Kent G. 2018. "Communities of Persistence: The Study of Colonial Neighborhoods in the Fort Ross Region of Northern California." In *Forging Communities in Colonial Alta California*, edited by Kathleen L. Hull and John G. Douglass, 214–33. Tucson: University of Arizona Press.

Lightfoot, Kent G., and Rob Q. Cuthrell. 2015. "Anthropogenic Burning and the Anthropocene in Late Holocene California." *The Holocene* 25 (10): 1581–87.

Lightfoot, Kent G., and Sara L. Gonzalez. 2018. "The Study of Sustained Colonialism: An Example from the Kashaya Pomo Homeland in Northern California." *American Antiquity* 83 (3): 427–43.

Lightfoot, Kent G., and Valentin Lopez. 2013. "The Study of Indigenous Management Practices in California: An Introduction." *California Archaeology* 5 (2): 209–19.

Lightfoot, Kent G., and Otis Parrish. 2009. *California Indians and Their Environment: An Introduction.* Berkeley: University of California Press.

Lightfoot, Kent G., and William S. Simmons. 1998. "Culture Contact in Protohistoric California: Social Contexts of Native and European Encounters." *Journal of California and Great Basin Anthropology* 20 (2): 138–70.

Lightfoot, Kent G, Rob Q. Cuthrell, Chuck J. Striplen, and Mark G. Hylkema. 2013a. "Rethinking the Study of Landscape Management Practices Among Hunter-Gatherers in North America." *American Antiquity* 78 (2): 285–301.

Lightfoot, Kent G., Lee M. Panich, Tsim D. Schneider, Sara L. Gonzalez, Matthew A. Russell, Darren Modzelewski, Theresa Molino, and Elliot H. Blair. 2013b. "The Study of Indigenous Political Economies and Colonialism in Native California: Implications for Contemporary Tribal Groups and Federal Recognition." *American Antiquity* 78 (1): 89–103.

Lindsay, Brendan C. 2012. *Murder State: California's Native American Genocide, 1846–1873.* Lincoln: University of Nebraska Press.

Lingenfelter, Richard E. 1967. *The Rush of '89: The Baja California Gold Fever & Captain James Edward Friend's Letters from the Santa Clara Mines.* Los Angeles: Dawson's Book Shop.

Loeb, Edwin M. 1932. "The Western Kuksu Cult." *University of California Publications in American Archaeology and Ethnology* 33 (1): 1–137.

Loeb, Edwin M. 1933. "The Eastern Kuksu Cult." *University of California Publications in American Archaeology and Ethnology* 33 (2): 139–232.

Lopez, Valentin. 2015. "Open Letter to Pope Francis." *News from Native California.* http://newsfromnativecalifornia.com/blog/amah-mutsuns-letter-to-pope-francis.

Lorimer, Michelle M. 2016. *Resurrecting the Past: The California Mission Myth.* Pechanga, CA: Great Oaks Press.

Luby, Edward M. 1995. "Preliminary Report on the Archaeological Investigations in the Sunol Valley, Alameda County, California." *Proceedings of the Society for California Archaeology* 8: 167–74.

Macarro, Mark. 2015. "Letter to Pope Francis." *Walk for the Ancestors.* http://walkfortheancestors.org/wp-content/uploads/2015/10/pechanga-letter-to-pope-francis.pdf.

Madley, Benjamin. 2008. "California's Yuki Indians: Defining Genocide in Native American History." *Western Historical Quarterly* 39: 303–32.

Madley, Benjamin. 2014. "'Unholy Traffic in Human Blood and Souls': Systems of California Indian Servitude under U.S. Rule." *Pacific Historical Review* 83 (4): 626–67.

Madley, Benjamin. 2016. *An American Genocide: The United States and the California Indian Catastrophe.* New Haven: Yale University Press.

Madley, Benjamin. 2019. "California's First Mass Incarceration System: Franciscan Missions, California Indians, and Penal Servitude, 1769–1836." *Pacific Historical Review* 88 (1): 14–47.

Magaña Mancillas, Mario Alberto. 1999. "Las Misiones Dominicas en Baja California: Santo Domingo de la Frontera, 1775–1875." *Colonial Latin American Historical Review* 8 (2): 185–206.

Magaña Mancillas, Mario Alberto. 2001. "Acculturation and Inequality in Power among the Native Groups of Baja California." *Pacific Coast Archaeological Society Quarterly* 37 (4): 11–15.

Magaña Mancillas, Mario Alberto. 2005. *Ni Muy Tristona, ni Muy Tristona: Testimonios de Mujeres Paipai y Kumiai de Baja California*. Mexicali: Instituto de Cultura de Baja California.

Mancini, Jason. 2015. "'In Contempt of Oblivion': Censuses, Ethnogeography, and Hidden Indian Histories in Eighteenth-Century Southern New England." *Ethnohistory* 62 (1): 61–94.

Mason, William M. 1978. "A Strategic Mission: Santa Catalina." *Journal of California Anthropology* 5 (2): 277–87.

Mathes, W. Michael. 2011. "Violence in Eden: Indigenous Warfare in Peninsular Baja California." *Pacific Coast Archaeological Society Quarterly* 45 (1 & 2): 1–12.

May, Ronald V. 1973. "An Archaeological Survey of Mission Santo Tomás, Baja California." *Pacific Coast Archaeological Society Quarterly* 9 (1): 48–64.

McKusick, M. B., and A. T. Gilman. 1959. "An Acorn Grinding Site in Baja California." *University of California, Los Angeles, Archaeological Survey Annual Report 1958–1959*: 47–58.

Medina, Vincent. 2015. "Our Cemetery, Our Elders: Hope and Continuity at the Ohlone Cemetery." *News from Native California* 29 (1): 16–19.

Meigs, Peveril III. 1935. *The Dominican Mission Frontier of Lower California*. University of California Publications in Geography 7. Berkeley: University of California Press.

Meigs, Peveril III. 1939. *The Kiliwa Indians of Lower California*. Ibero Americana, vol. 15. Berkeley: University of California Press.

Meigs, Peveril III. 1972. "Notes on the La Huerta Jat'am, Baja California: Place Names, Hunting, and Shamans." *Pacific Coast Archaeological Society Quarterly* 8 (1): 35–40.

Meigs, Peveril III. 1974. "Field Notes on the Sh'un and Jat'am, Manteca, Baja California." *Pacific Coast Archaeological Society Quarterly* 10 (1): 19–28.

Meigs, Peveril III. 1977. "Notes on the Paipai of San Isidoro, Baja California." *Pacific Coast Archaeological Society Quarterly* 13 (1): 11–20.

Mendoza, Ruben G. 2014. "Indigenous Landscapes: Mexicanized Indians and the Archaeology of Social Networks in Alta California." In *Indigenous Landscapes and Spanish Missions: New Perspectives from Archaeology and Ethnohistory*, edited by Lee M. Panich and Tsim D. Schneider, 114–34. Tucson: University of Arizona Press.

Merriam, C. Hart. 1967. "Ethnological Notes on Central California Indian Tribes." *Reports of the University of California Archaeological Survey* 68, part III.

Michelsen, Ralph C. 1991. "La Territorialidad del Indígena Americano de la Tierra Alta del Norte de la Baja California." *Estudios Fronterizos* 24/25: 151–60.

Michelsen, Ralph C., and Roger C. Owen. 1967. "A Keruk Ceremony at Santa Catarina, Baja California, Mexico." *Pacific Coast Archaeological Society Quarterly* 3 (1): 33–41.

Miller, Mark Edwin. 2004. *Forgotten Tribes: Unrecognized Indians and the Federal Acknowledgment Process.* Lincoln: University of Nebraska Press.

Milliken, Randall. 1995. *A Time of Little Choice: The Disintegration of Tribal Culture in the San Francisco Bay Area, 1769–1810.* Menlo Park, CA: Ballena Press.

Milliken, Randall. 2002. "The Indians of Mission Santa Clara." In *Telling the Santa Clara Story: Sesquicentennial Voices,* edited by Russell K. Skowronek, 45–63. Santa Clara, CA: Santa Clara University and City of Santa Clara.

Milliken, Randall. 2007. "Ethnohistory of the Ohlone People, Part 1: The Ohlone People of the Santa Clara Valley in the 1770s." In *Santa Clara Valley Prehistory: Archaeological Investigations at CA-SCL-690, The Tamien Station Site, San Jose California,* by Mark Hylkema, 47–60. Center for Archaeological Research at Davis, no. 15, University of California, Davis.

Milliken, Randall. 2008. *Native Americans at Mission San Jose.* Banning, CA: Malki-Ballena Press.

Milliken, Randall T., and James A. Bennyhoff. 1993. "Temporal Changes in Beads as Prehistoric California Grave Goods." In *There Grows a Green Tree: Papers in Honor of David A. Fredrickson,* edited by Greg White, Pat Mikkelsen, William R. Hildebrandt, Mark E. Basgall, Mildred Dickemann, and Thomas M. Origer, 381–95. Center for Archaeological Research at Davis, no. 11, University of California, Davis.

Milliken, Randall T., Richard T. Fitzgerald, Mark G. Hylkema, Randy Groza, Tom Origer, David G. Bieling, Alan Leventhal, Randy S. Wiberg, Andrew Gottsfield, Donna Gillete, Viviana Bellifemine, Eric Strother, Robert Cartier, and David A. Fredrickson. 2007. "Punctuated Culture Change in the San Francisco Bay Area." In *California Prehistory: Colonization, Culture, and Complexity,* edited by Terry L. Jones and Kathryn A. Klar, 99–124. Lanham, MD: Altamira Press.

Milliken, Randall, Laurence H. Shoup, and Beverly R. Ortiz. 2009. *Ohlone/Costanoan Indians of the San Francisco Peninsula and their Neighbors, Yesterday and Today.* Report to the National Park Service, Golden Gate National Recreation Area, San Francisco.

Minnich, Richard, and Ernesto Franco Vizcaíno. 1998. *Land of Chamise and Pines: Historical Accounts of Northern Baja California's Vegetation.* University of California Publications in Botany, vol. 80. Berkeley: University of California Press.

Miranda, Deborah A. 2013. *Bad Indians: A Tribal Memoir.* Berkeley, CA: Heyday.

Mixco, Mauricio J. 1977. "Textos para la Etnohistoria en la Frontera Dominicana de Baja California." *Tlalocan* 7: 205–26.

Mixco, Mauricio J. 1983. *Kiliwa Texts: "When I Have Donned My Crest of Stars."* University of Utah Anthropological Papers 107, Salt Lake City.

Mixco, Mauricio J. 2006. "The Indigenous Languages." In *The Prehistory of Baja California: Advances in the Archaeology of the Forgotten Peninsula,* edited by Don Laylander and Jerry D. Moore, 24–41. Tallahassee: University Press of Florida.

Montenegro, María. 2019. "Unsettling Evidence: An Anticolonial Archival Approach/Reproach to Federal Recognition." *Archival Science.* DOI: 10.1007/s10502-019-09309-9.

Moore, Jerry D., and Mary J. Norton. 1992. "'I Solemnly Baptize': Religious Conversion and Native Demography in Northern Baja California." *Journal of California and Great Basin Anthropology* 14 (2): 201–15.

Mrozowski, Stephen A., Holly Herbster, David Brown, and Katherine L. Priddy. 2009. "Magunkaquog Materiality, Federal Recognition, and the Search for a Deeper History." *International Journal of Historical Archaeology* 13: 430–63.

Muehlmann, Shaylih. 2013. *Where the River Ends: Contested Indigeneity in the Mexican Colorado Delta*. Durham, NC: Duke University Press.

Nelson, Edward W. 1921. "Lower California and Its Natural Resources." *Memoirs of the National Academy of Sciences* 16: 1–194.

Nelson, Nels C. 1909. "Shellmounds of the San Francisco Bay Region." *University of California Publications in American Archaeology and Ethnology* 7: 309–56.

Nelson, Peter A. 2017. "Indigenous Archaeology at Tolay Lake: Responsive Research and the Empowered Tribal Management of a Sacred Landscape." PhD diss., University of California, Berkeley.

Nelson, Peter A. 2019. "Indigenous Refusal of Settler Colonialism in Nineteenth-Century Central California: A Caseform the Tolay Valley, Sonoma County." In *Indigenous Persistence in the Colonized Americas*, edited by Heather Law Pezzarossi and Russell N. Sheptak, 169–85. Albuquerque: University of New Mexico Press.

Newell, Quincy D. 2009. *Constructing Lives at Mission San Francisco: Native Californians and Hispanic Colonists, 1776–1821*. Albuquerque: University of New Mexico Press.

Nieser, Albert B. 1960. "The Dominican Mission Foundations in Baja California, 1769–1822." PhD diss., Loyola University, Chicago.

NoiseCat, Julian Brave. 2018. "'It's About Taking Back What's Ours': Native Women Reclaim Land, Plot by Plot." *The Huffington Post*. https://www.huffingtonpost.com/entry/native-women-oakland-land_us_5ab0f175e4b0e862383b503c.

Nordhoff, Charles. 1888. *Peninsular California: Some Account of the Climate, Soil, Production, and Present Condition Chiefly of the Northern Half of Lower California*. New York: Harper and Brothers.

North, Arthur W. 1908. "The Native Tribes of Lower California." *American Anthropologist* 10: 236–50.

North, Arthur W. 1910. *Camp and Camino in Lower California*. New York: Baker & Taylor.

Norton, Jack. 1979. *When Our Worlds Cried: Genocide in Northwestern California*. San Francisco: Indian Historian Press.

O'Brien, Jean M. 2010. *Firsting and Lasting: Writing Indians out of Existence in New England*. Minneapolis: University of Minnesota Press.

Office of Federal Acknowledgment. 2002. *Summary under the Criteria and Evidence for Final Determination against Federal Acknowledgment of the Muwekma Ohlone Tribe*. Washington, DC: United States Department of the Interior.

Oland, Maxine, Siobhan M. Hart, and Liam Frink, eds. 2012. *Decolonizing Indigenous Histories: Exploring Prehistoric/Colonial Transitions in Archaeology*. Tucson: University of Arizona Press.

O'Neil, Dennis H. 1992. "The Spanish Use of Glass Beads as Pacification Gifts Among the Luiseño, Ipai, and Tipai of Southern California." *Pacific Coast Archaeological Society Quarterly* 28 (2): 1–17.

Ortiz, Beverly O. 1994. "Chocheño and Rumsen Narratives: A Comparison." In *The Ohlone Past and Present: Native Americans of the San Francisco Bay Region*, edited by Lowell John Bean, 99–163. Menlo Park, CA: Ballena Press.

Owen, Roger C. 1962. "The Indians of Santa Catarina, Baja California Norte, Mexico: Concepts of Disease and Curing." PhD diss., University of California, Los Angeles.

Owen, Roger C. 1963. "Indians and Revolution: The 1911 Invasion of Baja California, Mexico." *Ethnohistory* 10: 373–95.

Owen, Roger C. 1965. "The Patrilineal Band: A Linguistically and Culturally Hybrid Social Unit." *American Anthropologist* 67: 675–90.

Palóu, Francisco. 1926. *Historical Memoirs of New California, Volume IV*. Edited and translated by Herbert Eugene Bolton. Berkeley: University of California Press.

Panich, Lee M. 2009. "Persistence of Native Identity at Mission Santa Catalina, Baja California, 1797–1840." PhD diss., University of California, Berkeley.

Panich, Lee M. 2010a. "Missionization and the Persistence of Native Identity on the Colonial Frontier of Baja California." *Ethnohistory* 57: 225–62.

Panich, Lee M. 2010b. "Spanish Missions in the Indigenous Landscape: A View from Mission Santa Catalina, Baja California." *Journal of California and Great Basin Anthropology* 30 (1): 69–86.

Panich, Lee M. 2011a. "Collaboration and the Education of an Archaeologist." *News from Native California* 24 (4): 30–32.

Panich, Lee M. 2011b. "Continuities in a Time of Change: Lithic Technology at Mission Santa Catalina, Baja California." *Pacific Coast Archaeological Society Quarterly* 45 (1 & 2): 13–30.

Panich, Lee M. 2013. "Archaeologies of Persistence: Reconsidering the Legacies of Colonialism in Native North America." *American Antiquity* 78 (1): 105–22.

Panich, Lee M. 2014. "Native American Consumption of Shell and Glass Beads at Mission Santa Clara de Asís." *American Antiquity* 79 (4): 730–48.

Panich, Lee M. 2015. "'Sometimes They Bury the Deceased's Clothes and Trinkets': Indigenous Mortuary Practices at Mission Santa Clara de Asís." *Historical Archaeology* 49 (4): 110–29.

Panich, Lee M. 2016a. "After Saint Serra: Unearthing Indigenous Histories at the California Missions." *Journal of Social Archaeology* 16 (2): 238–58.

Panich, Lee M. 2016b. "Beyond the Colonial Curtain: Investigating Indigenous Use of Obsidian in Spanish California through the pXRF Analysis of Artifacts from Mission Santa Clara." *Journal of Archaeological Science: Reports* 5: 521–30.

Panich, Lee M. 2017. "Indigenous Vaqueros in Colonial California: Labor, Identity and Autonomy." In *Foreign Objects: Rethinking Indigenous Consumption in American Archaeology*, edited by Craig N. Cipolla, 187–203. Tucson: University of Arizona Press.

Panich, Lee M. 2018. "Death, Mourning, and Accommodation in the Missions of Alta California." In *Franciscans and American Indians in Pan-Borderlands Perspective: Adaptation,*

Negotiation, and Resistance, edited by Jeffrey M. Burns and Timothy J. Johnson, 251–64. Oceanside, CA: American Academy of Franciscan History.

Panich, Lee M. 2019. "'Mission Indians' and Settler Colonialism: Rethinking Indigenous Persistence in Nineteenth-Century Central California." In *Indigenous Persistence in the Colonized Americas*, edited by Heather Law Pezzarossi and Russell N. Sheptak, 121–44. Albuquerque: University of New Mexico Press.

Panich, Lee M., and Tsim D. Schneider, eds. 2014. *Indigenous Landscapes and Spanish Missions: New Perspectives from Archaeology and Ethnohistory*. Tucson: University of Arizona Press.

Panich, Lee M., and Tsim D. Schneider. 2015. "Expanding Mission Archaeology: A Landscape Approach to Indigenous Autonomy in Colonial California." *Journal of Anthropological Archaeology* 40: 48–58.

Panich, Lee M., and Michael Wilken-Robertson. 2013. "Paipai Pottery Past and Present: Evolution of an Indigenous Ceramic Tradition." *Pacific Coast Archaeological Society Quarterly* 48 (1 & 2): 75–95.

Panich, Lee M., Helga Afaghani, and Nicole Mathwich. 2014. "Assessing the Diversity of Mission Populations through the Comparison of Native American Residences at Mission Santa Clara de Asís." *International Journal of Historical Archaeology* 18 (3): 467–88.

Panich, Lee M., Érika Moranchel Mondragón, and Antonio Porcayo Michelini. 2015. "Exploring Patterns of Obsidian Conveyance in Baja California, Mexico." *Journal of California and Great Basin Anthropology* 35 (2): 257–74.

Panich, Lee M., M. Steven Shackley, and Antonio Porcayo Michelini. 2017. "A Reassessment of Archaeological Obsidian from Southern Alta California and Northern Baja California." *California Archaeology* 9 (1): 53–77.

Panich, Lee M., Rebecca Allen, and Andrew Galvan. 2018a. "The Archaeology of Native American Persistence at Mission San José." *Journal of California and Great Basin Anthropology* 38 (1): 11–29.

Panich, Lee M., Ben Griffin, and Tsim D. Schneider. 2018b. "Native Acquisition of Obsidian in Colonial-Era Central California: Implications from Mission San José." *Journal of Anthropological Archaeology* 50: 1–11.

Panich, Lee M., Emilie Lederer, Ryan Phillip, Emily Dylla. 2018c. "Heads or Tails? Modified Ceramic Gaming Pieces from Colonial California." *International Journal of Historical Archaeology* 22 (4): 746–70.

Panich, Lee M., Sarah Peelo, and Linda Hylkema. 2018d. "Archaeological Insights into the Persistence of Multiscalar Native Communities at Mission Santa Clara de Asís." In *Forging Communities in Colonial Alta California*, edited by Kathleen L. Hull and John G. Douglass, 191–213. Tucson: University of Arizona Press.

Panich, Lee M., Tsim D. Schneider, and R. Scott Byram. 2018e. "Finding Mid-19th Century Native Settlements: Cartographic and Archaeological Evidence from Central California." *Journal of Field Archaeology* 43 (2): 152–65.

Parker, J. C. 1876. *Vocabulary of Santa Tomás Mission Indians, Lower California*. MS 1137. Washington, DC: Smithsonian Institution National Anthropological Archives.

Pattie, James O. 1930. *The Personal Narrative of James O. Pattie of Kentucky*. Chicago: Lakeside Press.

Peelo, Sarah. 2009. "Baptism Among the Salinan Neophytes of Mission San Antonio de Padua: Investigating the Ecological Hypothesis." *Ethnohistory* 56 (4): 589–624.

Peelo, Sarah. 2010. "The Creation of a Carmeleño Identity: Marriage Practices in the Indian Village at Mission San Carlos Borromeo del Río Carmel." *Journal of California and Great Basin Anthropology* 30 (2): 117–39.

Peelo, Sarah. 2011. "Pottery-Making in Spanish California: Creating Multi-Scalar Social Identity through Daily Practice." *American Antiquity* 76 (4): 642–66.

Peelo, Sarah, Linda Hylkema, John Ellison, Clinton Blount, Mark Hylkema, Margie Maher, Tom Garlinghouse, Dustin McKenzie, Stella D'Oro, and Melinda Berge. 2018a. "Persistence in the Indian *Ranchería* at Mission Santa Clara de Asís." *Journal of California and Great Basin Anthropology* 38 (2): 207–34.

Peelo, Sarah, Lee M. Panich, Christina Spellman, John Ellison, and Stella D'Oro. 2018b. "Marriage and Death in the Neophyte Village at Mission Santa Clara: Preservation of Ancestral and Elite Communities." In *Forging Communities in Colonial Alta California*, edited by Kathleen L. Hull and John G. Douglass, 162–88. Tucson: University of Arizona Press.

Pérez, Erika. 2018. *Colonial Intimacies: Interethnic Kinship, Sexuality, and Marriage in Southern California, 1769–1885*. Norman: University of Oklahoma Press.

Phillips, George Harwood. 1993. *Indians and Intruders in Central California, 1769–1849*. Berkeley: University of California Press.

Phillips, George Harwood. 2010. *Vineyards and Vaqueros: Indian Labor and the Economic Expansion of Southern California, 1771–1877*. Norman, OK: Arthur H. Clark Company.

Pilloud, Marin A., Al W. Schwitalla, and Terry L. Jones. 2014. "The Bioarchaeological Record of Craniofacial Trauma in Central California." In *Violence and Warfare among Hunter Gatherers*, edited by Mark W. Allen and Terry L. Jones, 257–72. Walnut Creek, CA: Left Coast Press.

Popper, Virginia S. 2016. "Change and Persistence: Mission Neophyte Foodways at Selected Colonial Alta California Institutions." *Journal of California and Great Basin Anthropology* 36 (1): 5–25.

Porcayo Michelini, Antonio. 2013. "Ceramics from Northern Baja California." *Pacific Coast Archaeological Society Quarterly* 48 (1 & 2): 55–73.

Porcayo Michelini, Antonio. 2018a. "Chronological Reordering of the Yuman Complex in Baja California." *Pacific Coast Archaeological Society Quarterly* 54 (3 & 4): 35–55.

Porcayo Michelini, Antonio. 2018b. "The Vesicular or Egyptian Rectangle as an Analytical Tool: Demonstrating the Persistence of Yuman Ceramic Production Through the Increasing Proportional Height of Vessels." *Journal of California and Great Basin Anthropology* 38 (2): 191–206.

Porcayo Michelini, Antonio, and Juan Martín Rojas Chávez. 2018. *"Keruk* tratamiento mortuorio entre los norbajacalifornianos." *Arqueología Mexicana* 154: 36–43.

Powers, Stephen. 1877. *Tribes of California*. Contributions to North American Ethnology 3. Washington, DC: U.S. Geological and Geographic Survey of the Rocky Mountain Region.

Preston, William. 1996. "Serpent in Eden: Dispersal of Foreign Diseases into Pre-Mission California." *Journal of California and Great Basin Anthropology* 18 (1): 2–37.

Preston, William. 1997. "Serpent in the Garden: Environmental Change in Colonial California." *California History* 76 (2 & 3): 260–98.

Radding, Cynthia. 1997. *Wandering Peoples: Colonialism, Ethnic Spaces, and Ecological Frontiers in Northwestern Mexico, 1700–1850.* Durham, NC: Duke University Press.

Radding, Cynthia. 2005. *Landscapes of Power and Identity: Comparative Histories in the Sonoran Desert and the Forests of Amazonia from Colony to Republic.* Durham, NC: Duke University Press.

Raibmon, Paige. 2005. *Authentic Indians: Episodes of Encounter from the Late-Nineteenth-Century Northwest Coast.* Durham, NC: Duke University Press.

Ramirez, Renya K. 2007. *Native Hubs: Culture, Community, and Belonging in Silicon Valley and Beyond.* Durham, NC: Duke University Press.

Rareshide, Elisabeth A. 2016. "Tongva Ritual Practice on San Clemente Island: Exploring the Origins of the Chinigchinich Religion." Master's thesis, California State University, Northridge.

Rawls, James J. 1984. *Indians of California: The Changing Image.* Norman: The University of Oklahoma Press.

Reddy, Seetha N. 2015. "Feeding Family and Ancestors: Persistence of Traditional Native American Lifeways during the Mission Period in Coastal Southern California." *Journal of Anthropological Archaeology* 37: 48–66.

Reddy, Seetha N., and John G. Douglass. 2018. "Native Californian Persistence and Transformation in the Colonial Los Angeles Basin, Southern California." *Journal of California and Great Basin Anthropology* 38 (2): 235–59.

Reid, Joshua L. 2015. *The Sea Is My Country: The Maritime World of the Makahs.* New Haven, CT: Yale University Press.

Reyes, Bárbara O. 2004. "Race, Agency, and Memory in a Baja California Mission." In *Continental Crossroads: Remapping U.S.-Mexico Borderlands History*, edited by Samuel Truett and Elliott Young, 97–120. Durham, NC: Duke University Press.

Reyes, Bárbara O. 2009. *Private Women, Public Lives: Gender and the Missions of the Californias.* Austin: University of Texas Press.

Ringelstein, Austin. 2016. "Galleons, Temples, and Beads: An Investigation of a Colonial Archaeological Assemblage from the Tongva Village of Nájquqar at Two Harbors, Pimu Santa Catalina Island, California (CA-SCaI-39)." Master's thesis, California State University, Northridge.

Ritter, Eric W. 2014. "Integration of Spanish galleon artifacts into Native American Indian lifeways along Baja California's Pacific coast." In *Memorias: Balances y Perspectivas de la Antropología e Historia de Baja California* 15: 61–70. Mexicali: Centro INAH Baja California.

Rizzo, Martin A. 2016. "No Somos Animales: Indigenous Survival and Perseverance in 19th Century Santa Cruz, California." PhD diss., University of California, Santa Cruz.

Robinson, Alfred. 1851. *Life in California.* London: H. G. Collins.

Robinson, David. 2013. "Polyvalent Metaphors in South-Central California Missionary Processes." *American Antiquity* 78 (2): 302–21.

Robinson, William W. 1948. *Land in California: The Story of Mission Lands, Ranchos, Squatters, Mining Claims, Railroad Grants, Land Scrip, Homesteads.* Berkeley: University of California Press.

Rodríguez Tomp, Rosa Elba. 2002. *Cautivos de Dios: Los Cazadores Recolectores de Baja California durante la Colonia.* México DF: CIASAS.

Rogers, Malcolm J. 1936. "Yuman Pottery Making." *San Diego Museum Papers* 2. Museum of Man, San Diego.

Rojas Chávez, Juan Martín, and Antonio Porcayo Michelini. 2015. "Archaeological Investigations at the Mission of San Fernando Velicatá, Baja California." *Boletín: Journal of the California Mission Studies Association* 31 (1): 132–44.

Rojo, Manuel Clemente. 1972. *Historical Notes on Lower California, with Some Relative to Upper California Furnished to the Bancroft Library by Manuel C. Rojo, 1879.* Baja California Travels Series 26, edited and translated by Philip O. Gericke. Los Angeles: Dawson's Book Shop.

Rojo, Manuel Clemente. 2000. *Apuntos Históricos de la Frontera de la Baja California.* Colección de Documentos sobre la Historia y la Geografía del Municipio de Ensenada 1. Ensenada: Museo de Historia.

Rosenthal, Jeffrey S. 2011. "The Function of Shell Bead Exchange in Central California." In *Perspectives on Prehistoric Trade and Exchange in California and the Great Basin*, edited by Richard E. Hughes, 83–113. Salt Lake City: University of Utah Press.

Rubertone, Patricia. 2000. "The Historical Archaeology of Native Americans." *Annual Review of Anthropology* 29: 425–46.

Rubertone, Patricia. 2012. "Archaeologies of Colonialism in Unexpected Times and Unexpected Places." In *Decolonizing Indigenous Histories: Exploring Prehistoric/Colonial Transitions in Archaeology*, 267–81. Tucson: University of Arizona Press.

Ruiz, José Manuel. 1797. *Letter to Gobernador Diego de Borica, September 13.* C-A 8:396. Bancroft Library, University of California, Berkeley.

Ruiz, José Manuel. 1799a. *Letter to Gobernador Diego de Borica, March 18.* C-A 10:267. Bancroft Library, University of California, Berkeley.

Ruiz, José Manuel. 1799b. *Letter to Gobernador Diego de Borica, July 10.* C-A 10:278. Bancroft Library, University of California, Berkeley.

Ruiz, José Manuel. 1804. *Letter to José Joaquín de Arrillaga, May 9.* C-A 11:391–392. Bancroft Library, University of California, Berkeley.

Russell, Matthew A. 2011. "Encounters at *tamál-húye*: An Archaeology of Intercultural Engagement in Sixteenth Century Northern California." PhD diss., University of California, Berkeley.

Sales, Luis. 1956. *Observations on California, 1772–1790.* Early California Travels Series 37, edited and translated by Charles N. Rudkin. Los Angeles: Dawson's Book Shop.

San Francisco Call, The. 1904. "Life of Noted Indian Ends." 96 (119): 4. Sept. 27.

Sandos, James A. 1985. "Levantamiento!: The 1824 Chumash Uprising Reconsidered." *Southern California Quarterly* 67 (2): 109–33.

Sandos, James A. 2004. *Converting California: Indians and Franciscans in the Missions*. New Haven, CT: Yale University Press.

Sandos, James A., and Patricia B. Sandos. 2014. "Early California Reconsidered: Mexicans, Anglos, and Indians at Mission San José." *Pacific Historical Review* 83 (4): 592–625.

Santa María, Vicente. 1971. "The Journal of Father Vicente de Santa María, 1775." In *The First Spanish Entry into San Francisco Bay 1775*, edited by John Galvin, 12–76. San Francisco: John Howell Books.

Sauer, Carl, and Peveril Meigs. 1927. "Lower California Studies: I. Site and Culture at San Fernando de Velicatá." *University of California Publications in Geography* 2 (9): 271–302.

Schaefer, Jerry. 2012. "Archaeological Evidence of Native American Participation in the Casa de Bandini Household, Old Town San Diego State Historic Park." *Proceedings of the Society for California Archaeology* 26: 137–54.

Scharlotta, Ian. 2015. "Determining Temporal Boundaries and Land Use Patterns: Hunter-Gatherer Spatiotemporal Patterning in San Diego County." *California Archaeology* 7 (2): 205–44.

Scheiber, Laura L., and Mark D. Mitchell. 2010. *Across a Great Divide: Continuity and Change in Native North American Societies, 1400–1900*. Tucson: University of Arizona Press.

Schenck, W. Egbert, and Elmer J. Dawson. 1929. "Archaeology of the North San Joaquin Valley." *University of California Publications in American Archaeology and Ethnology* 25 (4): 289–413.

Schlictmann, Margaret, ed. 1988. *The Journals of Jesus M. Estudillo*. Fredericksburg, TX: Awani Press.

Schmidt, Peter R., and Stephen A. Mrozowski, eds. 2013. *The Death of Prehistory*. Oxford: Oxford University Press.

Schneider, Khal. 2010. "Making Indian Land in the Allotment Era: Northern California's Indian Rancherias." *Western Historical Quarterly* 41 (4): 429–50.

Schneider, Tsim D. 2007. "The Role of Archived Photographs in Native California Archaeology." *Journal of Social Archaeology* 7 (1): 49–71.

Schneider, Tsim D. 2015a. "Envisioning Colonial Landscapes Using Mission Registers, Radiocarbon, and Stable Isotopes: An Experimental Approach from San Francisco Bay." *American Antiquity* 80: 511–29.

Schneider, Tsim D. 2015b. "Placing Refuge and the Archaeology of Indigenous Hinterlands in Colonial California." *American Antiquity* 80: 695–713.

Schneider, Tsim D. 2018. "Making and Unmaking Native Communities in Mission and Post-Mission Era Marin County, California." In *Forging Communities in Colonial Alta California*, edited by Kathleen L. Hull and John G. Douglass, 88–109. Tucson: University of Arizona Press.

Schneider, Tsim D. 2019. "Heritage In-Between: Seeing Native Histories in Colonial California." *The Public Historian* 41 (1): 51–63.

Schneider, Tsim D., and Lee M. Panich. 2014. "Native Agency at the Margins of Empire: Indigenous Landscapes, Spanish Missions, and Contested Histories." In *Indigenous*

Landscapes and Spanish Missions: New Perspectives from Archaeology and Ethnohistory, edited by Lee M. Panich and Tsim D. Schneider, 5–22. Tucson: University of Arizona Press.

Schneider, Tsim D., and Lee M. Panich. 2017. "Toms Point Archaeology: Investigating Native American History at Tomales Bay." *The Ardeid* 7–9.

Schneider, Tsim D., and Lee M. Panich. 2019. "Landscapes of Refuge and Resiliency: Native Californian Persistence at Tomales Bay, California, 1770s–1870s." *Ethnohistory* 66 (1): 21–47.

Schneider, Tsim D., Anneke Janzen, GeorgeAnn M. DeAntoni, Amanda M. Hill, Alec J. Apodaca, and Rob Q. Cuthrell. 2018. "Indigenous Persistence and Foodways at the Toms Point Trading Post (CA-MRN-202), Tomales Bay, California." *Journal of California and Great Basin Anthropology* 38 (1): 51–73.

Schwitalla, Al W., Terry L. Jones, Marin A. Pilloud, Brian F. Codding, and Randy S. Wiberg. 2014. "Violence among Foragers: The Bioarchaeological Record from Central California." *Journal of Anthropological Archaeology* 33: 66–83.

Scott, James C. 2009. *The Art of Not Being Governed: An Anarchist History of Upland Southeast Asia*. New Haven, CT: Yale University Press.

Serra, Junípero. 1955. *Writings of Junípero Serra*, vol. 1. Edited by Antonine Tibesar. Washington, DC: Academy of American Franciscan History.

Serra, Junípero. 1956. *Writings of Junípero Serra*, vol. 2. Edited by Antonine Tibesar. Washington, DC: Academy of American Franciscan History.

Shackley, M. Steven. 1998. "Patayan Culture Area." In *Archaeology of Prehistoric Native America: An Encyclopedia*, edited by Guy Gibbon, 629–31. New York: Garland Publishing.

Shackley, M. Steven. 2000. "The Stone Tool Technology of Ishi and the Yana of North Central California: Inferences for Hunter-Gatherer Cultural Identity in Historic California." *American Anthropologist* 102 (4): 693–712.

Shackley, M. Steven. 2004. "Prehistory, Archaeology, and History of Research." In *The Early Ethnography of the Kumeyaay*, edited by M. S. Shackley, 12–35. Berkeley, CA: Phoebe Hearst Museum of Anthropology.

Shanks, Ralph C., and Lisa Woo Shanks. 2006. *Indian Baskets of Central California: Art, Culture, and History: Native American Basketry from San Francisco and Monterey Bay North to Mendocino and East to the Sierras*. Novato, CA: Costaño Books.

Shaul, David L. and John M. Andresen. 1989. "A Case for Yuman Participation in the Hohokam Regional System." *Kiva* 54: 105–26.

Shaul, David L., and Jane H. Hill. 1998. "Tepimans, Yumans, and other Hohokam." *American Antiquity* 63 (3): 375–96.

Shipek, Florence C., ed. 1965. *Lower California Frontier: Articles from the San Diego Union 1870*. Baja California Travels Series 2. Los Angeles: Dawson's Book Shop.

Shipek, Florence C. 1977. "A Strategy for Change: The Luiseño of Southern California." PhD diss., University of Hawaii.

Shipek, Florence C. 1982. "Kumeyaay Socio-Political Structure." *Journal of California and Great Basin Anthropology* 4 (2): 296–303.

Shipek, Florence C. 1988. *Pushed into the Rocks: Southern California Indian Land Tenure, 1769–1986*. Lincoln: University of Nebraska Press.

Shipek, Florence C. 1993. "Kumeyaay Plant Husbandry: Fire, Water, and Erosion Management Systems." In *Before the Wilderness: Environmental Management by Native Californians*, edited by Thomas C. Blackburn and M. Kat Anderson, 379–88. Menlo Park, CA: Ballena Press.

Shoup, Laurence H., and Randall T. Milliken. 1999. *Inigo of Rancho Posolmi: The Life and Times of a Mission Indian*. Novato, CA: Ballena Press.

Silliman, Stephen W. 2004. *Lost Laborers in Colonial California: Native Americans and the Archaeology of Rancho Petaluma*. Tucson: University of Arizona Press.

Silliman, Stephen W. 2009. "Change and Continuity, Practice and Memory: Native American Persistence in Colonial New England." *American Antiquity* 74: 211–30.

Silliman, Stephen W. 2010. "Indigenous Traces in Colonial Spaces: Archaeologies of Ambiguity, Origin, and Practice." *Journal of Social Archaeology* 10 (1): 28–58.

Silliman, Stephen W. 2012. "Between the Long Durée and the Short Purée: Post-Colonial Archaeologies of Indigenous History in Colonial North America." In *Decolonizing Indigenous Histories: Exploring Prehistoric/Colonial Transitions in Archaeology*, edited by Maxine Oland, Siobhan Hart, and Liam Frink, 113–31. Tucson: University of Arizona Press.

Silliman, Stephen W. 2014. "Archaeologies of Indigenous Survivance and Residence: Navigating Colonial and Scholarly Dualities." In *Rethinking Colonial Pasts through Archaeology*, edited by Neal Ferris, Rodney Harrison, and Michael V. Wilcox, 57–75. Oxford: Oxford University Press.

Skowronek, Russell K. 1998. "Sifting the Evidence: Perceptions of Life at the Ohlone (Costanoan) Missions of Alta California." *Ethnohistory* 45 (4): 675–708.

Skowronek, Russell K. 2006. *Situating Mission Santa Clara de Asís, 1776–1851, Documentary and Material Evidence of Life on the Alta California Frontier: A Timeline*. Berkeley, CA: Academy of American Franciscan History.

Skowronek, Russell K., Jelena Radovic Fanta, and Hugo Morales, eds. N.d. *By All Accounts . . . The Mission Santa Clara de Asís Ledger Book, 1770–1828*. Manuscript on file, University of Texas Pan American, Edinburg.

Smith, Erin M., and Mikael Fauvelle. 2015. "Regional Interactions between California and the Southwest: The Western Edge of the North American Continental System." *American Anthropologist* 117 (4): 710–21.

Smoak, Gregory E. 2006. *Ghost Dances and Identity: Prophetic Religion and American Indian Ethnogenesis in the Nineteenth Century*. Berkeley: University of California Press.

Sousa, Ashley Riley. 2015. "'An Influential Squaw': Intermarriage and Community in Central California, 1839–1851." *Ethnohistory* 62 (4): 707–27.

Spicer, Edward H. 1962. *Cycles of Conquest: The Impact of Spain, Mexico, and the United States on the Indians of the Southwest, 1533–1960*. Tucson: University of Arizona Press.

Spicer, Edward H. 1971. "Persistent Cultural Systems." *Science* 126: 795–800.

Stanger, Frank M., and Alan K. Brown. 1969. *Who Discovered the Golden Gate? The Explorers' Own Accounts*. San Mateo, CA: San Mateo County Historical Association.

Stein, Gil J., ed. 2005. *The Archaeology of Colonial Encounters: Comparative Perspectives*. Santa Fe, NM: School of American Research Press.

Stephens, Michele M. 2018. *In the Lands of Fire and Sun: Resistance and Accommodation in the Huichol Sierra, 1723–1930*. Lincoln: University of Nevada Press.

Stephens, Scott L., Carl N. Skinner, and Samantha J. Gill. 2003. "Dendrochronology-based Fire History of Jeffrey Pine—Mixed Conifer Forests in the Sierra San Pedro Mártir, Mexico." *Canadian Journal of Forestry Research* 33: 1090–1101.

Stevenson, Robert Louis. 1910. *Across the Plains, with Other Memories and Essays*. New York: Charles Scribner's Sons.

Taylor, Alexander S. 1864. "Precis India Californicus." In *Hand-Book Almanac for the Pacific States: An Official Register and Business Directory*, edited by William H. Knight, 27–41. San Francisco: H. H. Bancroft and Company.

Thomas David Hurst. 1991. "Harvesting Ramona's Garden: Life in California's Mythical Mission Past." In *Columbian Consequences*, vol. 3, *The Spanish Borderlands in Pan-American Perspective*, edited by David H. Thomas, 119–57. Washington, DC: Smithsonian Institution Press.

Thomas David Hurst. 2014. "The Life and Times of Junípero Serra: A Pan-Borderlands Perspective." *The Americas* 71 (2): 185–225.

Thomas, David Hurst. 2015. "Bilocating the American Mission Borderlands with Saint Serra." *Boletín: Journal of the California Mission Studies Association* 31 (1): 5–34.

Thompson, Richard E., and Andrew A. Galvan. 2007. "Excavations at St. Joseph Catholic Community Rectory, 43148 Mission Boulevard, Fremont, California 94539." Draft report to Reverend Monsignor Manuel C. Simas, Fremont, CA.

Trafzer, Clifford E., and Joel R. Hyer, eds. 1999. *Exterminate Them! Written Accounts of the Murder, Rape, and Enslavement of Native Americans during the California Gold Rush, 1848–1868*. East Lansing: Michigan State University Press.

Treganza, Adan E. 1942. "An Archaeological Reconnaissance of Northeastern Baja California and Southeastern California." *American Antiquity* 8: 152–63.

Troncoso, Francisco. 1849. Untitled. In *Noticias Estadísticas de Sonora y Sinaloa*, created by José Agustín de Escudero, 13–23. México DF: R. Rafael.

Trouillot, Michel-Rolph. 1995. *Silencing the Past: Power and the Production of History*. Boston: Beacon Press.

United States Census. 1860a. *Population Schedules of the Eighth Census of the United States, Alameda County, California*. Washington, DC: National Archives of the United States.

United States Census. 1860b. *Population Schedules of the Eighth Census of the United States, Santa Clara County, California*. Washington, DC: National Archives of the United States.

United States Census. 1870a. *Population Schedules of the Ninth Census of the United States, Alameda County, California*. Washington, DC: National Archives of the United States.

United States Census. 1870b. *Population Schedules of the Ninth Census of the United States, Santa Clara County, California*. Washington, DC: National Archives of the United States.

United States Census. 1880. *Population Schedules of the Tenth Census of the United States, Alameda County, California*. Washington, DC: National Archives of the United States.

United States Bureau of the Census. 1910. *Thirteenth Census of the United States: 1910-Indian Population*. Washington, DC: National Archives of the United States.

Van Camp, Gena R. 1979. *Kumeyaay Pottery: Paddle-and-Anvil Techniques from Southern California*. Socorro, NM: Ballena Press.

Viader, José. 1799. *Letter Regarding Elections*. Mission Santa Clara Manuscript Collection, Archives & Special Collections. Santa Clara University Library, Santa Clara, CA.

Vizenor, Gerald. 1999. *Manifest Manners: Narratives on Postindian Survivance*. Lincoln: University of Nebraska Press.

Vizenor, Gerald. 2008. "The Aesthetics of Survivance: Literary Theory and Practice." In *Survivance: Narratives of Native Presence*, edited by Gerald Vizenor, 1–23. Lincoln: University of Nebraska Press.

Von der Porten, Edward. 2019. *Ghost Galleon: The Discovery and Archaeology of the San Juanillo on the Shores of Baja California*. College Station: Texas A&M University Press.

Voss, Barbara L. 2008. *The Archaeology of Ethnogenesis: Race and Sexuality in Colonial San Francisco*. Berkeley: University of California Press.

Wade, Lizzie. 2017. "On the Trail of Ancient Mariners." *Science* 357 (6351): 542–45.

Wade, Maria F. 2008. *Missions, Missionaries, and Native Americans: Long-Term Processes and Daily Practices*. Gainesville: University Press of Florida.

Wade, Sue A. 2004. "Kumeyaay and Paipai Pottery as Evidence of Cultural Adaptation and Persistence in Alta and Baja California." Master's thesis, San Diego State University.

Wagner, Henry R. 1929. *Spanish Voyages to the Northwest Coast of America in the Sixteenth Century*. San Francisco: California Historical Society.

Walder, Heather, and Jessica Yann. 2018. "Resilience and Survivance: Frameworks for Discussing Intercultural Interactions." *Midwest Archaeological Conference Occasional Papers* 2: 1–18.

Warren, Claude N. 1984. "The Desert Region." In *California Archaeology*, edited by Michael Moratto, 339–430. Orlando: Academic Press.

Warren, Louis S. 2015. "Wage Work and the Sacred Circle: The Ghost Dance as Modern Religion." *Western Historical Quarterly* 46: 141–68.

Waters, Michael R. 1982. "The Lowland Patayan Ceramic Tradition." In *Hohokam and Patayan: Prehistory of Southwestern Arizona*, edited by Randall H. McGuire and Michael B. Schiffer, 275–97. New York: Academic Press.

Watkins, Joe. 2017. "Can We Separate the 'Indian' from the 'American' in the Historical Archaeology of the American Indian?" In, *Historical Archaeology Through a Western Lens*, edited by Mark Warner and Margaret Purser, 113–37. Lincoln: University of Nebraska Press and the Society for Historical Archaeology.

Webb, Edith B. 1952. *Indian Life at the Old Missions*. Los Angeles: Warren F. Lewis Publisher.

Welch, John R. 2017 "Cycles of Resistance." *The SAA Archaeological Record* 17 (1): 17–21.

White, Raymond C. 1963. "Luiseño Social Organization." *University of California Publications in American Archaeology and Ethnology* 48 (2): 91–194.

Wiberg, Randy S. 2005. "Final Report: Archaeological Evaluation and Mitigative Data Recovery at CA-YOL069, Madison Aggregate Plant, Yolo County, California." Report to Solano Concrete Company, Inc., Fairfield, CA.

Wilcox, Michael V. 2009. *The Pueblo Revolt and the Mythology of Conquest: An Indigenous Archaeology of Contact*. Berkeley: University of California Press.

Wilken, Michael. 1987. "The Paipai Potters of Baja California: A Living Tradition." *The Masterkey* 60: 18–26.

Wilken, Michael. 1992. "Baja's Paipai Indians: People from an Ancient Time." *Baja Explorer* 2 (6): 28–34.

Wilken-Robertson, Michael. 2000. "I May Still Be Speaking: The Indigenous Oral Tradition of Northern Baja California." *Proceedings of the Literary History of San Diego and Northern Baja California, 1998–1999*. San Diego: The Congress of History of San Diego and Imperial Counties and the California Council for the Humanities.

Wilken-Robertson, Michael. 2018. *Kumeyaay Ethnobotany: Shared Heritage of the Californias*. San Diego: Sunbelt Publications.

Wilken-Robertson, Miguel, and Don Laylander. 2006. "Ethnography." In *The Prehistory of Baja California: Advances in the Archaeology of the Forgotten Peninsula*, edited by Don Laylander and Jerry D. Moore, 67–81. Tallahassee: University of Press of Florida.

Winter, Werner. 1967. "The Identity of the Paipai (Akwa'ala)." In *Studies in Southwestern Ethnolinguistics: Meaning and History in the Language of the American Southwest*, edited by Dell H. Hymes and William E. Bittle, 371–78. The Hague: Mouton.

Wolfe, Patrick. 2001. "Land, Labor, and Difference: Elementary Structures of Race." *American Historical Review* 106 (3): 866–905.

Zappia, Natale A. 2014. *Raiders and Traders: The Indigenous world of the Colorado Basin, 1540–1859*. Chapel Hill: University of North Carolina Press.

Zappia, Natale A. 2018. "Indigenous Food Frontiers in the Early American West." *Southern California Quarterly* 100 (4): 385–408.

Zárate Loperena, David A. 1993. "Nñait Jatñil, Soy Caballo Negro." *Estudios Fronterizos* 31–32: 81–100.

Zárate Loperena, David A. 1995. "Testimonios de Santo Tomás: La Muerte de Padre Eudaldo Surroca en 1803." In *Apuntes Para la Historia Regional: Antología de David A. Zárate Loperena*, 42–51. Tijuana: Universidad Autónoma de Baja California.

Index

About the Author

Lee M. Panich is an associate professor of anthropology at Santa Clara University, specializing in the archaeology and ethnohistory of colonial California, particularly the Spanish mission system. He is co-editor with Tsim D. Schneider of *Indigenous Landscapes and Spanish Missions*.